Fro[...]

to the Arctic Circle

From Vietnam to the Arctic Circle

Memoir of a Naval Officer in the Cold War

JACK WHITEHOUSE

McFarland & Company, Inc., Publishers

Jefferson, North Carolina

LIBRARY OF CONGRESS CATALOGUING-IN-PUBLICATION DATA

Names: Whitehouse, Jack, author.
Title: From Vietnam to the Arctic Circle : memoir of a naval
officer in the Cold War / Jack Whitehouse.
Description: Jefferson, North Carolina : McFarland & Company, Inc.,
Publishers, 2022 | Includes bibliographical references and index.
Identifiers: LCCN 2022013801 | ISBN 9781476688350 (paperback : acid free paper) ∞
ISBN 9781476646596 (ebook)
Subjects: LCSH: Whitehouse, Jack. | United States. Navy—Officers—Biography. |
Vietnam War, 1961-1975—Personal narratives, American. | Vietnam War,
1961-1975—Naval operations, American. | Arctic regions—Description and travel. |
Cold War. | Sayville (N.Y.)—Biography. | BISAC: HISTORY / Military / Naval
Classification: LCC V63 .W49 2022 | DDC 359.0092 [B]—dc23/eng/20220329
LC record available at https://lccn.loc.gov/2022013801

BRITISH LIBRARY CATALOGUING DATA ARE AVAILABLE

ISBN (print) 978-1-4766-8835-0
ISBN (ebook) 978-1-4766-4659-6

Front cover: *inset* the author standing on the bow of the USS *Chehalis*, 1971
(photograph by Elaine Kiesling Whitehouse); *background, bottom* USS *Chehalis*
(PG-94) underway in heavy seas (U.S. Navy photograph); *background,
top* map of Arctic region (Shutterstock/Peter Hermes Furian)

Printed in the United States of America

*McFarland & Company, Inc., Publishers
Box 611, Jefferson, North Carolina 28640
www.mcfarlandpub.com*

This book is dedicated to the citizen heroes who gave their young lives in the service of our country, especially:

Captain John Michael Gibbons, United States Army
Warrant Officer Willard Spencer Lund, United States
    Army
Captain Merrill Howard Masin, United States Air Force
Petty Officer Third Class George Daniel Miller, United
    States Navy
Ensign John Townsend Norton, Jr., United States Navy

Table of Contents

Table of Contents

Acknowledgments

Many people helped me during my research and while writing this book. Most of all I want to thank my wife and editor, Elaine Kiesling Whitehouse, for reviewing and correcting the manuscript numerous times and for her steadfast belief in my seeing the project through to completion. The book would not have been possible without her.

I want to thank my publisher McFarland and particularly editor Charles Perdue for giving me the opportunity to get the book into print.

I wouldn't have a book were it not for the actions of the men with whom I served. Many of their names are in the book. I want to thank them, and the many who are not mentioned by name, for their dedicated service. Some of the men were my dearest friends, men who, as Lincoln said at Gettysburg, gave to their country their last full measure of devotion. Those men are Captain Merrill Masin, Captain Mike Gibbons, Ensign John Norton, Warrant Officer Spencer Lund, and Seaman Apprentice Danny Miller. It is they who provided much of the inspiration to finish this book.

I want to acknowledge the example my father set for me with his service in the Western Pacific during World War II as a Navy pilot aboard the USS *Lunga Point* (CVE-94). Like so many men who served in World War II he rarely spoke of it, but from the faded cruise books and old family photo albums everyone in the family knew about his service. His ship received the prestigious Presidential Unit Citation, something he never mentioned, but which we all knew.

The World War II service of my Uncles Gilbert (Bud) and Henry (Hank) Whitehouse helped inspire my service, particularly the loss of twenty-one-year-old Bud in a March 1944 naval air training accident. My father-in-law, Frank Kiesling, who died much too young from cancer, received the Bronze Star and Purple Heart for his actions in the invasion of Salerno in September 1943. Like my father, he never spoke of his sacrifice, but his family knew what he had done.

Acknowledgments

Finally, I would like to say thank you to the people of my hometown of Sayville, New York, who through their example created the environment that made possible men like Merrill Masin, Mike Gibbons, Spencer Lund and Danny Miller. Thank you to all the teachers, the sports coaches, the clergy, the scout leaders, the veterans' organizations, the local newspapers, the shop owners and all the parents who were such positive influences in their children's upbringing.

Vietnam Vet

by Elaine Kiesling Whitehouse

Hell no, we won't go!
They won't go.
But he goes.

Get out of the Comfort Zone.
Get into the Combat Zone.

One two. One two.
When I grow up, what will I do?

You don't need a license to go to war.

Hell, no.

He sees fire and rain.
His two best friends are slain.
When he comes home,
He can never face their parents again.

When he gets home,
There is no heroes' welcome
(He did not win the World Series.)

But I thought I was serving my country...

There is no job—he didn't have a chance to get the license
like those who would not go.

But he gets to see a Wall.
And every time he makes eye contact with another Vet,
They Know.

Preface

Many excellent books have been written about Vietnam and the Cold War by some of America's best historians, among them *The Best and the Brightest* by *New York Times* Vietnam War correspondent David Halberstam, who masterfully depicts the major figures behind the prosecution of the conflict and the tragic mistakes made in the decade long struggle; *The Cold War* by Odd Arne Westad, who emphasized the global nature of the ideological confrontation and how much of it was fought in third-world revolutionary states such as Cuba; *The Sword and the Shield* by Christopher Andrew and Vasili Mitrokhin, revealing the Soviet KGB's unrelenting Cold War covert operations in almost every nation of the world, but always with the United States as its primary target; and *Blind Man's Bluff: The Untold Story of American Submarine Espionage* by Sherri Sontag and Christopher Drew with Annette Lawrence Drew about the mostly hidden history of submarine warfare in the Cold War.

My story is about those very same subjects but told from the perspective of a young, Ivy League-educated naval officer who served on a destroyer in Vietnam, spent four months on a gunboat doing sensitive ops out of Guantanamo Bay, and who for two years on Norwegian naval vessels helped defend Norwegian waters north of the Arctic Circle from Soviet submarine incursions. In books of this genre this one is unusual and important because of my disparate experiences on the front lines in three of the Cold War's hot spots—Vietnam, Cuba and Northern Norway. The story is also as personal as it is academic. It comes from someone who lost a number of his dearest, lifelong friends in Vietnam War violence during the period of his naval service.

I wanted to write a story that reveals both the sacrifice and the personal rewards that came with serving on the right side of the seemingly endless struggle between freedom and authoritarianism. I also wanted to show how serving in the U.S. military teaches life lessons no one can learn from a book or in a classroom. The study of civics, history and

1

philosophy can provide the vital basics of a liberal education, but serving in the American military provides the litmus test for what is real and what is academic fantasy, what is important and what is not.

While so many texts reveal the faults in American Cold War policies this book mostly sees the other side, how in the big picture unsung efforts by heroic young men in remote regions of the world helped stop authoritarian regimes' aggression and preserve the freedoms enjoyed in the Western world.

The story also reveals how the men who gave their last full measure of devotion in the Vietnam War—a war often believed to be a mistake— are not forgotten in the small towns from which they came. They are treasured patriots, remembered and celebrated as men who made possible the current generation of proud American warriors.

Introduction

I never planned to write this book. The process began years ago when I wrote down what I could remember and what I could find out about high school classmates who were killed in the war in Vietnam. It concerned me that several of my best friends had been killed in action, and so little had been made known about their sacrifice.

For years I had felt guilty about never having done anything to honor the memory of a fellow naval officer and close friend, Ensign John Norton. John and 73 of his shipmates died in the June 3, 1969, collision between the *Frank E. Evans* (DD-754) and the HMAS *Melbourne* (R21). I wrote about John, what I remembered of the tragedy and what I learned through research. I shared the piece with the Frank E. Evans Association, Inc. and they were kind enough to include it in their 2nd quarter 2019 Newsletter. I've included more about that heartbreaking loss in this book.

About a year ago, while cleaning out a corner of the cellar, I happened on a cache of personal letters between my wife Elaine and me, written from 1968 to 1975. There are hundreds of letters the content of which described in some detail our lives in the Navy, news of our military friends, the progress of the war and the politics of the day. Almost coincidentally, I found in the National Archives website the logbooks for the USS *Buck* (DD-761) for the years 1966–70.

At first, I wrote only about my time on the *Buck*, thinking of making little more than a personal journal. Then it expanded to my reasons for joining the Navy, what it took to obtain my commission, my service on the USS *Chehalis* (PG-94) and my time in the Norwegian Navy. But the heart of the story became the people with whom I worked from 1964 to 1975. The risks they assumed and the personal sacrifices they made without expectation of reward inspired me. In writing their story I felt honored to have been associated with all of them.

I made every effort to be as accurate as possible in my portrayal

Introduction

of the people and events of 45 to 55 years ago, but mistakes happen. Indeed, in writing my two other history books—*Sayville Orphan Heroes, the Cottages of St. Ann's* and *Fire Island, Heroes and Villains on Long Island's Wild Shore*—I learned much from readers' feedback that had been unavailable to me at the time of my writing.

1

Why Join the Navy?

Joining the Navy had not been a spontaneous decision but a goal that had evolved over time from a variety of influences. At some point later in life I came to understand that my family and friends, my schooling, my hometown community, and my geographic location near the water all combined to make joining the Navy something I had to do. I was a very good naval officer, and so I stayed for eleven years. I liked and respected the men who sailed on warships, and I gained a great deal of personal satisfaction from doing the right thing by serving the best country in the world.

The family influence began at the turn of the 20th century with a wealthy great-great-uncle on my mother's side named John B. O'Donohue ("J.B.," 1857–1918). J.B. owned a 27-foot sloop named the *Crescent*. Sailing was his sport. From a dock on his Sands Point estate in the heart of Long Island's Gold Coast, he raced in the waters off New York City and Long Island. He took my grandfather, John B. Catlin, on as crew, which is where my grandfather learned to love the water. In 1906 the Atlantic Yacht Club, of which O'Donohue was a prominent member, awarded *Crescent* a large, engraved sterling silver platter for the boat's victories in the season's races. Despite scratch and cut marks from regular use by the family over the years as a meat tray, today it sits in a place of honor in our home.

In 1949 my grandfather purchased a two-masted ketch named the *Sea Dawn*, which he docked behind his house at 70 Sunset Drive in Sayville. When I was around five years old, he took me along on regular weekend sails around the Great South Bay. The Great South Bay, actually a lagoon, is situated between the Atlantic barrier beach known as Fire Island and the south shore of Long Island. Off Sayville it is approximately four miles wide. The depth of the water varies but has a maximum of about twenty feet. My Grandfather loved to sail to Fire Island, especially the two beach communities of Cherry Grove and Fire Island Pines for a day on the ocean shore.

From Vietnam to the Arctic Circle

Fire Island is a place of legends, from Dutch settler discovery to pirate refuge, buried treasure, hundreds of shipwrecks and much more. Fire Island is still one of the most beautiful and wild locations anywhere in the U.S. and was even more so when we visited in the late 1940s and early 1950s. Today it is a national park, and a group of people is working to name Fire Island a World Heritage Site.

As a youngster in the 1930s my mother was an avid sailor racing Snipes—a small, two person, Marconi rigged sloop—with a Sayville area sailing organization known as the Wet Pants. As soon as I was old enough, my mother enrolled me in Wet Pants sailing classes. After completing the three-summer program, she bought me an old, 18-foot, Cape Cod Knockabout, referred to as a CC, complete with a badly warped wooden mast, tattered sails and a hull with so many leaks it could have been used to drain spaghetti.

I loved that old boat. I especially loved the feeling of independence sailing my own boat wherever I wanted to go. When I wasn't mowing lawns for spending money, I was sailing my boat all over the Great South Bay, usually with young Sayville friends Gavin Clowe and John Hayden as crew. Gavin grew up to become a math professor and John a lawyer. We sailed in all kinds of weather taking chances only young people will take, but learning a lot about boats, the wind and the water.

In the late 1950s and early 1960s there were about seven or eight other CCs in the Wet Pants, so on weekends we had a great time sailing in the club's competitive Saturday morning and afternoon races held off Sayville in the Great South Bay. I took racing very seriously and wouldn't tolerate Gavin and John not putting everything they had into holding the trim of the sails, or managing the spinnaker, or whatever else there was to do while I handled the tiller. Physically bigger and stronger than both of them, I was loud and demanding, a Simon Legree who rarely if ever thanked either of them.

About halfway through the first summer of racing my two friends calmly explained that their parents had told them they no longer needed to crew for me because I behaved so badly towards them. I was astonished. I had no idea my friends didn't appreciate me for wanting us to win at almost any cost. I apologized and assured them I'd change—finding kids willing to crew was not easy. I asked if they would give me another chance and keep sailing with me. They agreed to continue, but only so long as I didn't threaten them anymore. So, as a twelve-year-old, I got my first slap-in-the-face lesson in personnel management. Don't act like a jerk or you're going to lose more than the race. The lesson stayed with me.

1. Why Join the Navy?

When I was 16 the Wet Pants hired me to teach their children's sailing program, which I happily did for three summers with two fellow instructors, Kathy Huus and Carolyn James. The pay wasn't great, but the girls were a lot of fun—especially the spirited Kathy Huus—and the kids were eager to learn.

Of course, the Great South Bay was not a kiddie pool. The Bay could be ferocious in stormy weather, dangerous in unexpected situations, completely different in each of the four seasons, and often unpredictable even in good weather. It even changed colors from light gray to deep blue depending on its mood. Several times the Bay came close to killing me, but each time it let me go, as if to say, "Okay, I'll let you go again, but I hope you learned from this."

One day in early June after junior high school let out for the day, local friend Steve Brennan asked John Hayden and me if we'd like to help him sail his new Sailfish—little more than a hollowed-out surfboard with a sail. It is easy to tip over and usually fairly easy to right simply by standing on the dagger board. We said sure!

The weather was warm and sunny but with a cold breeze from the north. That meant there would be little wave action in the northern part of the Bay—the water just off our south shore. We didn't even consider that the still very cold water of the early season might be a problem. We headed home, changed to bathing suits, pushed the Sailfish on its cart down to the bay, hoisted the sail and headed out. The three of us sort of knew what we were doing, but we'd never sailed Steve's Sailfish before. We soon found we were having trouble keeping the boat stable with the shifting weight of all three of us, the boat really designed for only one. The gusty north wind kept tipping us over which was a lot of fun—at first.

About a half mile from shore, the sun was starting to get low in the sky, the north wind was rising, and we were getting cold. As we tried to tack back to shore, we realized we couldn't keep the boat upright. The wind kept tipping us over. Worse, we were drifting further out. Hypothermia began to set in. We tried swimming while pushing the boat in front of us and that didn't work. We just kept getting colder with the waves pushing the boat farther from shore. Soon it was too far to swim back. As the thinnest of the three of us, I was the first to begin the uncontrollable shivering that characterizes hypothermia. We realized we had a big problem and there seemed to be nothing any of us could do about it.

At this time of day on a weekday, and this early in the season, there were no other boats out on the water. We began to feel a little desperate. But suddenly, seemingly from out of nowhere, a guy in a small motorboat appeared next to us and offered to help. He could see our predicament and pulled us to shore. We were too cold to talk to him and so never learned who he was or how he happened upon us when he did. Once on the beach we just lay in the still warm sand for a half an hour before feeling good enough to walk home. Once home I stood in a hot shower for a long time.

One very cold winter day a group of us decided to ice skate across the Bay to the Fire Island home of classmate David Lerner. Jack Meyer, a lifelong friend who eventually retired from the Coast Guard to this day talks about our risky adventure.

On the Saturday in question the Bay was frozen over, but the weather had been warming. The skate to the beach was without incident and with no signs of any potential problems. However, on the return, after a beautiful day of warm sunshine, things were noticeably different. We found puddles of water forming on the ice, and other spots we knew we had to avoid, the groaning ice seeming to be shifting as we skated. All went well enough until about a half-mile off the south shore, just west of Browns River. Suddenly somebody yelled, "Wow, look at that crack in the ice!" The wide crack paralleled the shore and seemed to go on forever, so there was no going around it. What to do? Well, we knew we had to get off the ice and we had to get home, so we made a decision born of youthful arrogance and the conviction that nothing could harm us. One by one we got a running start and, skates flashing, leapt over the widening crack. Somehow God saved all of us from ending up in the water, to this day I don't know how. As kids, none of us had any idea of the risk we had taken. Today we know.

One summer day, Kathy Huus and I decided to sail her CC over to the beach. Kathy was a cute girl but tough. Like most guys, she enjoyed horsing around and this day was no different. About three quarters of the way to the beach and after I had teased her about something, I got up to grab a jib sheet. The next thing I knew I was in the water. I treaded water as I watched Kathy sail off laughing all the way. I wasn't a bad swimmer but after a while in the choppy waves I began to tire. Finally, yelling loudly and insistently, I convinced her she had to come back and pick me up, now! She acquiesced, but by the time she got the boat alongside me so I could pull myself aboard, I was completely out of energy. Male pride—there used to be such a thing—kept me from letting her know I had come close to going under.

1. Why Join the Navy?

One Wet Pants race day there was a strong, gusty wind out of the north. Sailing in such winds is always tricky. It can be calm one minute and blowing forty knots the next. If you're not quick with letting out the sails, you can flip the boat. Sure enough, a young girl and her friend sailing a Blue Jay didn't react in time and flipped their boat. Never slow to assist girls in distress, we sailed over to help. Her mast was pounding into the bottom of the bay and with the sails secured in place it was impossible to even partially right the boat. Leaving the CC to my crew, I decided to jump in the water and dive down to loosen the sheets and/ or halyards to loosen the sails. Once under water I felt one of the lines begin to wrap around my legs. Suddenly I couldn't swim, the more I kicked the more the line seemed to tighten. Fortunately, I didn't panic. I went into a crouch position and with my last breath managed to unwind the line from my legs. I was gulping for air by the time I reached the surface.

The above-described incidents didn't frighten me, in fact just the opposite. They gave me the increased confidence to believe I could overcome whatever the water could throw at me. As a kid I remember thinking that you just have to not give up, work at it, keep going and you'll be okay. I don't know that I'd see it the same way today as I did then.

In the late 1950s and early 1960s, the media was vastly different than what it is today. Back then most popular prime time TV shows extolled the virtues of bravery, honesty and traditional family values. People watched *I Love Lucy, Gunsmoke, Wagon Train, The Andy Griffith Show, Ozzie and Harriet, Bonanza,* and *The Untouchables,* all featuring solid citizen heroes and heroines. In the late 1950s and early 1960s we even had patriotic shows emphasizing core values boys could try to emulate, shows like *Men of Annapolis, West Point, Navy Log* and *The Silent Service.* I remember watching those shows at the age of eleven or twelve and being strongly influenced by them, wanting to be like the heroic young men they portrayed, and I was not alone. In real life for kids growing up in the late '50s and early '60s what better sports heroes could I have had than Army's Pete Dawkins, track star Wilma Rudolph, the Navy's Roger Staubach, and pitcher Sandy Koufax as well as the many other non-sports heroes like President Dwight Eisenhower, President Jack Kennedy, Medal of Honor recipient Audie Murphy, John Wayne, and so many more. These people espoused positive and patriotic causes virtually every young American aspired to support, me included.

A few of my teachers and coaches taught me the value of working hard and staying with it, George Zeller, my calculus teacher and freshman football coach among them. George coached freshman football all by himself and never lost a single game in the many years he held the position. The reason he never lost a football game was the same reason no one ever failed his math regents. George made it crystal clear that losing in football or failing an important math test was not an option. The only way to avoid losing at either endeavor was to work for it and want it more than anything else. George Zeller was our Vince Lombardi before there even was a Vince Lombardi.

My chemistry teacher and varsity football coach, Charlie Carpenter (also a sailor) had a more subtle approach. He would inspire the kids with quiet words about the hard work they had done to get to where they were and how they could be the best if they just kept confidence in themselves and continued to play up to their God-given abilities. He was smart, young and active, a good athlete, and we believed what he had to say about doing and being our best. In the Navy and later in life the lessons learned from the Great South Bay, Zeller and Carpenter taught me and other classmates to stay with it and not give up when things got tough.

Teachers in earlier grades kindled my interest in me in American history and the Navy. A social studies teacher, Larry Fanjoy, was a diminutive history geek who, despite his physical stature, the kids respected more than any other junior high school teacher. He believed what he taught us about the value of thinking things through, not judging people on appearances, and respecting the great things patriotic Americans had accomplished. A science teacher and later junior high school principal, Laurier (Pete) Begnoche, was the one who encouraged me to seek a U.S. Navy ROTC scholarship and apply to Brown University. I don't know why, but my parents wanted me to go Union College and stay out of the Navy, but several times Begnoche met with the family and insisted I go for the Navy scholarship and admittance to Brown. My mother said she thought Brown would be too much for me but eventually both my parents agreed to support the idea. Had it not been for Pete's remarkable extra efforts shepherding me through the process I probably wouldn't have gone to Brown and maybe missed out on serving in the Navy.

So, in the late summer I packed up and headed for Providence to begin my Ivy League education as a freshman at Brown and my Navy career as a first-year midshipman. By early September 1964 I was still two months away from turning 18 and a proud 4th class midshipman in Brown's Naval Reserve Officer Training Corps (NROTC) unit.

1. Why Join the Navy?

My NROTC program began in historic Lyman Hall on Brown's main campus on the first day of the school year. I was one of thirty-six 4th class midshipmen. At the beginning of our first session the instructor, Lieutenant Robinette, told us to look at the man sitting to either side, because neither of those men would be attending the commissioning ceremony a little less than four years hence. Everyone registered surprise. Securing a scholarship that covered Brown's high tuition, textbooks, lab fees, uniforms, paid $50 a month and provided a six-week summer job aboard a warship was highly competitive and a very valuable award. Giving it up would mean having to find a new source of funding, probably in the form of sizeable student loans. But the Lieutenant was precisely correct, of the thirty-six that began, only 18 received their commissions.

Reasons for dropping out of the NROTC program varied but included the difficulty in taking five courses per semester instead of the standard four for all other students, the inability to handle the physical and mental requirements of each summer's six-week training regimen, not being able to adapt to the military culture, and the requirement to pass two semesters of math, two semesters of physics and a semester of celestial navigation. The course requirements may not sound particularly difficult, but the devil was in the details. First, in the mid–1960s grades were highly competitive meaning you had to earn your grade in competition with several very intelligent students. No one got a "C" or even a "D" just for showing up to class, it wasn't difficult to fail a course. There was no such thing as a "pass-fail" option. Also, midshipmen who were linguists and writers, but not particularly great science and math students had a tough slog with the competitive math and physics material. Finally, if a midshipman played a sport like football as I did, and/or worked part time for spending money as I did in the cafeteria, the lack of free time became burdensome.

Generally speaking, good grades were harder to come by in the 1960s than they are today. Richard Vedder, an Ohio University professor emeritus of economics and a historian, author and columnist wrote the following in an op-ed in the April 11, 2019, *Wall Street Journal.*

> As economists Philip Babcock and Mindy Marks have demonstrated, students in the middle of the 20th century spent nearly 50% more time—around 40 hours weekly—studying. They now lack incentives to work very hard, since the average grade today—a B or B plus—is much higher than in 1960 when the average grade-point average of around 2.5 implied a typical grade of B-minus or C-plus.

From Vietnam to the Arctic Circle

I'm part of the problem: I've been teaching for 55 years, and I assign far less reading, demand less writing, and give higher grades than I did two generations ago.

In the spring semester of 1968 at Brown, I took a great one-semester course on modern American history taught by former CIA Executive Director Lyman B. Kirkpatrick. It had a required—not recommended, required—reading list of eighteen books!

So, adding an extra, fifth, course at Brown made a difference. Also, the NROTC program required two hours a week of "drill" in uniform meaning an additional time commitment of at least four hours per week. Drill consisted of a variety of activities including marching, personnel inspections, parades, lectures and other such formal military work all while dressed in uniform. Finally, participation in an after-hours program such as the drill team or the pistol team or similar was strongly encouraged adding an additional two hours or so a week. Five courses, the Navy unit's "after-hours" time requirements, playing a sport such as football for three hours a day, and working part time in the cafeteria for spending money made time the midshipman's most precious commodity. Oh, and with a little luck, a social life could be had from 8–12 p.m. on Saturday night. For some it was too much, and so they left the program.

Interestingly, once in the fleet and speaking with successful officers the near-unanimous opinion was that the NROTC training program was inversely related to the success of the fleet officers it produced. In other words, many of those who did the best in school did the least well in the fleet. Of course, there are exceptions. Vice Admiral Richard Mayo, a friend, a Brown University NROTC classmate and a Delta Phi Omega fraternity brother of mine is certainly one. Presaging things to come, his nickname in our fraternity was "Admiral." But in many cases getting superior grades in classroom programs and activities had precious little to do with ship handling, underway watch standing, personnel management, endurance, and other skills and traits needed by officers aboard ship. NROTC classroom discussions, drill programs, and "participation politics" seemed to produce officers more suited to shore-based jobs than ship-based.

2

A Life Changing Event

In early June 1968, Elaine Kiesling and I graduated from college, she from SUNY Oswego and I from Brown University. I received my commission as an ensign in the U.S. Navy in a ceremony directly following graduation. The world-famous comedian Bob Hope spoke and presented me with my certificate of commission. I thought that was pretty special. As only youth will allow, Elaine and I managed to attend both graduation ceremonies by driving all night in two cars from Oswego in upstate New York to Providence, Rhode Island—at least a nine-hour drive.

Truth be told, I almost never made it to my commissioning; in fact, I almost never made it through my first semester at Brown. In midsemester 1964 an event unfolded that almost changed my life forever.

The weather on Saturday evening, October 10, 1964, was cool and clear, a perfect night for two freshmen to go out and see the sights on campus and maybe get invited in to one of the many parties in full swing in the fraternities and dormitories around the quads. Meeting girls was always high on the priority list.

My friend Hank Stevens and I left our freshman dorm that evening dressed in the 1964 Ivy League Saturday night uniform, a good sports jacket, dress shirt—no tie—and pants with the ubiquitous and always very shiny penny loafers.

So partying for me was something done only lightly on Saturday night. Hank and I were not out that night looking to do much more than have a beer and relax, perhaps with a couple of new friends if we got lucky.

Hank and I headed out toward the central dormitory quadrangle, known as Wriston Quad, wherein stood the refectory and many of the fraternities. Physical security was important even back in 1964. Brown had long suffered from occasional negative interactions between some of the less fortunate Providence area youths and their more advantaged Brown University peers. However, Brown "men" also found some of the interaction a definite plus. On Saturday nights, local girls would put on

13

their tightest sweaters and pants, fluff up their hair and in groups of two to four girls per car, drive around Wriston Quad and the surrounding streets looking to meet guys from Brown and maybe get invited to a frat or dorm party. For their part, the Brown boys would walk the sidewalks looking for cars filled with girls to invite to parties in hopes of finding what guys are looking for in such meeting arrangements. Some guys were particularly adept at this street meet and greet process and could literally populate a party with reasonably attractive and eager young ladies in no time at all. The ritual was generally referred to by one and all as "street meet" with most of the Brown boys preferring a slightly altered spelling of the second word in the phrase. Not always a one-night-stand arrangement, my friend Hank eventually married a local girl named Bobbi he met through the process.

All of the above to say that around 8:30 that Saturday evening, as Hank and I approached the arched brick main entrance to Wriston Quad, we were intercepted on the street by a well-dressed, pretty young girl of about 18 years of age who was trying to find the Phi Kappa Psi fraternity house to meet up with a boyfriend. We offered to show her the way, an offer she accepted.

As we approached the fraternity from the main gate, we could see a small crowd in the patio area just outside the fraternity front door. There appeared to be a party in full swing with music, laughing and yelling and people having a good time. The downstairs windows were open because the weather was so nice, and the rooms could quickly fill up with cigarette smoke.

Hank and I walked the girl up a couple of steps, onto the patio and then the thirty or so feet to the front door. The girl went in, and we turned to leave. As we were walking back toward the patio entranceway and the main sidewalk in front of the frat house, I noticed a small knot of four or five "townies," as the university people sometimes referred to young, local Providence males.

As we descended the two steps to the main sidewalk, one of the townies stepped right in front of me. Without so much as a word, the townie put his face within inches of mine.

I knew in that instant that there was going to be a fight, and so felt my body prepare for that first hit and the fistfight that would surely follow. I was taller than the "townie" and in good shape from football, so I wasn't particularly alarmed. What I did not know was how utterly devastating that first hit would be.

The next thing I knew I felt as though I was waking up from a sleep, but I was in a standing position, standing on a lawn with a big brick fraternity house directly in front of me. My eyes focused on the open windows of the fraternity house with people hanging out and yelling and pointing at me. Then I realized I felt warm and wet. My first thought was that someone must have thrown a water balloon at me from a high floor, and it landed on my head soaking me in warm, soapy water and that people in the windows were pointing and laughing at me because of it. What a stupid thing to do I thought, although Brown "men" were always doing things like that as pranks.

And then I felt something hanging on my face, maybe part of the balloon I thought. But it was not; whatever it was, it was attached to my face. Then I realized it was my face. I looked down and in the reflected light from the fraternity house I saw I was a sheet of crimson from my chest to my still brightly shined shoes. It was then that it started to dawn on me that maybe I had a bigger problem than a direct hit from a water balloon. I felt my face again and on the left side there was a big piece missing.

By this time my friend Hank had gotten to me. The look on Hank's face did absolutely nothing to reassure me that everything would be fine. Fortunately, despite his look of horror, Hank had the presence of mind to suggest I needed to get to the infirmary—only about two hundred yards away—immediately.

So the two of us began a fast walk toward the infirmary with me beginning to feel a little woozy probably from shock and also from loss of blood. I remembered almost passing out right under the main gate entranceway, but after a brief rest, felt stronger and returned to a fast walk. I remembered seeing people on the walkway staring at me in disbelief and then hiding their eyes or turning away at the sight of the blood and gore.

When we reached the infirmary, there was only one elderly nurse on duty. She too seemed repulsed, almost ready to go into a state of shock. She managed to hand me a large wad of gauze to hold over the left side of my face while she called emergency services.

In the infirmary there was a bathroom cabinet over a sink with the standard, face level mirror. I pulled the saturated gauze away from my head and for the first time saw the mess that had been the left side of my face. The sight was devastating; my left cheek from my ear to the tip of my chin was hanging down, I could see my jawbone and facial muscles and tendons hanging in ragged swatches. Still in shock, I remembered thinking, "If I live, this is going to be with me forever."

From Vietnam to the Arctic Circle

Soon a Providence Fire Department rescue vehicle arrived. Two firemen in full regalia—I don't think they had EMTs in those days—applied a bandage, wrapping almost my entire head in gauze. I looked something like a movie land zombie with blood all over me, and not much of my head visible other than eyes, nose and mouth.

The firemen walked me out to their truck, one on each side. It was like a police perp walk. No gurney, no wheelchair, the three of us walked the fifty feet or so from the front door out to the small fire truck. By that time a crowd of perhaps a hundred people had gathered to catch a glimpse of the "bloody monster." It seemed very strange to be the focus of so much attention, but not as a human being, more like I was some sort of weird Halloween display piece.

For whatever reason, the two firemen made me ride between them in the front seat for the approximately fifteen-minute drive to Providence General. They also made it obvious they didn't appreciate being called out at 9:00 p.m. on a Saturday night to ferry some messed up Ivy League brat to the hospital. Even in my state of shock, I found their attitude both surprising and disappointing. While the two firemen obviously didn't know the story behind what had happened, that didn't stop them from deciding the spoiled rich kid must somehow have been at fault for his injury.

Not long after getting to the emergency room, two Providence Police Department detectives came up and introduced themselves and asked what had happened. I related the above story about how I came to be outside the fraternity house and how a young man I had never seen before approached me. The young man tried to intimidate me by putting his face as close as possible to mine. I told the officers that at that point I expected a fistfight but had no idea the guy had a knife. I said I never saw the knife coming but as I got hit, I brought my arms up to try and fend off the attack, but too late. I recalled punching the kid away with both hands, saw stars and then the lights went out. I remembered nothing after that until I was standing some twenty feet away. After I gave them a physical description the detectives said they would be in touch.

By about 1 a.m. I was in surgery to fix as much of the damage as possible. The lead surgeon was a plastic surgeon who did a first-rate job sewing up the remnants of the left side of my face. For hours I lay on my right side on the operating table, watching the clock on the wall go from one hour to the next and the next. One thing the surgeon did not do, for whatever medical reason, was properly sew up the sliced-through salivary glands. In the future this would come to be a significant problem.

2. A Life Changing Event

Four hours after going in, and some 99 stitches later, I came out of surgery a repaired man in serious but stable condition.

So began the healing process. My parents came to see me on Sunday afternoon having received a phone call the night before from a university official who told them their son had been seriously wounded in a stabbing on campus, but that he was expected to survive. My surgeon came in and explained that I was one of those cases where I actually might think of myself as having been lucky. If the cut had been made slightly lower, it would have sliced through the jugular vein resulting in near instantaneous death. Had the blade hit an inch or so back, it would have gone into my ear, an inch or so forward into my eye. The blade also just missed severing the main facial nerve, and while I may have some permanent left-side facial paralysis, it will be nothing like what it would have been if the main nerve been cut.

Freshmen friends from Brown also came to visit with two dormitory friends being the most helpful. Two who had graduated from local Providence schools enjoyed an amazing network of Providence area buddies. They told me they would find out who did this. I didn't believe them at first, but I came to learn that these two sophisticated, intelligent kids also knew the local streets and had friends who would know, or who could find out, who had done this.

After the stabbing the university did almost nothing. The dean of the college met with my parents for an hour or so on the Sunday they visited and assured them he and the university would do everything they could to help. And, as far as I know, that was the last I, or they, ever heard from the dean. My parents, who were impressed with the dean's senior position at the university, would forever after tell me the dean was a wonderful gentleman who was very nice to them. In fairness to my parents, they too were in something of a state of shock and had four other children, two of them twin toddlers, to care for at home. They were not in position to initiate much follow-up with the dean. I was also disappointed that no one from the coaching staff of the football team visited or even sent a card.

After a couple of days at the hospital, I was released to the custody of the university infirmary. There, in a second-floor ward with a fellow frosh by the name of Grosvenor (Grove) Burnett, a lanky, athletic Southerner whose father was a professor at the University of North Carolina, I worked on adjusting to my new world. Grove became a good friend and with his sense of humor made my initial recovery much smoother.

The first few days I spent learning to speak intelligibly through a wired shut jaw, and sucking down a variety of medicinal potions and pureed nourishment through a fat straw. I had no real pain other than some soreness from the internal bruising because a good part of the left side of my face was numb.

Of significant help in my immediate recovery were the get-well cards and letters sent by my Sayville High School classmates, their parents and other local friends. Never before had I received anything like the handwritten, deeply meaningful messages I got that first week after the assault. I am not one normally given to outward expressions of love or affection, but those heartfelt written words from my friends gave me something I had not experienced before, something I might not otherwise ever have found. The memory of how I felt after reading those letters has stayed with me always. One of the writers became my wife.

By Thursday that week, the detectives were back. Acting on information provided by my Providence friends, they had picked up the perpetrator. The detectives brought him up to my bed in the infirmary and asked if he was the one who had stabbed me. I identified him on the spot.

In hindsight my reaction to that first face-to-face meeting after the incident surprised me a little. I found my thoughts channeling to one idea and that was to attack with the intent of doing as much harm as possible. It wasn't an emotional, "I'm going to kill him!" response, but a slower, stronger, deep inside desire to destroy him completely. The feeling was something like a surge of adrenalin but with controls, a feeling like you're very powerful and near invincible, able to inflict damage you could not normally do regardless of who or what tried to stop you. I mention it because I've never had that same feeling again.

His name was (I'll call him Freddy Kreuger), 16 years old. He had an arrest record for about as much trouble as a 16-year-old kid can get into. He told the cops that, on that evening, he and his buddies had been outside the fraternity house in question, having a verbal altercation with some of the fraternity brothers who were in the house. When they saw me come down the fraternity walkway, they thought I was one of the fraternity members with whom they had been fighting, and so Kreuger attacked me. The weapon was not a knife but the top half of a broken beer bottle he had picked up off the street.

After the cops left the infirmary, their handcuffed prisoner in tow, the hardest part of what would prove to be a lengthy ordeal began slowly to unfold.

At the time Brown did not have a "gentleman's C" for any course, except maybe a couple of courses in classics taught by a professor with a deep love for Brown hockey and the hockey team members. So it was important to attend lectures and keep up with the course work. By Saturday I had missed three lessons in each of my five classes along with the many hours of study and homework associated with those classes. Not being a genius-level student like many of my classmates, I was going to have to hustle to catch up.

On Monday of the week following the incident, my head bandaged and my jaw beginning to function more or less properly, I got permission from the doctors to return to the fray. My first order of business was an appearance at the courthouse down the hill from the campus. I had to testify before the Grand Jury to secure an indictment against Freddy Kreuger, meaning I had to again describe the scenario of the attack. The prosecutor ran me through the questioning. The Grand Jury eventually handed down an indictment against Kreuger for assault with a dangerous weapon; the exact wording of the charges escapes me.

I returned to campus to take up the next order of business, a meeting with my psychology professor about taking a mid-term test I had missed the previous week. The professor, a PhD psychologist himself, was very nice about it, offering to put the test off for a while until I had regained my strength. At one point the professor said, "You have been through something very traumatic and you will need time to recover from that." I may have needed time, but it wasn't available.

It was the first and only time anyone addressed the mental impact of the attack and so the professor's words stuck with me for a long time. In fact, until that conversation I had not thought about the assault in that way; I tended to think of it more like a football injury, a physical setback, something that would take me out of the game for a while but from which I would recover soon enough with no real lasting consequences. Still, the professor's words had made me at least think about the injury in a broader context and what the future might hold. I took the test the next day and got a "C," not as good a grade as I had hoped.

Talk to someone who has been through a serious illness or injury, and they almost always relate stories about the silly, sometimes even atrocious, things people say when they're trying to make you feel better. "Oh, you look much better than I'd heard," or, "I'm sure that horrible scar will look better with some make-up," or "I know a couple of people who have been able to compensate for that handicap you have."

And so, I got those sorts of comments, and I also got the jokes and the teasing that kids that age provide to their peers for any appearance that's an exception to the rule. I became known to one and all on campus as "Football Head" not from my prowess on the football field but the obvious resemblance of my swollen head with its outsized stitches to a football.

Two weeks went by and the swelling in my face had subsided hardly at all. The bandage I wore covering the left side of my face hid much of the bulge, but still the puffiness was very noticeable. The university-employed doctor treating me decided that most of the swelling appeared to be coming from a continuing fluid build-up, the source of which was uncertain. Most likely it would go away if allowed to drain, and so the doctor opened a small hole in my cheek. The doctor was able to cut open the hole without anesthetic because of the continuing numbness.

The doctor's theory proved mostly correct; i.e., the hole allowed fluid to flow out of the wound, and the swelling diminished. The problem was that the treatment didn't keep the fluid from continuing to flow freely. Most of the fluid turned out to be saliva from my severed salivary gland. The saliva was not flowing into my mouth as it should, but out the side of my face.

At mealtime I was like a large drooling dog, only instead of the drool coming out of my mouth it flowed through the wound, out the side of my face, down the jaw line and off my chin to the table forming little pools of yellowish liquid. I couldn't feel anything, so the first indication of the leakage was always the small puddle forming on the table in front of me. Whenever I ate I had to remove my bandage and hold napkins to my face to soak up the substantial flow.

Between the still raw scar, the hole in my cheek, the flowing saliva, and wads of soaked napkins, my mealtime appearance was such that no one would eat anywhere near me. So I ate my meals alone in a corner of the cafeteria. Once in a while, I would try to sit at a table with other people, but with limited success. Almost always my dining companions were too polite to just get up and leave, but they always seemed to eat very little more and left as quickly as possible. For his part, the doctor said I should just ignore the social stigma and continue to let the saliva flow and the gland would eventually heal eliminating the inconvenient leakage.

Not long after the indictment of Freddy Kreuger by the Grand Jury, Kreuger got his first appearance in court. I had asked the District Attorney's office to let me know when Freddy would be in court, and so off I went one morning, by myself, to follow the proceedings. It wasn't much to watch. Nothing happened. Kreuger and his lawyer appeared before the bench but by prearrangement his case was immediately postponed for some obscure legal reason. About a month or so later basically the same scenario unfolded, with the case postponed once again.

This time, on my way back up the hill to the Brown campus, I heard someone calling my name from down the hill, not far from the steps of the courthouse. I turned and saw Freddy Kreuger running up the hill toward me. It was just the two of us again, on the street, face-to-face. I couldn't believe this was happening, that there should be some law against being attacked a second time—and outside the court no less! Once again, I braced myself for what was to come.

Only this time he was in a jacket and tie and didn't have a weapon in his hand; it was the first thing I looked for. But what Kreuger said shocked me almost as much as a hit. Short of breath from running up the hill, he blurted out, "What are you doing this to me for? Why do you want to hurt me? Why don't you tell them you want to drop the case?" He offered no words of apology or regret. His attitude seemed to be one of disbelief that I would not accede to his demand and agree to drop my complaint on the spot. I remember thinking that things might have turned out differently for both of us if the system had disciplined him for his previous brushes with the law.

My spontaneous reaction was to turn the left side of my face to him and point to the scar and bandages. I said, "You see this? This is what you did to me. I'm going to have this forever. I want you to pay for this."

And without further word the conversation was over. An expressionless Kreuger turned and walked back down the hill.

But Freddy Kreuger wasn't the only one who thought I was being too hard on Freddy Kreuger. Not long after I returned to campus, I got a phone message that Brown's Dean of Students would like to see me at 10 a.m. the next morning. So, off I went to the dean's office at the appointed hour. The dean said he was disappointed that I seemed to have some sort of personal vendetta against this Providence youth. The dean wanted to know if I thought it was the right thing to do to pursue this case to the point where I might possibly send him to jail for a considerable period. Wasn't that something I would like to avoid? I should think seriously about how difficult that would be for the already underprivileged young man. I responded with basically what I had said to Freddy. After that our conversation was over and I was told I could leave. That was the last I ever heard from the Brown University Dean of Students, or any other dean for that matter.

21

From Vietnam to the Arctic Circle

Thinking about this meeting years later I could only conclude that someone in the public defenders' office or some related local government entity had leaned on the university to get me to rescind my complaint against Kreuger. The university went to great lengths to be seen contributing to the Providence community and particularly to the less fortunate within the community. The ardent prosecution of a poor local lad for a "fight" with a Brown football player obviously wouldn't help the Brown image among many local residents.

Meanwhile I was about to get a new shock. The Navy was not quite as sanguine about my recovery as my university doctor and let me know they were considering what to do about a 4th class midshipman who was now damaged goods. Navy physicians had read my medical reports and by December had decided that the damage to my face might be permanent. If that were the case, then they would have to rescind my scholarship. Just before the Christmas break the NROTC unit yeoman informed me I would have a physical exam sometime early in the New Year, with a Navy physician at the Newport Naval Station infirmary. At that time a determination would be made as to my continued medical suitability for the NROTC program.

So, I returned to my hometown of Sayville for the Christmas break in less than great spirits. I took a Greyhound bus from downtown Providence to the Port Authority Bus Terminal in Manhattan and then the Long Island Rail Road to Sayville. The five-hour bus ride was always a learning experience, but this time the learning came after I got to Manhattan.

I traveled in old jeans, worn leather boots, a favorite old fleece-lined rawhide leather jacket and, of course, the bandage on my still nasty looking wound. Thin from not being able to eat properly for a long time, I looked far more like a runaway than an Ivy League student on his way home at Christmas break.

It was early evening. I was hungry, so I decided to get a burger in a small and somewhat rundown diner near the Port Authority terminal. After wolfing down my meal, I reached into my pocket for a couple of dollars to leave on the counter. The waitress, a tough looking woman of about forty-five years of age, leaned over the counter put her face down close to mine. She said in a whisper, "Keep your money, just go. And you be careful out there."

If you are ever the subject of such an act of kindness, it has a way of staying with you for a long time.

During the Christmas break I went to a New Year's Eve party at a friend's house and so did Elaine. We had stopped seeing one another not long after high school graduation.

I think she missed me, and I missed her. At first, I was slow to approach her, certain like everyone else she would find me less than attractive because of my face. But her mind was on a more serious problem. Her father was at home in the final stages of cancer. He would be gone in three months' time. In the torture of watching her poor father withering away she seemed to barely notice my disfigurement. I learned a lot from that and after that night we would remain together forever.

Two things happened in the New Year that finally brought closure to what had begun on that terrible Saturday night in October. The first was that Freddy Kreuger finally appeared before a judge who accepted from him a plea of *nolo contendere*. I had to look it up after I got back from the courthouse to find out what it meant. The judge sentenced him to 4 years in detention, although where he served time and how much time he actually served I have no idea.

The second and more important thing was the promised physical exam at the U.S. Naval Station in Newport. By early February 1965, the saliva finally had stopped flowing out of my face, but there remained a considerable swelling in the middle of my jaw. My facial nerves also seemed improved with more feeling returning to the left side of my face, but still, the apparently near permanent swelling was not good and not having all the feeling come back was also a negative.

The Navy doctor I saw concentrated strictly on the physical damage to my face. He said the swelling concerned him and so he palpitated the wound localizing the apparent problem in the approximate center of the scar and the hole that still allowed a little of the fluid to flow out. He then opened the hole on both sides of the scar and drained the wound.

The swelling immediately and markedly diminished. More importantly, the doctor appeared convinced the wound would eventually heal completely including any residual facial numbness. Not only did I pass the physical, the left side of my face, except for the immediate vicinity of the mean red scar, finally looked relatively normal again. I would get to keep my NROTC scholarship and continue my education at Brown.

Years later I asked my parents why they had not sued or in some way sought compensation from Brown for what had happened that night. They said, "Back then decent people didn't do that sort of thing." I believed then that their answer described part of the price I had to pay for being brought up in a decent middle-class American family.

3

Midshipman Tough

Before talking about life as a junior officer in the U.S. Navy aboard a U.S. Navy destroyer in the Pacific in the late 1960s, I should mention a little about the intensive education and training that went into making it possible. Those of us who went through the four-year NROTC program were NOT 90-day wonders. The Navy saw to it that we were thoroughly vetted and well trained in almost every aspect of naval service.

Despite the attack, my serious wound, and the aftermath, I managed to finish my first year at Brown with adequate grades. Following exams in late May 1965, I traveled the short distance to Boston where, along with 93 other 3rd class NROTC midshipmen, I reported aboard the aircraft carrier USS *Wasp* (CVS-18). The *Wasp* would be the venue for my first shipboard experience, my 3rd class midshipman cruise.

It was late May 1965 when I reported aboard the *Wasp* along with two Brown University 3rd Class midshipman classmates, Ted Hand and Rick Miles. It was the first time any of us had been aboard ship and the first time I experienced that aroma found in every U.S. Navy ship. It is a scent unique to U.S. Navy warships derived from a combination of oil paint, Navy Standard Fuel Oil (NSFO), linoleum (the decks of every ships' internal spaces are linoleum tiles), cooking food, salt air, cleaning agents, coffee, operating machinery and sailors. I've never found anything even close to that smell anywhere else in the world. If you blindfolded a sailor and put him aboard a U.S. Navy ship and asked him where he was, he'd know from the smell.

All 93 of the midshipmen on board got assigned to the same birthing compartment, a large dormitory-like room directly below the hangar deck toward the aft end of the ship. Probably the compartment had been repainted a stark white color a couple of times since the ships commissioning in November 1943, but otherwise it had remained unchanged.

Racks for sleeping stood four high from the deck to the overhead and took up virtually the entire space. I had the top rack. I measured the distance between my rack and the overhead at 16 inches! These sleeping units were nothing more than man-size aluminum frames strung on chains fastened to the overhead. Serving as a mattress was a rectangular patch of canvas strung with cotton cord to the aluminum frame. Everyone shared one large "head" located adjacent to the berthing compartment outfitted with showers, sinks and urinals. The plumbing, like the racks, was early 1940s shipboard technology.

Privacy for 3rd class midshipmen was non-existent but not strictly necessary, because no one wanted to use their very limited free time for anything other than sleep. Life aboard ship for 3rd class middies meant nothing but hard, physical labor doing everything from chipping paint to cleaning bilges to standing boiler watch. A lot of the work was in non-air-conditioned areas, or spaces with only limited air conditioning, which is tough in the tropics in June. The idea was to give these officers-to-be a taste of what it's like being low man on the totem pole, a junior seaman or a fireman whose life at sea can be one of pure, and usually unappreciated, drudgery. Senior enlisted men assigned to manage us made sure we got the idea.

We stayed out of trouble for the most part but not always. One evening after chow Ted, Rick and I went out on the hangar deck fantail to get some air and watch the sun sink into the sea. We sat ourselves on the flat tops of a large bitt—a bitt being a pair of metal posts mounted on the deck used to secure mooring lines—just inboard of the lifelines. Close by and mounted on the lifeline next to a life ring was what looked to us to be a rectangular wooden canister one end of which held a finger ring attached to a wire leading into the canister. As we talked Ted absentmindedly started playing with the canister, swinging it back and forth from the finger ring and wire. Suddenly the wire came out and the canister crashed to the deck. Then smoke started coming out, and then it started smoking like crazy. We suggested Ted throw whatever it was overboard, just in case things got a lot worse. He did as we recommended and while we were all safe and unhurt, there was no doubt where the ship had been when Ted threw his canister overboard.

Ted's toss resulted in a large plume of gray smoke rising from the sea behind the carrier. We had never been briefed on smoke bombs or their availability at various locations around the ship for marking the location of a man overboard or similar event. So we couldn't know what we didn't know, but nonetheless we knew enough not to fool around with things we didn't know anything about. Long story short, within five minutes Ted had been summoned over the ship's loudspeaker to report immediately to the bridge. He went unpunished for his mistake, but for the remainder of the summer he was affectionately referred to by one and all as Smoke Bomb Hand. Ted was a mentally tough guy and so took his new appellation in stride.

The *Wasp* had been assigned the mission of picking up the Gemini IV space capsule carrying astronauts James A. McDivitt and Edward H. White II, both U.S. Air Force officers. McDivitt commanded the mission with White his copilot. I was excited at the prospect of being on scene and participating in the recovery. Today space flight seems routine, but in May of 1965 it had been only a little over three years since John Glenn in his Mercury space capsule had made America's first orbital space flight. Such heroics were still a big deal and front-page news. In fact, in 1967 the U.S. Government even commemorated the Gemini IV flight by issuing a pair of 5-cent stamps.

The Gemini IV flight proved to be the United States' longest flight up to that time lasting all of 4 days, 1 hour, 56 minutes and 12 seconds. It also featured America's first spacewalk. On June 3 Edward White became the first American to walk in space, floating in the ether outside the Gemini spacecraft for about 23 minutes. White was attached to the spacecraft by a 25-foot umbilical line and a 23-foot tether line.

After 62 revolutions around the Earth, the GT-4 spacecraft splashed down at 12:12 p.m. on June 7, approximately 400 miles east of Cape Canaveral and about 50 miles from the expected splash down point where the *Wasp* was waiting. The weather was fairly clear and bright with relatively calm seas, but unfortunately the ship was nowhere near close enough for the crew to be able to see the parachuting capsule come down, or the splash when it hit the water. The commanding officer had been good enough to allow those men not on duty to scan the horizon in anticipation of the landing, but to no avail.

We later learned that White was the first to be hoisted into the recovery helicopter while McDivitt waited in the life raft below. With the astronauts safely aboard the chopper and on their way back to the carrier flight deck, divers closed the spacecraft hatch to make sure everything stayed safe. Meanwhile the carrier proceeded at full speed to the spacecraft's location for its safe retrieval.

White and McDivitt were greeted on the flight deck of the *Wasp* by commanding officer Captain J. W. Conger; and Rear Adm. W.M. McCormick, commander, Carrier Division 14, Atlantic Fleet. A large number of the officers and men of the *Wasp* also cheered them aboard, me among them. In fact, I stood right next to the well-known CBS news reporter Dallas Townsend.

The most interesting part was the recovery of the spacecraft, a scene I witnessed from just behind the elevator bay of the starboard side hangar deck where the capsule got hoisted aboard. It impressed me how small the capsule was, just a speck in the ocean, really. The colors were vivid with a bright yellow green dye surrounding the capsule looking so striking painted against the azure blue of the open ocean. I was able to see the capsule up close in the hangar deck after it was lifted aboard. It looked more like an oddly shaped brown buoy than a space vehicle. There seemed barely enough room inside for one man let alone two. I was moved by the courage of these two astronauts. It is something I will never forget. The Gemini 4 capsule is now on display at the National Air and Space Museum in Washington, D.C.

On June 9, on our way to U.S. Naval Station Mayport, Florida, to drop off the astronauts, the midshipmen on the *Wasp* challenged the ship's U.S. Marine detachment to a tug of war. The midshipmen easily won the first round. USAF Major and astronaut James McDivitt had been watching the action and volunteered his services to rally the marines for a second try. The midshipmen won again anyway. Major McDivitt then congratulated a good number of us before he was called away. His simple gesture was a real morale builder for all of us.

From Mayport it was a slow ride back to Boston arriving on the 23rd. By the 24th of June I was at the Naval Air Station (NAS) Brunswick Maine and its Fleet Air Wing Five for a week's introduction to naval air patrol. NAS Brunswick flew P-2V Neptunes and P-3A Orions, U.S. Navy long-range anti-submarine warfare, reconnaissance and surveillance aircraft. The P-2V was a twin-engine aircraft with a crew of nine being replaced by the P-3A, a four-engine turboprop carrying a crew of twelve. I had one long patrol flight in a P-2V where we flew far out into the Atlantic to check Soviet ships in the area as well as the identities of other ships. We also conducted anti-submarine warfare (ASW) training exercises including dropping sonobuoys in sub-tracking patterns and then taking the readings. The nose of the P-2V was clear glass. To sit in the nose as the pilot dropped steeply from a several thousand feet to a few hundred feet off the water was like being on the beak of a hawk in a dive after prey!

Another opportunity I recall to this day was to fly on a Grumman S-2 Tracker ASW aircraft off the deck of the *Wasp*. We didn't do anything in particular except fly around the area and then land back on the ship. But two things stayed with me. One was the unique feeling of being catapulted into space off the carrier deck and the second was looking down at the carrier from a few thousand feet up and being amazed at how tiny it seemed in that huge expanse of ocean.

By the 4th of July, Ted, Rick and I were back on the *Wasp* and counting the days until mid–July when the cruise concluded, and we could all go home for summer break.

The 2nd class midshipman cruise took place during the summer of 1966. It was not really a cruise at all as it had almost nothing to do with boats or ships. The navy planned to provide us with an introduction to naval aviation with three weeks at the Naval Air Station in Corpus Christi Texas, followed by exposure to the Marine Corps with three weeks training at the Naval Amphibious Base in Little Creek, Virginia.

By the end of the first week in Corpus Christi with a 14-to-16-hour a day schedule the instructors had us flying airplanes. We flew the T-34, the Navy's two-seat trainer, with the student pilot in the front seat and the instructor in the back seat. Each flight lasted an hour and a half and included everything from simulated engine failure to spins and barrel rolls. By the fourth flight we had to be able to start the aircraft, taxi it to the end of the runway, make a good takeoff and land it safely. Of course the instructor was there for advice and guidance, but basically they had us flying within a week. After that we practiced take offs and landings, stalls, spins, barrel rolls and even Cuban eights, which are something like figure eights in the air. We graduated to the Navy's twin-engine TS-2A, which in its fleet configuration was used for ASW. Because it was a far more complex aircraft than the T-34, students were limited in how much we could actually fly the aircraft. The instructors did most of the flying.

One of our training sessions involved an altitude chamber. We put on oxygen masks and the air pressure within the chamber was lowered to what it would be at 25,000 feet. We were ordered to take off the masks. After about two minutes we started to get dizzy and by two and a half minutes we began to lose some vision. At three minutes we were ordered to put the oxygen masks back on. The instructor explained that if we had left the masks off for five minutes or longer, we would begin to die from hypoxia.

Another "hands-on" demonstration took place with the aircraft ejection seat simulator. The instructor straps you into a mock-up pilot seat attached to two rails that go up about thirty feet in the air. Once you're strapped in the instructor hits the eject button and instantaneously you're at the top of the two rails beginning a slow descent. The force exerted on you is about five Gs over a sixth of a second. If you ejected from an actual jet the G force would be much greater. It was another training experience that stayed with me.

I got selected to go for an hour-long jet training flight. This particular flight was for advanced student pilots and involved two planes. The idea was for the student pilot's plane to pursue an instructor's plane to be in position to shoot down the instructor's plane. The instructor's job was to maneuver in such a way as to make it as difficult as possible for the student's plane to attack him successfully.

I was assigned the front seat of the two-seater jet. My instructor pilot, a captain in the Marine Corps, was to be in the back seat. When I got to the plane the Marine Corps officer looked me up one side and down the other and asked if I was going into the corps or the navy. I said the navy. Big mistake. The next thing the marine asked was if I got airsick. I said no, to which the marine replied, well you will this time. He was right I did get airsick. Any normal human being would have gotten airsick.

The flight was the wildest ride you could possibly imagine. The pilot took us almost straight up pulling G-forces so strong they gave me tunnel vision. Tunnel vision is where your peripheral vision gradually disappears giving you only vision straight ahead. The feeling is similar to passing out. Your vision narrows so that it seems as though you are looking at things from the end of a darkened tunnel. Another unpleasant reaction that occurs when climbing at a very high rate of speed is that the sweat from the top of your head pours down in sheets, not unlike standing in a shower.

After climbing near vertically we then dropped almost straight down. The rest of the hour brought flying upside down at low altitude, screeching to a halt (a jet fighter can be made to decelerate so fast it feels practically like you're hitting a brick wall), stomach churning high-speed barrel rolls, and much more—anything and everything a jet fighter can do without coming apart. After all that we never did get in position to "fire" on the plane we were chasing. I had never been much interested in choosing naval aviation in the first place, and this ride did nothing to change my mind.

Another Corpus Christi event was qualifying as a "swimmer" meaning you had to pass a swim test or face remedial classes. As I recall it, you began by jumping from a height into the deep end of the pool, then had to swim 50 yards non-stop using any stroke, then float for 5 minutes face down pivoting at the neck to inhale through your mouth, and finally, while floating take off and inflate your trousers to create a makeshift flotation device good enough to keep you afloat. Basically, the test was to ensure a man could stay afloat and survive in open water long enough to be rescued if he fell overboard. I passed, but it wasn't easy.

The instructors had to compile a ratings list of the 120 or so midshipmen at Corpus Christi, with each man to be assigned a number from 1 to 120 for his three-week performance. Everyone considered it essential to do well, and so I too looked for ways to try to excel. Part of the training was an obstacle course, which, while it wasn't especially difficult, was demanding enough in the bright sun, high humidity and over 100-degree Fahrenheit temperatures typical in South Texas in the summertime. This was before anyone worried about heat exhaustion other than to maybe pop salt pills, which, without water, did more harm than good. No quarter was given for the excessive heat and humidity; it was all part of the training regimen to weed out the weak and those without at least a modicum of grit. Thinking back, it's a wonder there weren't cases of heat exhaustion if not heat stroke.

At the end of the three weeks the midshipmen, who were divided up into companies, competed against one another in the obstacle course to see which was the best company. All individuals were timed, and the lowest composite time determined the winning company. I completed the course in excellent time and then volunteered to run the approximately two miles back to the barracks to relieve the watch stander there so he could compete as well. Thanks to my extra effort the watch stander, who happened to be the best athlete in the company, made it to the obstacle course in time helping to ensure their company's overall high ranking. The only problem with my "heroics" was that I came very close to heat exhaustion. My genetic make-up rebelled against running an obstacle course at three in the afternoon followed by a two-mile run under those harsh South Texas conditions. I had to lie down on my top bunk in my non-air-conditioned barracks for almost an hour before recovering.

We finished up our three weeks of training just before the 4th of July weekend and then decided to take a couple of days to see what Mexico was all about. On Tuesday, July 5, I wrote the following in a letter to Elaine about the 4th of July weekend I spent with a group of midshipmen visiting the Mexican border town of Reynosa:

> Did you get my card from old Mexico? Somehow I doubt you will. I really don't know where to start. What would you like to hear about first, bullfights, "Boys Town," the grossest floorshows in existence, extreme

poverty, or great Mexican food and drink? I might as well start at the beginning.

On Friday we finished up at 7:30 p.m. with sunset parade. Everyone was in formation on the parade ground in dress whites, there was a flyover by some T-34s, and two admirals made speeches before the show was over.

As soon as we were dismissed we ran back to the barracks, changed into our civis, and piled into a couple of rental cars. The border town of Reynosa is about 180 miles from Corpus so we didn't get to the American side of the border until 2 a.m. After renting a couple of motel rooms we decided to cross the border and visit Reynosa just to see what the near legend of a border town looked like.

It was like going into a different world. We had to pay ten cents each to cross over this narrow, rickety steel bridge across the Rio Grande into Mexico. That was the extent of formalities, no showing IDs or anything else. Even in the dark we could see how totally poverty stricken the place was. The stench was more than noticeable, the buildings for the most part in disrepair, and the air thick with dust from the unpaved streets and God knows what else. We had seen enough in the first five minutes to know we'd better return across the border and come back in the daylight.

The customs checks for getting back into the U.S. were about the same as getting into Mexico: nonexistent. On leaving we each had to pay one cent instead of ten cents, but that was the only difference.

On Saturday morning we parked the cars on the American side because we had learned from the desk clerk that if you're ever in an accident in Mexico all is lost unless you have Mexican insurance. The town looked worse in the daylight than in the dark. We found one decent looking restaurant that seemed okay so we stopped in to try a margarita and ended up having a few. After the drinks we went to see what "Boys Town" looked like. We had heard so much about Boys Town from the local guys in Corpus Christi that our curiosity was killing us. Basically it is the town's red light district with lots of bars where whores can be bought for fees of from $1 to $7.

Like most places in Reynosa, the streets in Boys Town are unpaved. They're nothing but mud or dust. Shack after shack lined the streets inhabited by a single woman apparently anywhere from thirty to forty years old. They usually sat in the doorways yelling vulgar offers in broken English to join them. One old woman came running up to a hole in the wall of her shed, which served as something of a window, and made every obscene gesture in the books trying to entice us to come and play. Enough was enough so we decided to go back to the U.S. side and maybe come back to the town that night to see what life was like then.

We were back in Reynosa by about 7 p.m. and ate dinner at "Sam's Restaurant and Bar," the place where we had the margaritas earlier. We were there for almost three hours drinking, singing, and eating. The food was great! We had venison, some kind of fish, dove, partridge, and every kind of Mexican food imaginable. My total bill was $3.

31

From Vietnam to the Arctic Circle

After dinner we were ready for more and so we decided to take in a floor-show or two in Boys Town. The first "floorshow" I am at a loss to describe to you. After a couple of beers and a few of the "acts," we decided to move on and try another seemingly more conventional place. The second place had a mixed audience of about 100 people so we thought it might be a little less in your face. Wrong. They enticed some drunken cowboy to get up on the "stage" so some poor female could engage him in every act imaginable. The crowd cheered along. Meanwhile lots of young women, some of them barely 18 years old, mingled in the audience trying to seduce any customer who looked at them. We all just sort of marveled at what was going on before deciding it was time to wander back to the good old U.S. of A.

Elaine you wouldn't believe how poor, dirty and pitiful so many of these people are. Legions of filthy little kids barely dressed run around in the streets trying to sell you sticks of gum, and old men on every corner offer to introduce you to their "sister," or sell you dirty pictures, or "aphrodisiacs," or all three.

Sunday we went to the bullfight. It cost $1.60 for a pretty decent seat. I don't think I've seen anything so gory. There were some pretty wretched looking matadors who, by the time they killed a bull, had turned the poor creature into walking hamburger. It's really too much to describe to you in a letter. We watched four bulls get killed this way before once again deciding enough was enough. All of us were very happy to be returning to the other side of the border with no plans to return any time soon.

On the 6th of July the navy had to ship all the midshipmen from Corpus to Little Creek, and the only economical way to do that was by plane. The planes of choice were C-47s (civilian DC-3s) with a passenger capacity of around 25 men. The day before we were to fly out of Corpus the plane assignments were posted on the barrack's bulletin board. Much to the dismay of most of the guys they discovered their classmates were divided up among all the planes. We asked the lieutenant in charge if we couldn't switch planes so we could make the long flight with our buddies. The answer was no and the reason was that a plane had crashed a few years back killing all onboard and all were from the same NROTC unit. Since then, the navy has had a standing order not to allow everyone from one unit on one flight.

Much of our time at Little Creek was spent learning how to be a "grunt." It had nothing to do with pigs or hogs; a grunt was a low-ranking marine infantryman or foot soldier. The days were filled with close order drill, long marches, loud and in-your-face sergeants, taking apart your M-1 rifle and putting it back together again, backpack packing, inspections and preparing for inspections. Some weapons firing, amphibious tactics, and learning how to storm a beach were also covered.

3. Midshipman Tough

For me, the Marine Corps experience in Little Creek proved somewhat less interesting if not a little more painful than flight training in Corpus. I was still a good football player despite giving it up in college after being stabbed. And so, in Little Creek I sometimes played in a local pick-up game in the evening after all the drills. One evening I fell the wrong way on my left wrist and broke it. I tried to ignore the pain hoping it was just a bad sprain but by that night it had swollen up and was causing me significant pain. At the dispensary the doctors gave me some pain pills, put me in a plaster cast and told me my "Marine Corps" days were over for the time being. I was forced to watch as the other midshipmen performed their landing on the beach from troop transports just off the coast, the exercise a culmination of our training.

One activity I could participate in was the evening dress ball given for the 650 midshipmen and comparable number of single young ladies from the Tidewater area. In the beautiful summer evening light, it was quite a show. There was even a complete orchestra. The midshipmen came to the affair in their dress whites while the girls wore mostly colorful strapless evening gowns. By this time the guys had done nothing but hard physical training for the past six weeks and the chance to associate with beautiful young girls in inviting dresses in a soft evening light came as quite a change. An abundance of male and female chaperones saw to it that everyone behaved like ladies and gentlemen.

In the summer of 1967, my first class cruise was six weeks aboard the USS *Corry* (DD-817) home ported in Norfolk, Virginia. It proved basically uneventful, but it was the celestial navigation class that preceded it in the second semester of my junior year that almost proved my undoing. For those of you unfamiliar with celestial navigation, it is the science (and art) of using celestial bodies such as the sun, the moon, the planets and the stars to determine your ship's position at sea. The algebra, calculus, geometry, trigonometry and physics involved can make calculations complicated. If math is not your strong suit, the course is tough sledding.

At Brown's NROTC unit, the final exam in the course carried the most weight, and so it was imperative to do well. If you failed the final, the chances were good you'd fail the course and out you would go. The instructor did his students no favors by creating a very difficult final. Of course, I did the best I could but came away worried, convinced I would need a lot of both good luck and good will on the part of the instructor to survive with a passing grade.

However, when the instructor posted everyone's grades for the course it came with the explanation that the first question on the final exam had contained an error, making it impossible to calculate the correct answer. Because the rest of the test was predicated on getting the first question correct, all the test results had to be thrown out and the course work for the semester accepted as the final grade. So, through great good fortune, I passed the course! Had the instructor not screwed up the final exam I'm fairly certain I would have come close to failing and maybe even losing my scholarship.

4

Catastrophes of 1968

Elaine's and my junior year in college was not one of the less stressful. Elaine and I had been close for some time constantly looking for opportunities to see one another. With little or no spending money, travel back and forth between Providence, Rhode Island, and the State University of New York at Oswego had to be done on the cheap. Once in a while I could ride with one of my Delta Phi Omega fraternity brothers, Skip Falbo or Doug Blatz, who also had girlfriends at Oswego, and once in a while I would take the Greyhound bus, but most often I hitchhiked. Regardless of the mode of travel, door-to-door, it took about ten hours, and for a weekend visit that didn't leave us much time. Of course, we always thought it well worth the effort. Getting older makes you forget the magic of being young and the great efforts young people will make for but a few minutes with one another.

Today, few would hitchhike anywhere for any reason, but back then it wasn't that unusual. Most of the time I could do it with no more than about three to four different hitches, with most of the rides coming just outside the major highway entrances. In the mid-winter it could get cold. I vividly remember freezing nearly to death standing for a long time in a light snow and strong wind in the middle of the Massachusetts Turnpike. I hadn't taken the time to dress for the cold weather and that proved a big mistake. Finally, some truck driver spotted me, took pity and picked me up. In hindsight I'm sure other drivers thought I must have been truly nuts doing what I was doing and didn't want to take a chance picking me up.

The ride I most remember was with a young guy just back from Vietnam driving a canary yellow 1967 Camaro Super Sport with a huge engine that could generate well over 400 horsepower. Today, people forget that GM brought out the first Camaro in the 1967 model year to try to take market share from Ford and its super-successful Mustang, the pony car they had introduced in 1964. In any case, the guy who was no more than a couple of years older than me picked me up. He wanted to talk to someone about his experiences in Vietnam.

From Vietnam to the Arctic Circle

Several times he floored his Camaro, reaching speeds of well over 100 mph. He explained he bought the car with all the money he had saved from his 13-month tour of duty. He had picked it up as soon as he got back and since then had spent all his time just driving. He was having trouble adjusting to being back home. He could not leave the war behind. Driving the muscle car fast seemed to help. I don't believe many people knew much about post-traumatic stress disorder (PTSD) back then, including me, but certainly this poor vet suffered from it.

People driving alone were always the ones to pick me up. I'm sure it was for the companionship. One truck driver told me that the reason he picks up hitchhikers like me is because he feels as though he can talk freely. He feels free to say virtually anything he wants without having to worry about ever seeing or hearing from the hitchhiker again. The trucker didn't offer anything particularly odd or alarming, he just rambled on at length about his family and friends and life's troubles. In fact, in all my hitchhiking adventures I never experienced a problem of any sort with anyone; most went out of their way to be helpful.

By Elaine's and my senior year in college (1967–1968) the country seemed on the verge of a nervous breakdown. The war in Vietnam had become an issue of great importance and there were other major problems.

On January 23, 1968, North Korea captured the USS *Pueblo* (AGER-2) in international waters killing one U.S. sailor and holding captive the remainder of the crew. I was driving with friends to see Elaine at Oswego when I heard the news on the radio. At the time I wondered, as did many others, how it could be that the U.S. could allow this to happen and not retaliate, and then thinking retaliation must be in the planning stages.

In the coming days the North's refusal to return the ship, combined with its sickening abuse and torture of the ship's crew, created a major international crisis including worsening tensions with the Soviet Union and China. The crisis also demoralized and angered many Americans—I was among them—who saw the U.S. as impotent in the face of a military threat from a tiny nation. For those who cared deeply about U.S. leadership in the world, it was also infuriating. Finally, after eleven months of mistreatment, the North allowed the crew to leave. To this day, the USS *Pueblo* is moored on the Pothong River as an exhibit in Pyongyang's Victorious War Museum.

On January 30, the Viet Cong (VC) and the North Vietnamese launched the Tet Offensive, their biggest attack of the war against the

South Vietnamese and their allies including the U.S. The Battle of Hue lasted more than a month resulting in the destruction of the city and loss of thousands of lives. The famous Battle of Khe Sanh was another significant bloodbath.

While the Tet Offensive was considered a military loss for the North and the VC, it also shocked the American public into reconsidering support for the war. News media photos and TV footage of the Tet battles flooded American homes with graphic photos of men, women and children being wounded, maimed and killed. Periodicals carried the portraits of hundreds of young American soldiers who had been killed, the text of the articles driving home that such men were continuing to die in ever growing numbers.

The Tet Offensive resulted in a significant loss of confidence on the part of the American public that the war could even be won. It was Tet that caused the respected CBS News anchor Walter Cronkite to pronounce the war as "mired in stalemate," causing President Lyndon B. Johnson reportedly to say that if he'd lost Cronkite, he'd lost Middle America.

The final words of Cronkite's prescient statement on the war came on his evening news program of February 27, 1968:

> For it seems now more certain than ever that the bloody experience of Vietnam is to end in a stalemate. To say that we are closer to victory today is to believe, in the face of the evidence, the optimists who have been wrong in the past.
>
> To say that we are mired in stalemate seems the only realistic if unsatisfactory conclusion. On the off chance that military and political analysts are right, in the next few months we must test the enemy's intentions, in case this is indeed his last big gasp before negotiations.
>
> But it is increasingly clear to this reporter that the only rational way out then will be to negotiate, not as victors, but as an honorable people who lived up to their pledge to defend democracy, and did the best they could.
>
> This is Walter Cronkite. Good night.

In February 1968, U.S. Defense Secretary Robert McNamara left the Pentagon, replaced by Clark M. Clifford. It was McNamara who, on June 17, 1967, created the Vietnam Study Task Force the purpose of which was to write the complete history of U.S. involvement in the war in Vietnam from 1945 to 1967. He kept the existence of the study secret from President Johnson, then Secretary of State Dean Rusk and National Security Advisor Walt Whitman Rostow. On June 13, 1971, the *New York Times* began publishing that study. It came to be known as the

Pentagon Papers, revealing the duplicitous, shocking behavior of many of the most senior U.S. Government officials from the Truman through the Johnson administrations that had kept the U.S. involved in the Vietnam War.

In early March, in response to the Tet Offensive, General William Westmoreland, the commander of the U.S. Military Assistance Command in Vietnam, called for increasing U.S. troop presence in South Vietnam by more than 200,000 men. His shocking request helped fuel a rapidly growing anti-war, anti-draft and anti-military movement on college campuses and elsewhere. Even many of President Lyndon Johnson's closest advisors began to doubt the wisdom of further escalation. Finally, the Tet Offensive helped to convince President Lyndon Johnson he did not have the public support to run for reelection in 1968. On March 31, President Johnson stunned the world with the announcement at the conclusion of a nationally televised speech about the war that he would not be a candidate for re-election. I recall watching the speech on TV and being greatly surprised by Johnson's announcement. It reinforced in my mind that the war effort was beginning to unravel.

I thought the pictures of the war shown in magazines, newspapers and the evening news channels were horrible. To this day I can vividly recall a *Life Magazine* photograph of the face of an innocent young soldier near death as he was being transported from the battlefield. No one, not even the war hawks, could look at such photos and not be "against war" if not "against the war." With those haunting images as a backdrop, no one could listen to senior U.S. military men or politicians argue for a larger effort without a growing concern for where it would all end. Those who were of draft age, and those with a son or a brother or a boyfriend who could be drafted, became more than quietly concerned, they began to protest loudly.

By 1968 friends in college and in my Long Island hometown of Sayville, New York, were talking not about ball scores, girls or jobs, but how to avoid being drafted, or which service to join to avoid serving in Vietnam, or even leaving the country. Not everyone wanted to escape serving. Plenty of young men signed up willingly and spoke with disdain for those who actively encouraged others to oppose the government, the military and the war. It was impossible not to feel sympathy for close friends who were in anguish over what path to choose.

Some felt as William Shakespeare wrote hundreds of years ago in the St. Crispin's Day speech in *Henry V*:

4. Catastrophes of 1968

That he which hath no stomach to this fight,
Let him depart; his passport shall be made
And crowns for convoy put into his purse:
We would not die in that man's company
That fears his fellowship to die with us.

Most of Elaine's and my friends supported their country and the American military, but they could also see the futility of the war effort. Some believed they were just not physically or mentally up to slugging it out for a year with a vicious enemy in the distant jungles of Vietnam. Others found little to no support for joining the military among immediate family members or close friends.

There existed numerous, easy to understand reasons why young men did not want to join the U.S. military of the late 1960s, but at the time many of these same young men were greatly conflicted with the thought of trying to avoid serving. In choosing to actively avoid military service, they had to pay the price of shame, to themselves, their family and friends. If they chose to opt out with a faux injury or condition, or by fleeing to another country, they would have to live with the dishonor of that decision for the rest of their lives. A *1975 Macrohistory and World Timeline* article said that an August 4, 1972, Gallup poll found that 60 percent of the voting-age public opposed an unconditional amnesty for men who evaded the draft by leaving the country. To this day, former President Donald Trump occasionally hears derogatory comments about his bone spurs and Senator Richard Blumenthal (D-CT) about his claim to have served with the Marines in Vietnam when he did not. However, today there seems to be a shift in the collective mentality about serving in the military during the Vietnam War. Because many now see the war as a huge mistake, they are more ready to excuse those who actively avoided serving.

According to a May 28, 2019, article in SFGATE on the complicated legacy of Vietnam, presidential historian Douglas Brinkley said the Vietnam War carries an emotional wallop more than four decades later. "Vietnam is still with us," Brinkley said. "It was a defining, seminal moment, and older voters especially are curious about whether you were a hawk or a dove, or how you dealt with Vietnam when our country was divided."

Today we hear how polarized the country is, but during the late '60s and early '70s, it was worse. I will describe some of that divisiveness from a personal perspective later in this book.

On April 4, James Earl Ray shot and killed the Rev. Dr. Martin

Luther King, Jr. In the days following the shooting most American cities with significant black populations experienced violent protests. City blocks burned, inner cities suffered looting and physical violence. Many citizens were killed or injured with authorities arresting thousands.

The assassination also caused further radicalization of some who even before the incident had been moving away from King's path of non-violence. For some the murder prompted a move to become more vocal and more politically active in attempts to overcome the hatred and violence in many places in the country. Perhaps most importantly, the assassination drove a giant wedge into race relations making the everyday lives of both blacks and whites more difficult in the years that followed.

Two months after the King assassination the nation was rocked yet again by violence against a major political figure. On June 5, a Palestinian with Jordanian citizenship, Sirhan Sirhan, shot President John F. Kennedy's younger brother, U.S. Senator Robert F. Kennedy, in Los Angeles. Sirhan's motivation was Kennedy's support for Israel and the Jewish people.

In the weeks prior to his assassination Kennedy had been gaining in popularity and looked to be on track to eventually win the Democratic Party's nomination for the presidency. Kennedy had the "it" factor as the handsome younger brother of JFK, and he was beginning to ride the wave of increasing anti-war protest. With Robert Kennedy's death, Hubert Humphrey gained the Democratic nomination, losing to Richard M. Nixon in the 1968 general election. It is entirely possible that had Kennedy lived he would have gotten the nomination and then with his anti-war stance and Kennedy charisma, beaten Nixon in November.

5

Graduate, Marry
and Join the Fleet

A few days after graduation in late spring of 1968 and a few weeks before having to report for duty in San Diego, I finally proposed to Elaine. Among my shortcomings is an inability to display much of a romantic nature, so my proposal to Elaine might be described as being in character. Nevertheless, to this day I'm somewhat embarrassed when she reminds me how I blurted out, "Will you marry me?" in a small parking lot behind Frances' Sweet Shop in our hometown of Sayville, New York. Fortunately, Elaine, unperturbed by my blunt approach, overlooked the total absence of a romantic venue, and said yes, she would.

We agreed the wedding should take place before I was to leave for my first Navy assignment in San Diego on July 6. So that meant there was just a little over three weeks to make all the arrangements. It also meant Elaine had to back out of a teaching position with Sayville schools leaving her essentially unemployed and with a big student debt. The superintendent of Sayville schools, Dr. Harry B. Spencer, registered dismay at her rejection of his offer for her to teach at the brand-new Sunrise Drive School.

Somehow, within the very brief three-week window of time from my proposal to our departure for San Diego, we arranged a complete wedding with all the traditional parties, fanfare and celebration. My step-grandfather and longtime minister of the beautiful and historic St. Ann's Church in Sayville, the Rev. Joseph Bond, officiated. The ceremony took place on July 5, 1968, with the bride and groom departing via New York City for San Diego that same evening.

Elaine's mother, Ingrid (her father Frank had died of cancer three years before) and my parents, Betty and John, all knew the demands of the military. Ingrid had waited for two and a half years for Frank who had served as a combat medic in North Africa, Italy, France and Germany during World War II. He won the Bronze Star and also the Purple

Heart for almost having his left leg blown off in the September 9, 1943, Allied assault on the beaches at Salerno, Italy. Betty had waited for my father for eighteen months while he served as a pilot on an escort carrier (CVE-94) in some of the biggest battles in the Western Pacific. John had also endured the trauma of losing his younger brother Gilbert ("Bud") in a Naval air training accident. At the conclusion of the war John's ship was awarded the highly prestigious Presidential Unit Citation.

Indeed, the parents understood the prospects for some trying times for their still naïve 21-year-old children. But for my parents with four younger children to raise and Elaine's mother with two kids to bring up on her own, there wasn't much time for elaborate farewells or follow-up parental guidance. As my father said in his usual succinct fashion, "You're twenty-one, out of school, and so now you're on your own. Good luck." It really wasn't meant to be as dismissive as it might sound. When my father graduated from high school at age eighteen, the director of St. Ann's orphanage in Sayville where he grew up told him bluntly—as she had his brother Hank and other orphans before him—it was time for him to leave and fend for himself.

Before I reported for duty at San Diego's 32nd Street Naval Station, we found a studio walk-up apartment in the Seton Arms, an old downtown building located on the corner of 10th Avenue and "C" Street. We had one window overlooking a busy intersection and a brightly lit all-night gas station. What sold the place was that it came complete with an old Murphy bed, perfect for newlyweds with no furniture. For transportation we purchased a used four-door white Ford Galaxie 500.

After a couple of Navy courses in the San Diego area, I reported aboard the USS *Buck* (DD-761), an aging *Sumner* class, Fram II (Fleet Rehabilitation and Modernization Program) destroyer, dry-docked at the Hunter's Point Naval Shipyard in San Francisco. The ship was named for United States Navy Civil War Medal of Honor winner James Buck. Buck served as a quartermaster on board the USS *Brooklyn* during the 24 and 25 April 1862 attack on Forts Jackson and St. Philip in the Union's successful battle to take New Orleans from the Confederacy. He was cited for remaining at his post for many long hours despite being severely wounded.

Workers at Bethlehem Steel in San Francisco put down the *Buck*'s keel on February 1, 1944; she was launched on March 11, 1945—sponsored by Miss Mary Nimitz, daughter of the famous Fleet Admiral Chester W. Nimitz—and she was commissioned on June 28, 1946. Thus, she was not a new ship and needed shipyard overhauls and a lot

The author on 10th street in downtown San Diego, leaning proudly against his biggest purchase ever—a 1966, 4-door Ford Galaxie 500. It was a lemon with all kinds of problems. Elaine replaced it a year later with a brand new, standard shift, Hula Blue Ford Maverick (courtesy Elaine Kiesling Whitehouse).

of maintenance to keep her going. But in 1968, the 376–foot long, 36 knot ship with six 5-inch/38 guns, six torpedo tubes and an assortment of other weaponry including the Drone Anti-Submarine Helicopter (DASH) armed with two torpedoes was still a powerhouse. She

A model of the destroyer USS *Buck*. Weapons systems included the Mark 37 gunfire control system on the signal deck, just behind the bridge, that controlled the three, twin 5-inch/38 caliber gun mounts, and the AN/SPS-40 long range air search radar located near the top of the mast. In addition, the ship carried 50 caliber machine guns and a variety of small arms. Anti-submarine weapons included the SQS-23 sonar—the sonar dome is attached to the hull underneath the forward gun mount—two anti-submarine Hedgehog launchers mounted port and starboard immediately behind the second gun mount, and two Mark 32 torpedo tubes with three launchers each, mounted port and starboard amidships. The torpedo storage room and DASH hangar stand behind the second stack. The flight deck shows the DASH, capable of dropping two MK 44 torpedoes. The Variable Depth Sonar is mounted on the stern. A portable electronic intelligence box sits between the torpedo tubes (courtesy Elaine Kiesling Whitehouse).

could play a number of important roles in the still intensifying war in Vietnam.

The Captain of the *Buck* was Commander Paul J. Mode, a stickler for detail, a tough taskmaster and some might even go so far as to say a tyrant. His fiercest critics described his management style as an amalgam of James Cagney in *Mister Roberts*, Captain Ahab in *Moby Dick* with maybe a little Humphrey Bogart in *The Caine Mutiny* thrown in. Those more appreciative of his style would say he never failed to get results, his ship performed remarkably well on all of its assigned missions, and none of his men ever suffered any personal injury that might have been prevented through more attentive management.

Six months before I reported aboard, Mode had taken command from Commander Emil Roth on January 27, 1968, in Sasebo, Japan. Roth's departure followed the *Buck*'s October 2, 1967, collision with the USS *Hassayampa* (AO-145) during an attempted refueling. While alongside the *Hassayampa* the *Buck* experienced a steering problem causing her to collide with the much larger ship. Lt. (j.g.) Bob Martin, who had been in charge of the mid-ships refueling station at the time of the collision, told me the *Buck* had to execute an emergency breakaway. The procedure entailed immediately severing all lines connecting the two ships. Bob said the two ships crashed together three times before permanently separating.

Refueling, or replenishment, is one of the more dangerous tasks a ship can undertake. Being alongside another ship at 12 to 15 knots at only about 100 feet apart requires both ships to precisely maintain their course and speed. The conning officer must constantly focus on maintaining precisely the same heading as the refueling ship and at precisely the same speed. Even a slight steering error on the part of one of the ships can quickly lead to a collision. Bernoulli's theorem explains that when two ships are moving in very close proximity, a decrease in static pressure in the water between them results, while pressure on the outer side of the ships remains higher. This pressure differential can drive the ships together.

The collision resulted in the DASH controller's platform being pushed up about 20 degrees, some lifeline stanchions being bent and a number of relatively minor scrapes and dents. However, the impact also drove the *Buck*'s port anchor through the side of the ship into the chiefs' quarters. Bob said the damage could have been worse, and fortunately no one was injured, but the ship was out of commission for about three weeks.

Bob commented that as far as he knows, the actual cause of the steering problem was never fully explained. Initially some said there might have been a mechanical failure, or possibly some error by the helmsman, or even a ship handling error by the conning officer. Bob recalls that it was Captain Roth who had the conn at the time of the collision. Commander Mode replaced Captain Roth approximately 17 weeks after the accident.

* * *

The *Buck* was almost ready to return to her homeport of San Diego when I reported aboard in September of 1968. Lt. (j.g.) Richard Armitage, later to become the Deputy Secretary of State in 2001 under President George Bush, was the Officer of the Deck when I walked up the gangway for the first time and saluted the flag.

Armitage was the ship's damage control assistant (DCA). A 1967 U.S. Naval Academy graduate, he was a barrel-chested man with a raspy voice and a quick smile. He was personable with everyone and generally well-liked by his men and his fellow officers. He left not long after I reported aboard for an assignment in-country in Vietnam.

On the *Buck,* Armitage worked for the Chief Engineer, a Bostonian native and feisty Irishman named Joe Mulkerin. Joe took his work very seriously but could have a good time when encouraged. I recall one Saturday night ashore in Hawaii Joe and I decided we could hula dance better than most. After a remarkable display of flexibility and numbness to pain, we ended up winning the evening's big hula-dancing contest at the main officers' club in Pearl—the Hickam Air Force Base Officers' Club. Fellow officers claimed the club's large, very popular, and can't-be-duplicated-anywhere Mai Tais played a significant role in bringing home the trophy. The Mai Tais came in large tumblers and featured two flavors of rum in generous quantity combined with the juice of fresh pineapples, a pineapple slice and orange slice topped with a maraschino cherry. We learned they could be delicious any time of day.

In 1968 there was a quaint Navy custom—perhaps there still is— that called for the captain of a ship and his wife to make a social call at the home of all the new junior officers. Leaving a calling card on a table by the front door was a part of the formalities. So, one Saturday afternoon a month or so after I joined the ship Captain Mode and his wife Claire called on us at our tiny one bedroom furnished apartment in Chula Vista. We had moved from the downtown San Diego "C" Street walk-up only a month or so before. The only "furniture" we owned at the time was a portable record player I had received for my birthday some years before. Both of the Modes proved very pleasant and sociable, he surprisingly so given his comportment aboard ship. His wife was a lovely, intelligent person who went out of her way to help the younger wives of which Elaine was one. The whole idea of such a visit today seems like an event more appropriate to 1919 than 1969. But, as anyone who has served in the Navy knows, tradition is, and surely always has been, an important part of Navy life. It contributes greatly to camaraderie, pride in belonging to a venerable American institution, and is an integral part of what makes the Navy as successful a fighting force as it is.

6

Classmates Lost

In the late summer of 1968, immediately prior to reporting aboard, I was sent on temporary duty (TDY) to attend the ten-week long Drone Anti-Submarine Helicopter (DASH) School on San Clemente Island off the coast of Southern California. At DASH school I met fellow Ensign John Norton who was assigned to a destroyer nearly identical to the *Buck*. John had recently graduated from college, at about the same time I had from Brown. We enjoyed comparing stories of student activism on our respective campuses and whose campus had the most effective anti-military rallies. John had a majored in geology and wanted to go back to school to get an advanced degree after completing his years in the service. Tall, slim and handsome, John had a quick smile and a warm, quiet but outgoing personality. He made friends quickly and easily. Something about him radiated honesty and integrity; you knew immediately he was a man you could trust. Elaine and I saw a lot of John. In a matter of months, the three of us became best friends, as though we had known each other all our lives. John's ship deployed to WESTPAC only a few weeks or so before the *Buck*'s April 1969 deployment. Little did we know then that something dreadful was lurking in our future.

On November 11, the *Buck* began Refresher Training (Reftra) with Fleet Training Group, San Diego. Reftra is one of the most tortuous exercises the navy ever devised. The ship's crew spends six weeks on endless drills closely observed and critiqued by the training staff, exercises designed to prepare for every action the ship may be expected to undertake. All facets of the ship's capabilities—from precision anchoring to shore bombardment to the prosecution of sonar contacts to refueling—must be done to the trainers' satisfaction. Days begin as early as 0430 and end as late as 2230. It is a physically and mentally exhausting process. Finally on December 20, the ship satisfactorily completed Reftra and we could enjoy some down time in port in San Diego.

From mid–January 1969 through March the *Buck* took part in a variety of at-sea exercises from 1st Fleet training ops such as acting as an ASW school ship to taking part in exercises with names only the military could dream up such as COMPTVEX9–69, Operation Gold One and Operation Bell Jangle in the waters around San Diego.

*　*　*

In late March 1969 Elaine and I learned of the death in South Vietnam of our high school classmate, 22-year-old Warrant Officer Willard Spencer Lund (Spencer), an AH-1G Cobra helicopter gunship pilot with the B Troop, 3rd Squadron, 17th Cavalry Division of the 1st Aviation Brigade.

The 3rd Squadron, 17th Cavalry Regiment had arrived in Vietnam on 30 October 1967 and was assigned to the 12th Aviation Group, 1st Aviation Brigade, primarily stationed at Di An Base Camp, just northeast of Saigon. It was responsible for air cavalry support in the western part of III Corps. The support included attack missions, reconnaissance, air assault, and resupply.

On March 18, 1969, Spencer and his crewman, 1st Lt. Hardy E. Calloway, were seeking enemy targets of opportunity in the Plain of Reeds when they encountered approximately 90 sampans on the Bobo Canal. They engaged the enemy force and called in for infantry support. After expending ordnance and fuel, they withdrew to Tan An to rearm and refuel. Returning to the battle, they attempted to engage the enemy again at which point they encountered enemy fire, suffered a rotor separation, crashed, and caught fire. Both Spencer and 1st Lt. Calloway suffered fatal injuries in the crash. The site of the crash was not far to the northwest of where a few months later the *Buck* would provide thousands of rounds of Naval Gunfire Support.

We remembered Spencer as a quiet man with a penchant for helping others while never asking anything for himself. He had grit, was tough when he needed to be, his excellence as a high school wrestler a testament to both his athleticism and his personality.

In April Elaine and I received a letter from our high school classmate and dear friend Dave Lerner who was serving as a Navy Aviation Ordnanceman 3rd class with attack squadron VA-105. Dave wrote about Spencer's death, the two of them having been close friends. Dave said,

> I have some very sad news. Maybe you've already heard. Spencer Lund was killed in Viet Nam March 18th. Needless to say I'm very sad. Spencer and I were very good friends. We grew up together on Fire Island. What a horrible waste. I hate to think Spencer died in vain, but someone please tell me what are we fighting for?

48

6. Classmates Lost

Spencer was our second high school classmate to die in the war. In July of 1967, 22-year-old Aviation Fire Control Technician Third Class George Daniel Miller ("Danny") was serving with Attack Carrier Air Wing 17, Squadron VF-74 flying F-4B Phantom IIs aboard the USS *Forrestal* (CVA-59). Danny died on July 28, along with 133 other men in explosions and a massive fire. Another 161 men were wounded in the incident.

During mid-morning combat flight operations on Yankee Station an accidental rocket launch from one aircraft on the *Forrestal*'s flight deck hit the aircraft in front of it resulting in explosions and a raging inferno. The fire became particularly well known in subsequent years because of the involvement of Lt. John McCain's fighter jet. Danny was initially declared missing by the Navy. His body was not found until days after the fire was finally extinguished.

Elaine and I both knew Danny as the epitome of someone people would call a "nice guy." He always had a smile or a kind word for everyone. Losing Danny was to lose a good man, a first-class citizen who would have contributed great things to his hometown.

Our Sayville High School class of 1964 would lose more good men before the war was over. The class would also have many who served and who managed to survive, but the war would hurt all of us who served and touch most who did not. As Argentinean author José Naroski wrote, "In war there are no unwounded soldiers."

In the letter to us from Dave Lerner cited above, Dave also said another classmate, Jimmy Mussler, who was co-captain of the high school football team with me, was entering the Navy's Officer Candidate School program in June. I saw him in the summer of 1970 in the Gulf of Tonkin when the *Buck* refueled from the AO on which he was serving.

Elaine and I discussed with local Sayville folks why one high school class with only 168 graduating members contributed so much to such an unpopular war, even suffering four of its best killed in combat. Our discussions might be summed up in words from the 20th-century British writer, poet and philosopher G.K. Chesterton who said:

> A soldier fights not because he hates what is in front of him.... He fights because he loves what he left behind.

Like other Americans in many small towns across the country, the decent, caring people in the Long Island hamlet of Sayville raised children like Spencer and Danny. It is not hackneyed to say that these small-town American men and women provided their children with love, honesty, respect and discipline through family, churches, schools, sports teams and community organizations.

People still love the little town of Sayville today and for the very same reasons. They, too, want their children and grandchildren to love what they someday may have to leave behind.

7

Deployment to Westpac

On Wednesday morning April 16, 1969, the USS *Buck* departed San Diego in the company of the carrier USS *Oriskany* (CVA-34) and the remainder of Destroyer Division (DesDiv) 72, the USS *Wiltsie* (DD-716), the USS *John W. Thomason* (DD-760) and the USS *Perkins* (DD-877), all bound for Pearl Harbor. The deployment was scheduled to last six and a half months.

Saying goodbye and leaving your new bride on the pier is not an easy thing to do. The long separations are one of the toughest aspects of military life. In hindsight, the separation for younger, just married people is probably more difficult than for those with more time together as a couple. I once commented to a married old salt with near-grown children that the Navy must have ruined a lot of marriages to which he replied, "Well, that could be, sir, but it probably saved just as many."

In 1969 aboard ship or even in foreign ports we had virtually no commercial phones or other such means of electronic communication with people in the states. Aboard ship mail could take as long as a week to a month in one direction. So when the men deployed, they were almost completely cut out of the family picture. Family decisions that needed to be made often had to be made without their input. I recall the frustration of reading a letter from Elaine about her moving us to a different, more expensive apartment, one I had never seen, in an area of San Diego with which I was unfamiliar. Similarly, another letter announced she had purchased a new 1969 Hula Blue, standard shift Ford Maverick for $1,995. She hadn't even hinted to me about it beforehand! That came as a real jolt to my male apple cart. In the American culture of today such a purchase by a spouse wouldn't raise an eyebrow, but in the late 1960s men were still expected to have a lot to do with such family decision-making. The worst part was that I had never learned to drive a standard shift and so would now have to take lessons from Elaine in order to drive my own car!

On the other hand, I welcomed Elaine's independence, ability to make decisions and take necessary actions on her own. (The apartment Elaine moved us into with its beautiful Pacific Ocean views proved to be our all time favorite residence—and we had many.) These qualities had brought us together and would help keep us married through long periods of separation. During long deployments many young wives returned home to their parents, some permanently.

Absence may make the heart grow fonder, but it also makes life a lot harder for both partners. Spousal relationships could and often did suffer irreparable harm during long deployments. Young men who received "Dear John" letters from a long-time girlfriend, fiancée or a wife were often caught off guard and usually devastated by the news. It was especially tough knowing there was absolutely nothing they could do about it from the waters of the western Pacific. Tears, perhaps more out of frustration than a broken heart, were not unusual. In the absence of any available religious or mental health counselor it usually fell to the officer for whom a sailor worked to console him and make suggestions about family issues. Just listening probably did more good than any attempted words of wisdom.

A second problem area for a number of the younger sailors—many were still teenagers—was personal finances. For many their Navy paycheck was their first real income and at first it seemed like a fortune. It was easy to overspend on a car or some other big purchase. Then came the letters from the car companies or debt collection agencies; some young sailors were at a loss to know what to do. They needed explanations, reassurance and especially guidance on what options were available to them. A few never seemed to learn and had collection agencies regularly pursuing them.

A third trouble was the availability of drugs. Illegal drugs had not yet become a major societal problem in the U.S., but the scourge had begun to rear its head on campuses and neighborhoods in many places. By 1968–69, a few in the Navy had begun to succumb to the attraction of marijuana, cocaine and other such illegal substances that were often far cheaper and more readily available in some foreign ports than at home. Fortunately, illegal drugs were not at all common aboard the *Buck*, or most ships in the fleet, but neither were they unheard of. When something was discovered, authorities from outside the ship's complement handled the matter promptly removing anyone involved. Shipboard life could be dangerous enough without mixing in drugs.

Transiting the Pacific in company with the *Oriskany* and several other destroyers meant lots of time for inter-ship exercises. It also meant plenty of opportunities to fly the Drone Anti-Submarine Helicopter (DASH). Captain Mode saw to it that we took advantage of every one of them. He loved to fly the QH-50D aircraft. The Squadron Commander, ComDesDiv 72, who was aboard the *Buck* for this leg of the journey also loved to fly the DASH, so we spent a lot of time at flight quarters.

The DASH was a powerful weapon system for use against submarines. It could deliver two MK-44 torpedoes at a distance of more than 20 miles from the ship. Its major shortcoming proved to be reliability. In June 1970 the Navy reported that 746 QH-50C/D drones had been lost. Of that number, more than 80 percent were the result of a single-point

QH-50D DASH carrying a MK-44 practice torpedo (courtesy Peter Papadakos, Project Manager QH-50 DASH Weapon System).

failure of the electronics. Another 10 percent came from engine or airframe failures and 10 percent from pilot error. Two of the destroyers in company with us each lost a drone during the transit, but we were fortunate to experience no accidents or incidents.

Actually, flying the DASH could get a little boring, and so for some variation to the standard takeoff and landing exercises, the DASH crew decided we would test the torpedo release electronics and mechanisms by attaching some reasonably heavy unwanted pieces of junk to the undercarriage. We would then fly the drone out to some prearranged or marked spot on the sea surface and release "torpedoes." Eventually, when we had become proficient, Captain Mode said he wanted to try delivering packages to other ships by flying the drone over the stern of the other ship and releasing some kind of package like old newspapers, books or magazines. If successful, the practice might be considered for exchanging movies or other such things instead of having to pull alongside one another.

After finally finding another available ship willing to let us try our plan, we gave it a shot. We didn't want to come too close to our target ship because of the potential for having a problem—always a possibility with the finicky DASH avionics. The captain emphasized he did not want to have to explain how his DASH caused damage to another ship. That said, we still had to get close enough to be successful. The second destroyer positioned itself about a hundred yards off our starboard quarter as I flew the drone on an approach from behind the other ship. I slowed the forward motion of the drone as we eased over the target, which was the middle of the other destroyer's flight deck.

We found that from almost any distance, judging precisely where the drone was in relation to the target was difficult. After all, a destroyer's flight deck is less than 30 feet wide and at a distance appears quite small. The hard part turned out to be keeping the drone over the precise release point long enough to drop the packages. Lateral ship motion, minor ship speed fluctuations and varying wind speeds and directions meant the DASH moved around quite a bit relative to the target. Even so, we managed to hit a bullseye on one of the two items dropped, much to my happy surprise.

We learned that DASH transfers between ships did not really have an immediate future. It was doable, but it wasn't easy. However, with calm weather and a camera mounted underneath the drone such transfers could be done relatively easily. Today, almost fifty years later, we are beginning to see plans for the extensive use of drones for package delivery.

7. Deployment to Westpac

The idea of a TV camera underneath the drone did not originate aboard the *Buck*. In fact, in 1965 the Navy deployed an observation system called SNOOPY where drones outfitted with video cameras could be used as spotters for shore bombardment and for surveillance missions. With the video a Naval Gunfire Support (NGFS) ship could see in real time where the shells were landing and make range and bearing adjustments as necessary. Generally speaking, the system worked well but was not without problems. The biggest benefit was that it could provide spotting for NGFS without risking human life.

We were unaware of the SNOOPY program until an operator came aboard the *Buck* with videotapes from actual SNOOPY missions and described for us how the system worked. From the videos we could see that the TV camera did not always provide an optimal picture of the target. Factors affecting the presentation could include the forest canopy, less than ideal weather conditions and the camera's resolution. Second, while the drone is difficult to see or hear above a certain altitude, it's not impossible. As a result, the drone was vulnerable to ground fire. Finally, while a DASH was designed to operate at a distance of as much as 22 miles from the ship, we had found that control issues could grow with distance from the ship. I believe most SNOOPY flights over Vietnamese territory ended by 1970.

On April 22 the *Buck* moored to the pier in Pearl Harbor. Of all the harbors I've visited Pearl is one of the most uniquely beautiful with its deep blue sky dotted with billowing white cumulus clouds against the reddish-brown earth and bright green foliage on the hills leading to the azure blue water. For years I promised Elaine I would take her there one day so she could see the beauty of the harbor for herself. I'm still promising.

After only a couple of days we were underway again headed for Subic Bay in the Philippines with the rest of our task group. On April 29, we learned the Secretary of the Navy had nominated the *Buck* as one of three finalists for the 1969 Captain Edward F. Key Memorial Award for excellence in food service. The nomination alone was an outstanding achievement given how many ships were eligible for the award. (In 1969 the Navy had more than 300 surface warfare ships whereas today it's about half that.) Of course, the notification pleased Captain Mode but not that anyone could notice. He much preferred to manage without reward or kind word; in fact, Captain Mode rarely missed an opportunity to display an authoritarian demeanor, seemingly unmoved by an outstanding performance by officer or crewman.

Honor guard on the flight deck of the USS *Buck*, entering Pearl Harbor (author's collection).

Despite his management style, no one saw Captain Mode as mentally unbalanced. But at sea his penchant for firing his Navy issue .45 caliber semi-automatic handgun made everyone a little nervous. He kept it hanging at the ready on the back of his sea cabin door. When something particularly annoying or frustrating occurred, he ran in, grabbed the gun, ran out to the starboard wing of the bridge and rapid fired a full clip into the sea, usually at no particular target. To the best of my knowledge, he never fired off the port side, and no one ever had the courage to ask him why not. There must have been a reason he favored the starboard side—maybe it was simply because his cabin was on the starboard side, and he was in a hurry. But it seemed to help him cope when he got especially stressed. Everyone accepted it as just another one of his idiosyncrasies.

7. Deployment to Westpac

In early May we received orders to break off from our carrier group and steam independently for the naval base United States Fleet Activities Yokosuka located at the southwestern end of Tokyo Bay. Early on the morning of May 7, we arrived just outside the Uraga Channel at the southern third of Tokyo Bay. The approach to the base through this always-busy body of water was a ship and boat traffic nightmare. There were so many blips on the screen that it looked like there was something wrong with our surface search radar.

The greater Tokyo Bay area has played a role in American history since the early 1850s when Commodore Matthew Perry visited, effectively opening Japan to the outside world. In 1879 President Ulysses S. Grant arriving aboard the USS *Richmond* visited Tokyo and nearby Yokohama during his world tour. His visit was a resounding success. Of all the countries he had visited, Grant considered Japan his favorite. At the famous Zojoji Temple in Tokyo he planted a cedar tree that is still growing. The Japanese revere the old tree for all it represents.

Relations between Japan and the U.S. remained stable until the build-up to World War II and the outbreak of war on December 7, 1941. On April 18, 1942, bombs from Lt. Col. James B. Doolittle's famous raid caused minor damage in Yokosuka and elsewhere in the Tokyo area. On September 2, 1945, Tokyo Bay was the location for the signing of the Japanese Instrument of Surrender on the deck of the battleship USS *Missouri* (BB-63). General of the Army Douglas MacArthur led the signing, also attended by Fleet Admiral Chester Nimitz, and many senior military representatives of the Allied Forces. Just before the signing the U.S. Navy took over Yokosuka making good use of the base as its primary naval ship repair facility in the Far East. Yokosuka played a major role in the maintenance and repair of ships assigned to the U.S. Seventh Fleet, first during the Korean War and then the Vietnam War.

Tokyo has been a part of four generations of my family. My father was a pilot aboard the escort carrier USS *Lunga Point* (CVE-94), when it anchored in Tokyo Bay on October 18, 1945. He visited the Imperial Palace, the famous Ginza shopping district or what was left of it, and a lot more, but given the devastation and the suffering of the local population it could hardly be described as seeing the sights. The *Lunga Point* remained in Tokyo Bay for ten days before receiving orders to return to San Diego.

With the *Buck* in Yokosuka, I took the opportunity to visit Tokyo with a couple of other officers from the ship. We saw the rebuilt sites my father had visited 25 years before and also the iconic Tokyo Tower, a 1,092-foot-high structure built in 1958. Thirty-three years after my visit to Tokyo, my son John Henry Whitehouse III, also a United States naval officer, married a Japanese girl, Etsu Kahata. From 2014 to 2018 they lived in downtown Tokyo. Favorite leisure time activities included visiting the Tokyo Tower and the ancient Zojoji Temple with my grandson, Jack, to appreciate the Ulysses S. Grant cedar.

During World War II Etsu's paternal grandfather, Fusao Kahata, served in the Japanese Imperial Army in Manchuria, the huge land area west of the Korean Peninsula. The Japanese had taken over Manchuria in 1932 establishing a puppet state they called Manchukuo. In 1934 the famous Pu Yi, the last emperor of the Qing Dynasty, became "Kangde Emperor" of Manchukuo under the name Datong. He remained in place as "emperor" until the end of World War II with the invasion of Manchuria by Soviet forces.

Etsu's grandfather was still a teenager during his service, but he managed to receive flight training with the Japanese Army Air Force. He was almost certainly part of the Japanese 2nd Air Army headquartered in Hsinking in northern Manchuria. What action he may have seen is unknown, but both families have marveled at the irony of a marriage between the grandchildren of a Japanese Army pilot and an American Navy pilot, World War II mortal enemies.

In September 1945 when Japan surrendered, Etsu's grandfather traveled from Manchuria through Korea back to Japan via Nagasaki on the southernmost Japanese island of Kyushu, eventually traveling north back to his home in Hokkaido. The trip was daunting, the defeated Japanese soldiers being threatened and pelted with rotting food and garbage along the way. He once told my son John that he encountered victims of the Nagasaki atomic bomb explosion in his transit through the Kyushu area. He still had some food rations and gave them to starving Japanese civilians and bomb victims he encountered.

In another ironic twist to the story, John's paternal grandfather probably came within close proximity to Etsu's paternal grandfather in Nagasaki in mid–September 1945. Before arriving in Tokyo in October, the *Lunga Point* stopped in Nagasaki on September 17, 1945—possibly the precise time Etsu's grandfather was there. The atomic bomb had been dropped on the city less than six weeks earlier, on August 9. In mid–September the city was still a scene of total devastation. According to some accounts, bodies were floating in the harbor. The *Lunga Point* did not stay long. On September 19, after taking aboard 760 former American POWs she sailed for Okinawa before returning to Tokyo in October.

On May 10, 1969, after only a few days in Yokosuka, the *Buck* headed southwest into the East China Sea for an 0600 May 12 rendezvous with the USS *Enterprise* (CVAN-65). We were to refuel from the massive carrier. As we approached the *Enterprise,* we were all taken with what an immense and impressive man-o-war she was, carrying on her huge flight deck—more than three football fields in length—enormous firepower in the form of the world's most advanced fighter and bomber aircraft.

After refueling we headed further south and west to rendezvous with the USS *Kitty Hawk* (CVA-63) and her escorts, the *Black* (DD-666), the *Radford* (DD-446), the *Southerland* (DD-743), and the *Knox* (DD-742). We immediately got sent to picket station (a ship sent out a significant distance from the main force to warn of any approaching enemy) about 60 miles from the *Kitty Hawk.*

The next day, May 14, not far from the South Korean coast in the East China Sea, our sonarmen detected an unidentified submarine about 1100 yards off the starboard bow. Almost immediately we received high-level Navy interest in pursuing the contact, and pursue it we did. At 2230 the USS *Dale* (DLG-19) joined us to assist in prosecution of our contact. On the morning of May 15, the *Black* relieved the *Dale* with the *Radford* also assigned to help prosecute the unknown, but assumed to be enemy, sub.

Lt. John Simpson's Weapons Department, especially the antisubmarine warfare (ASW) officer Lt. (j.g.) Skip Leeson and his crew, tracked the sub round the clock for three days. The plotting table in Lt.(j.g.) Joe Johnson's always-darkened Combat Information Center (CIC) was their home away from home. Officers and specialists stared for seemingly endless hours at the plots of the sub's movement anticipating where it might go next. It was literally a cat and mouse game with the sub doing everything it could to ditch its pursuer. Given the level of sophistication of the sonar aboard the *Buck* and the constant attention required to keep track of the sub's movements, the ASW team did a remarkable job. Eventually the sub disappeared into the depths and the hunt came to something of an anti-climactic close.

There is something unique about the emotional and dramatic nature of tracking an enemy submarine. The unseen presence, the pinging sonar, the periods of silence, the long draining hours, the chess-match nature of the pursuit combine to make it an intense experience.

By May 17, the Navy seemed satisfied with the information gathered, and we were ordered to leave the area and move south toward Taiwan. As far as I know we never learned to whom the sub belonged.

8

Driving Ships
and Yankee Station

Early on Monday morning May 19, 1969, the *Buck* began its approach to the harbor in Kaohsiung, Taiwan. The busy port has a very narrow channel entrance and an array of anchor buoys for ships to secure to. Most large ships use a pilot. Maneuvering and securing the almost 376-foot long *Buck* to harbor buoy #21 fore and #22 aft in a small, crowded harbor with a good wind blowing and no bow thruster takes consummate ship handling skill. Captain Mode seemed to welcome the challenge and took the conn himself.

Whenever the ship is underway—meaning not anchored or moored to the pier—to "take the conn" means to have control of the ship's movements. Without getting too detailed, the officer on the bridge with the "conn" tells the helmsman what course to steer. He also tells the lee helmsman, a.k.a. the engine order telegraph operator, the number of revolutions of the ship's propellers, either forward or astern. The Navy is very formal about who has the conn, with a loud vocal announcement made to all on the bridge whenever there is a change in the conning officer. Entry is made in the ship's logbook of the name of the officer and the precise time he took the conn.

The ship handling talent and skills Mode demonstrated in this tight situation impressed both officers and crew. For an officer of the line, ship-handling skills are essential, but not many were as proficient as Mode. Being able to judge the effects of wind and current on the vessel's speed, knowing how and when to adjust the ship's speed and rudder angle for a safe and secure landing, and being able to perform under the close observation of much of the ship's crew are important skills. Sailors respect and put increased trust in a commanding officer proficient in ship handling. They take pride in seeing their ship handled well and gain reassurance in the commanding officer's competence and experience. This reassurance positively influences officers and crew in the performance of their own underway duties. They make better decisions knowing they have capable leadership backing them up.

Yet, at least in my day, no midshipman training course covered anything but the basics of how to handle a ship mooring or unmooring from a pier or buoy. No training activities were conducted in this vital performance area. Most officers got their first experience in the fleet watching more senior officers perform, and then eventually being allowed to try it themselves, under close supervision of course. Some officers proved so incompetent at maneuvering a ship alongside a pier that they could never master it. This was sometimes a problem for their long-term career advancement.

I recall one incident where we were moored alongside another destroyer. After swinging the stern out to starboard the conning officer failed to account for our port bow being too close in and forward of the starboard bow of the other destroyer. Putting both engines in reverse, the ship quickly picked up considerable speed as it slid backward past the other destroyer. Suddenly we felt a small jolt and heard a loud, sharp, cracking sound. Everyone's reaction was the same—what the hell was that?

A quick look off the port side of the foc'sle revealed that the crown of our port anchor apparently had caught the other destroyer's starboard anchor. Our anchor crown had been completely broken off. A *Sumner* class destroyer's anchor is a piece of steel weighing approximately 4,000 pounds. The force required to break off the top of it must have been considerable.

With massive forces at play, mooring and unmooring a big ship presents situations fraught with potential danger to humans as well as equipment. Navy mooring lines, usually braided nylon about 3" in diameter, were remarkably strong and could stretch a good deal, but they could snap under excessive pressure. A snapped mooring line behaves a lot like a snapped rubber band. The breakage occurs in a split second; there is no time to get out of the way. The force of a snapped line can literally cut a man off at the knees.

Dropping anchor could be extremely hazardous if not done right. Every Navy seaman who ever helped drop an anchor knows the story of the poor sailor who was standing too close to the anchor chain when the boatswain's mate tripped the pelican hook and the anchor was let go. His pant leg got caught in the rattling chain and down he went in an instant, through the hawse pipe, his mutilated remains on their way to the bottom of the sea. The image is so graphic no seaman who has watched the chain fly as the anchor drops and heard the story ever gets too close.

Another shipboard danger was the possibility of suffocation in secured watertight compartments within the hull of the ship. Gases can build up relatively quickly in these spaces and poison or suffocate any sailor who enters without a gas mask. A strict rule aboard ship is that anyone who plans to enter a long-secured space must get the air tested for possible lethal gases to make sure it is safe.

While the *Buck* never experienced anything even close to a situation where a sealed compartment imperiled a sailor's life, we did have one incident that put a number of sailors off chicken for a while. To explain: Taking on supplies while underway is a fast moving and operationally flexible undertaking. In the heat of the summer, most things have to move off deck, out of the sun and into storage quickly to ensure freshness. On one occasion a large pallet of frozen chicken pieces couldn't find its way below decks fast enough and so someone wisely ordered it stored temporarily in a free storage locker to keep it out of the sun. Whoever issued that order got tied up with other duties and apparently just forgot about his "temporarily" stored chicken. A month or so later a shipboard inspection of sealed and unused spaces required the opening of the locker "temporarily" storing the chicken. The inspection team literally choked on the paint-removing stench. Hazmat suits had to be issued to the men ordered to clean out the space. Even then those passing on deck anywhere near the port side of the ship found the smell unbearable.

The *Buck* got underway from Kaohsiung on the morning of May 20, 1969, headed for the Gulf of Tonkin and the famous point known as Yankee Station, a spot in the Gulf of Tonkin south of Hainan Island and just east of the Vietnamese coast. It was the location used by Task Force 77, the U.S. Navy's 7th Fleet aircraft carrier battle/strike force, to launch airstrikes into Vietnam. For years American destroyers spent countless hours assigned to plane guard duty on Yankee Station.

Plane guarding is one of the more dangerous jobs performed by a destroyer. A ship assigned lead plane guard duty is positioned as close as 500 yards behind the carrier. Thinking of the length of the carrier's flight deck as 300 yards, sitting only 500 yards behind provides a perspective on how close the destroyer is. A destroyer in this position provides the advantage of an additional point of reference for aircraft coming in for a landing. But most importantly, if a carrier aircraft ditches or crashes—while taking off, while approaching the carrier, or following a failed landing—the destroyer can quickly proceed to the downed aircraft and attempt to rescue the crew. Plane guarding destroyers might also pick up men lost overboard. The blast of a jet engine can send a human being hurtling off a carrier's flight deck, not an unheard of occurrence during the turmoil of combat flight ops.

Plane guarding is dangerous because aircraft carriers must often change speed and direction to maintain optimum takeoff and landing conditions for their aircraft. A lack of focus by the conning officer on the bridge of the destroyer, or an unannounced radical or abrupt maneuver by the carrier, brings the potential for catastrophe. Remaining in position 500 yards behind a carrier varying its course and speed at darken ship (almost no light emanating from the ship) in poor visibility can be very demanding. The OOD on the carrier was supposed to get on the radio and tell his escorts about any course and speed changes. Most of the time he did, but often enough he did not. When he didn't, the OOD on the destroyer had better be paying close attention or the situation could get dangerous in a hurry.

Plane guarding duty on Yankee Station was a unique experience for any officer assigned to watches on the bridge. It could get busy just keeping track of other ships' locations and ships' movements. There were often as many as three carriers, each with as many as three escorting destroyers, as well as a fleet oiler, all charging around in a relatively small area of the South China Sea often with torrential tropical downpours and resultant poor visibility.

Then there was the occasional Soviet "fishing" trawler with which to contend. In reality these trawlers were equipped with sophisticated sensors and communication equipment. The Navy officially designated these trawlers as Auxiliary, General Intelligence vessels, or AGIs for short. One bright spot was that no one had to worry much about hostile subs on Yankee Station as the relatively uniform sea temperature layers, flat sandy bottom, relatively shallow water and multitude of destroyers in the area made it all but impossible for any sub to go undetected.

Witnessing the courage and ability of the pilots coming back to their carrier from missions over North Vietnam could be breathtaking. To increase the element of readiness, the officers on the bridge of the *Buck* monitored the radio frequency used between the returning planes and the carrier. During one watch we listened as a pilot radioed that he had no fuel left, his plane was shot up and he had been hit in the legs with shrapnel. He requested a direct approach to land, saying even then he wasn't sure he was going to make it. Somehow, he made it.

Another time it was pouring rain with visibility near zero in the foggy darkness, and a pilot was coming in with holes in both wings. He, too, safely landed his aircraft. In all the incidents we monitored the voices in the radio exchanges were always remarkably calm. We never once experienced an aircraft not making it home, but there were many of these "just made it" stories. Those navy pilots risked and sacrificed a lot.

The origin of the effective North Vietnamese anti-aircraft weaponry was no mystery to any of us. We had known about it for years, but could do nothing about it except to understand the Soviet Union was the force behind the loss of our courageous pilots and represented the existential threat to the U.S.

Soviet military aid to Vietnam began after the Second World War to assist Ho Chi Minh and his forces in their battle against returning French rule. The Indo-China War effectively ended with the French loss to a large Viet Minh force in the May 1954 battle of Dien Bien Phu. (Ho Chi Minh formed the Viet Minh, or in English the "League for the Independence of Vietnam," in China in May 1941.) The Geneva Accords of July 1954 divided the country into North and South Vietnam. However, Soviet military aid continued to be funneled to the North Vietnamese in an effort to overthrow the non-communist South.

In 1964 the Soviets increased their military support to the North, providing aircraft, air defense systems, small arms, radar, ammunition and other related supplies. They also sent thousands of military advisors, the majority of which were air defense personnel. In the South, the North Vietnamese and their South Vietnamese cohorts, the Viet Cong, were handing South Vietnamese forces defeat after defeat. Then came the August 1964 Gulf of Tonkin Incident and President Lyndon Johnson's decision to use the episode to increase U.S. support for the war effort.

On February 13, 1965, the U.S. launched Operation Rolling Thunder, a massive military air campaign to bomb North Vietnamese targets. In response, by mid–1965 the Soviets were providing the North with battalions of SA-2 surface-to-air missiles (SAMs) manned by Soviet crews. By late 1966 the Soviets were also training North Vietnamese fighter pilots and training antiaircraft units in the use of their surface-to-air missiles.

The Soviet SA-2 was not state of the art technology, but it could be highly effective. The two-stage, 5,000-pound missile flew at more than four times the speed of sound, could reach an altitude of 90,000 feet and had a range of a little over 20 miles. It carried a fragmentation warhead that could obliterate anything within a range of 250–300-yards. Pilots famously said the missile, at 35 feet in length, looked much like a flying telephone pole.

In October 1967 it was an SA-2 that shot down Lieutenant Commander John McCain's A-4 Skyhawk while on a bombing mission over Hanoi. Injured as he ejected, he managed to parachute into a lake in Hanoi where he was captured and taken prisoner. McCain's aircraft had taken off from the USS *Oriskany* (CVA-34) on Yankee Station in the Gulf of Tonkin. Using SA-2s as well as radar-controlled anti-aircraft artillery, during the war the North Vietnamese shot down hundreds of U.S. Navy and U.S. Air Force warplanes flying missions over the North.

* * *

Duties at Yankee Station did not preclude our own flight ops aboard the *Buck*. By the end of May we had flown the DASH for 71 hours and done 260 landings. Captain Mode, who continued to love to fly the DASH, said he wanted to fly it for a total of 150 hours by the end of the deployment.

One day Captain Mode approached me and said he wanted to get some close-up photos of the *Buck* underway and that he wanted to take the pictures himself. Could we rig up a stretcher-like sling under the DASH and fly him around the ship a few times to take his pictures? While it's entirely possible Captain Mode's request stemmed from his occasionally odd sense of humor, he seemed perfectly serious. It was not unlike Mode to take risks, and he trusted our ability to fly the machine safely, so I think he was serious. His request may also have been Mode's way of telling me he thought the DASH crew was doing a good job without having to say so—Mode did not compliment anyone for anything. I also thought Mode must have been reasonably certain I would turn down his request which, of course, I did.

Then we got word of an engineering casualty aboard the USS *King* (DLG-10). On May 25, the *King* suffered a fire in the fire room while operating in the Gulf of Tonkin, killing four men. Yet one more example of how dangerous everyday shipboard life can be. We were ordered to provide what assistance we could to the *King*. There was not much we could do, and the *King* eventually sailed for Subic Bay under her own power.

Toward the end of May everyone was looking forward to a break from the Yankee Station routine and at least eight days in Subic Bay for maintenance and upkeep. On May 30, the *Buck* had been at sea for thirty-eight of the forty-four days since departing San Diego. Both ship and crew needed a little downtime. On June 5th we finally moored to the pier in Subic Bay.

9

Ensign John Norton
and the *Evans*

On June 3, we awoke to the news that earlier that morning the USS *Frank E. Evans* (DD-754) had collided with the Australian aircraft carrier HMAS *Melbourne* (R-21) while participating in Southeast Asian Treaty Organization (SEATO) exercises. We knew the *Evans* suffered casualties, but initial reports of the incident provided no identities of the lost. Over the next two days I spent every moment I could trying to find out the fate of Elaine's and my dear friend, the DASH officer aboard the *Evans*, Ensign John Norton. On the morning of the 6th, I was able to speak by radio with one of the surviving officers. He told me John along with 73 other American sailors did not make it.

The *Evans* was cut in two amidships as though struck by a gigantic knife; in fact, "the knife" weighed some 20,000-tons and was 700 feet long. When the accident happened, John was asleep in his bunk in a small and overcrowded compartment called "forward officers' quarters" located on the starboard side in the forward end of the ship. Immediately outside the single entrance to the forward officers' quarters space was a ladder leading to the main deck. When the collision occurred, the ladder became jammed against the one and only door to the space, trapping John and other junior officers inside. Survivors said they could hear John and the others were inside the compartment, but they could not budge the door because of the jammed ladder.

The forward end of the *Evans* sank within minutes, but remarkably, the aft end had remained afloat. A fleet tug towed the surviving half of the ship into Subic Bay arriving there on June 9.

I went to the pier to see for myself what was left of the ship. That evening I wrote the following to Elaine:

> I went to the *Evans*, or what is left of it, to look around and run things
> through my mind. It was more than an eerie feeling but eerie seems the only
> way to describe it, just looking at the partial remains of a U.S. Navy ship, a

Following the June 3, 1969, collision with the Australian carrier HMAS *Melbourne* (R-21), on June 9 the USS *Opelika* (YTB-798) maneuvered the stern section of the USS *Frank E. Evans* (DD-754) alongside a pier in Subic Bay Naval Station (copyright John Hoffman via Navsource.org).

ship just like ours, but with no sailors on it, and knowing it was the ship on which John was killed. It looks like somebody took a big knife and sliced it in two, leaving only a few dangling entrails. It is a miracle more men weren't killed, but I can't get my own words out of my mind, what I wrote to you yesterday about John and the horrific manner in which he and his fellow junior officers died. I hope I didn't upset you too much; maybe I should have left some of it out.

I walked up the gangway and spoke to a Lt. (j.g.) who was the Officer of the Deck. He and a seaman assistant were the only men aboard the broken ship. He introduced himself as Lt. (j.g.) Robert Hiltz, the ship's weapons officer, the man for whom John worked. He couldn't tell me anything more about the accident that I didn't already know. He told me he made it off without any bodily harm, thanking God for that. He said he spends his time now counting the days until he can get out of the Navy. He said that last week he had ninety men and three officers working for him and now he has only forty-five men and no officers. Lt. (j.g.) Hiltz reminded me of John Norton in his open and plain-spoken manner. We spoke for a while longer before I went to take a look around.

I went to the DASH hangar. The watertight door that provided access to the forward part of the hangar stood open. Entering I could see the hangar

9. *Ensign John Norton and the* Evans

door that opened on the flight deck was about a third of the way down allowing in just enough sunlight to see everything inside the hangar.

The experience was like walking into a nightmare. In the low light everything looked just like the DASH hangar aboard the *Buck*, but things were strewn around, wet, broken and trashed, as if a storm had hit the inside of the hangar. In the rubble I spotted a large dark blue garment bag with John's name on it. It was empty. John must have been storing it there, because there was so little room in forward officers' quarters. I thought to take it with me but ultimately decided not to because removing it seemed somehow disrespectful.

It remains difficult to explain how I felt in the fetid air of that rotting hangar, totally alone with so many thoughts and memories. My thoughts of John and the tragedy and horror of what happened to him seemed to block out everything else. I am not a religious man but a prayer for John came

The stern of the USS *Frank E. Evans* (DD-754) in the auxiliary repair dry dock USS *Windsor* (ARD-22) at Subic Bay Naval Station. The Union Jack is flying just forward of the after stack which is just forward of the DASH hangar. The photograph shows how cleanly the *Evans* was sliced in two by the force of the strike from the carrier's bow (official U.S. Navy photograph via Navsource.org).

unbidden. My close friend's tragic death also brought home the vivid realization it could have been me. The *Buck*'s junior officer's quarters were identical to the junior officers' quarters on the Evans, even down to the same single exit. The Buck might just as well have been assigned to participate in the SEATO exercise in the South China Sea instead of its mission on Yankee Station.

Such a moment does not turn your mind to hate for war, or the military or any individuals who may have been in part responsible; instead, you are overcome with a personal grief that makes other emotions impossible. Your thoughts are only of what has been lost, what could have been.

I first met Ensign John Norton on a Monday morning in the summer of 1968 in San Diego, on the flight line at the U.S. Naval Air Station North Island on Coronado. John and I were among about a dozen other officers selected to attend the ten-week long Drone Anti-Submarine Helicopter (DASH) School on San Clemente Island. Fleet Composite Squadron Three's San Clemente Island Detachment administered the program. The island, about 21 miles long and from two to four miles wide, sits about 40 miles off the coast of Southern California. The Navy had long used the island—barren except for three or four trees, some wild grass, a few goats, and a small herd of deer—for gunnery practice and programs such as the DASH school. The guys fed the deer their cigarettes. Back then almost everyone smoked; no one thought the worse of it.

The other notable activity to take place on San Clemente Island was the naval gunfire support practice of the USS *New Jersey* (BB-62). Her huge 16-inch guns made a deafening noise and bright flash even at a distance. And they should have been noisy! The heaviest shells weighed as much as 2,700 pounds, about the same as a Volkswagen Beetle, with a maximum range of almost 24 miles. No one could help but be impressed with a salvo from the *New Jersey*'s big guns.

Of all the *Iowa* class battleships (USS *Iowa*, USS *Wisconsin*, USS *Missouri*, USS *New Jersey*), only the *New Jersey* saw combat in Vietnam, from 1968 to 1969. The *New Jersey* fired nearly 6,000 sixteen-inch shells and almost 15,000 five-inch shells at enemy targets in Vietnam. She actually fired more rounds in Vietnam than she did during World War II. The scuttlebutt at the time was that the *New Jersey*'s gunfire never actually killed anyone because as soon as the VC saw her off the coast they'd pack up and run as fast and far away as they could. There probably was a good deal of truth to that.

John and I sat next to one another on that first weekly flight out to San Clemente aboard an old Douglas DC-3. The DC-3 in Navy parlance was called a C-47 or "Gooney Bird," dedicated in 1968 to such low-precedence supply and transport missions as ferrying ensigns out to San Clemente. A trip on the C-47 was always an adventure. Mid-way on one outbound trip, the plane's forward to aft antenna suddenly broke off at the tail end. The antenna slamming against the side of the plane made a deafening racket, like a giant woodpecker trying to crack open the fuselage. We were reassured after noticing the plane seemed to be flying as it had before the noise started, but John and I agreed it was a comfort to feel the plane's wheels hit the tarmac on San Clemente.

At the end of the ten weeks of DASH school, John placed first in the class and I placed second. Both of us were proud of the silver helicopter tie clasps we were awarded by the Gyrodyne Company. I still have mine somewhere, although years ago the rotors broke off and it became basically unrecognizable as a little silver DASH mounted on a tie clasp.

The *Evans* had a schedule very similar to that of the *Buck*. My recollection is that both ships had gotten a months-long overhaul in the summer and early autumn of 1968 before entering REFTRA (refresher training). It had to be one of the most grueling programs the Navy ever invented. For six weeks or more, life was a never-ending cycle of closely monitored exercises using every ship system, with days often starting at 0430 and ending after 2230.

When there was time, John came for drinks and dinner at our 10th Avenue apartment. The old place came with the semi-functioning Murphy bed I mentioned earlier, a big water heater in the middle of the kitchen and no air conditioning. But for $165 a month rent, including utilities and the use of the phone in the landlady's apartment, we thought it was a pretty good deal. With a car payment, student loan debt and a first-year ensign's pay, just having a place of our own seemed great. When we were all there together, we always had a wonderful time laughing, eating and drinking, often with other friends John and I had made at DASH school.

The *Evans* got underway from Pier 17 (mole pier) in Long Beach on Saturday, March 29, 1969, deploying less than three weeks before the *Buck*'s April 16, 1969, deployment from San Diego's 32nd Street Naval Station. John Norton spent part of his last weekend ashore in San Diego with Elaine and me; it was the last time either of us would see him. We clearly remember saying good-bye to him on the street in the early morning hours just north and west of the famous U.S. Grant Hotel. Even at the time, something about our good-byes made it seem as though it was to be the last one. I sometimes think people can see into the future if only slightly, not unlike seeing the vague outline of structures through a fog or mist, "through a glass darkly," as it says in the Bible.

The *Evans* was decommissioned on July 1, 1969, and sunk by the USS *John R Craig* (DD-885) on October 10, 1969.

10

DASH Ops and Bangkok

On June 18, after almost two weeks in Subic Bay, the *Buck* got underway once again for routine ops such as flying the DASH and conducting other independent exercises en route to multi-ship ASW exercises.

On June 20, we met up with a couple of other destroyers for the ASW exercises with the USS *Bugara* (SS-331). On June 21, we completed the exercises and set course to rendezvous with the *Bon Homme Richard* (CVA-31), aka the Bonnie Dick, the USS *Walke* (DD-723), and the USS *Noa* (DD-840) for more plane guard duty on Yankee Station.

Once in the routine of trailing carriers around the Gulf, there was not much to occupy Captain Mode other than details, and Captain Mode was excellent at focusing on details. In fact, underway or pier side, he had a penchant for calling out even the smallest of mistakes. If the deck wasn't cleaned to his standards, a flag not hoisted to the very top of the pole, a rat guard too loosely bound to a mooring line, or some similar indiscretion, someone was going to hear about it.

In the Navy, foul-ups are a part of everyday life, but Captain Mode spent much of his life aboard ship trying to do the impossible and make things perfect. Some said there was method in his madness: Take care of the little things and the odds become better that big things won't become a problem. At his angriest he could be almost comical in his complaints, jumping up and down, chest out, fists clenched and squawking loudly. If it were a game of charades, one would immediately have guessed Donald Duck. It was a highly effective act. Regardless of rank, the offending party or parties were usually shocked into compliance and the error not repeated again.

One of the enduring Mode stories was the time he became infuriated by something and came storming out of his at-sea captain's cabin, located just behind the bridge. No one could stomp around like Captain Mode. What Captain Mode didn't know was that one of the seamen was busy washing the deck with a bucket of hot soapy water positioned

73

just a few feet in front of his door. Mode's stomping right foot entered the bucket and went instantaneously to the bottom resulting in much of the water being forced up his pant leg. He stopped yelling, looked down at the bucket, slowly pulled out his foot, glared at the offending seaman and then, without uttering a word, turned and went back into his cabin. Standing about ten feet off to his right, I was the only one in position to be able to see Mode's face as he re-entered his cabin. To this day I believe I saw a hint of a laugh, or at least a smile, forming on his lips.

Nearing the end of June our DASH flight time was at 100 hours without an incident. Achieving one hundred accident-free hours with this skittish, electronics-heavy weapons system was a remarkable achievement. The DASH crew did not talk about our good fortune for the same reasons a pitcher and his teammates don't mention a no-hitter going into the late innings. We knew our luck could change in an instant.

Losing a drone could happen to anyone, not that Captain Mode saw it that way. In fact, unknown to me until recently was that the *Buck* had lost a DASH off Australia the morning of February 27, 1968, only about one month after Mode had taken command. The ship's log entry says electronic interference with the flight deck control system was the suspected cause. However, former DASH officer and later Navy helicopter pilot Bob Martin commented that he thought the DASH might have encountered a weather front severe enough to cause a rotor blade failure. He based his conclusion on firsthand experience in a helicopter in San Diego flying through a small, innocent-looking cloud.

Bob said neither the deck controller, Ensign Bruce McCamey, nor the CIC controller, Ensign John Roarke, could gain control of the drone, so it flew itself over the horizon. When the incident happened, Bob had the conn. A very agitated Captain Mode immediately relieved him and sent him into CIC to try and help out, but there was little he could do. Captain Mode was absolutely furious, but there was nothing he could do either. The *Buck* was in formation with other destroyers and could not break off to give chase. For whatever reason, Captain Mode never said a word to me about the loss of this drone.

During a 28 June flight, we were logging our 104th hour in the air when we developed a problem. An electronic connection somewhere within the control system came loose and so the drone began to respond erratically and incorrectly to the control stick. It began to go left all on its own, and then too far right when I corrected it, and then, just like a misbehaving dog, took off on its own, over the horizon beyond visual range.

10. DASH Ops and Bangkok

QH-50D DASH carrying two practice torpedoes, approaching the flight deck over the after 5-inch/38 gun mount (courtesy Peter Papadakos, Project Manager QH-50 DASH Weapon System).

Of course, we had kept the bridge and the CIC informed. About twenty minutes after the drone's disappearance, the surface search radar operator in CIC reported he believed he had spotted something on his scope that could be our drone about ten miles away. While the ship altered course to close the distance to the drone, the DASH crew brainstormed what we might do to try and fix the problem. We decided

75

the problem must be in the aft control station, and so maybe we could regain command if we transferred control to the secondary CIC station. The idea worked! Within ten minutes we had the drone back in visual contact.

The problem now became how we could land the thing on the flight deck because it was not possible to do it from CIC. In order to have any chance of saving the drone, we had to transfer control back to the probably still malfunctioning aft deck station. If control issues recurred, especially while I was trying to land it, then there could be a problem. A sudden loss of altitude or attitude control might even cause it to crash into the ship. The decision what to do was not mine to make. Captain Mode decided we'd go for it. He ordered General Quarters to have the ship buttoned up tight and the damage control parties at the ready just in case.

Ensign Phil Shullo, our CIC controller, brought the drone in close to the ship and we were ready to make the transfer. It was an odd feeling standing in the aft control station by myself, just the drone and me. Usually most of the DASH crew and a few who enjoyed observing stood nearby. We made the transfer back to the aft control station and nothing bad happened. So far so good. Out of nervousness, I suppose, I started talking out loud to it, encouraging it to relax and behave. We all hate it when inanimate objects behave badly and sometimes it seems to help by talking nicely to them. In any case, the drone seemed to respond to the soft talk and behave as it should. Everything stayed together as I settled it down on the flight deck as smoothly and steadily as possible. I think I cheered out loud after shutting down the engine and watching the rotors come to a stop.

Almost exactly one-half hour after losing control of the drone, the aircraft had been saved, the over 100-hours of safe flight record preserved, the emergency over, and General Quarters secured.

It came as a complete surprise that Captain Mode had the wardroom galley make a large cake with "Congratulations 100 Hours" written on the top. The captain had the cook deliver the cake to the DASH hangar just after we recovered the drone. I hate to think what he would have done with it had we lost the drone. So, we doubly enjoyed the attention and the cake only moments after that very fortunate landing.

Captain Mode shocked everyone by shaking hands, posing for pictures and congratulating the five-member DASH flight crew including EN1 Fred Homer, ETR2 Mike Winchester, AT3 Aaron Rivkin, Petty Officer Wilson, Airman Scott, myself and the *Buck*'s other DASH

Left to right: the author, Commander Paul J. Mode, and Lt (j.g.) Phil Shullo, pictured in the DASH hangar of the *Buck* in front of the cake celebrating more than 100 flight hours. One of the two drones is visible in the background (U.S. Navy).

qualified officer, Ensign Phil Shullo. In later years I came to find that most ships' captains provided a cake after 100 successful landings, something the *Buck* crew had accomplished many times over. We were all happy for the captain's recognition and fully enjoyed the moment.

On June 30, we experienced another bit of the unusual. One of the lookouts spotted something slowly bobbing up and down in the waves at a distance of some 500 yards. The *Buck* got the order to investigate. It proved to be the underside of an overturned junk. We saw no trace of its crew or any visible reason for why it had almost sunk. The captain made the decision to sink it completely thereby removing it as a navigation hazard. Within minutes there was no more obstruction to navigation, and anything left on board the junk consigned to Davey Jones' locker.

Finished ridding the sea of the old junk, we resumed plane guard duty, this time hooking up with TG 77.7 composed of the USS

The *Buck*'s DASH crew. Right to left: EN1 Fred Homer, AN Scott, Lt (j.g.) Phil Shullo, ETR2 Mike Winchester, the author, AT3 Aaron Rivkin, and PO2 Mike Wilson, pictured in front of the cake celebrating 100 accident-free hours flying time (U.S. Navy).

Ticonderoga (CVA-14), the USS *John R. Craig* (DD-845), and the USS *Hamner* (DD-718). On July 3, we were called on to recover what debris we could from a downed *Ticonderoga* aircraft. Fortunately, a helicopter from the carrier was able almost immediately to recover the pilot and save his life. We also got more good news that day with notification that the *Buck* had been named first runner-up for the Navy's prestigious Ney Award for food service excellence.

On July 5, we met up with the USS *John W. Thomason* (DD-760) for the transit through the Gulf of Siam headed for the Chao Phraya River and the port city of Bangkok. Bangkok is a beautiful river city. During the Vietnam War it was known as a sailor's (or soldier's, or airman's, or marine's) delight. While nowhere near as wild and crazy as the infamous Olongapo just outside the gates of the Naval Station in Subic Bay, Bangkok offered similar attractions, plus great sightseeing, good shops and restaurants, fine but relatively inexpensive jewelry, and more.

10. DASH Ops and Bangkok

I remember the 20-mile ride up the Chao Phraya River from the Bay of Bangkok. Along the shore, lined with small native homes on stilts, we saw people in their native clothing tending to their daily lives. Some of them bathed in the river wearing nothing at all.

When the *Buck* was there, the river close to the city was clogged with vegetation, flotsam and miscellaneous other junk. After we'd visited Bangkok, I heard a very sad story I've never been able to confirm. According to the story, one of my Brown University NROTC acquaintances on another destroyer drowned in the river while coming back off liberty. Reportedly, in the dark he somehow slipped out of the launch that ferried people from the pier to the ship and disappeared in the clogged and murky depths. Again, I don't know that it happened, but the condition of the river, possibly bad weather, the early hours of the morning, and the use of the ship's launch to and from the quayside makes such a tragic event plausible.

In part Bangkok was known for its countless brothels. According to a 2001 report by the World Health Organization, "The most reliable estimate is that there are between 150,000 and 200,000 sex workers (in Bangkok)." Other reports suggest this number is probably too low with the true number estimated to be as high as three quarters of a million people. The terrible misfortune was that many of these young people were attractive, intelligent—many were multi-lingual—with so much they could offer were they employed in productive lines of work. Often the reason these young people were sex workers was not to support a drug habit or an opulent lifestyle, but to provide support for their families living in remote, poverty stricken sections of Thailand. Isan, or northeastern Thailand, was just such a place. It remains home to one-third of Thailand's population of 67 million but provides only ten per cent to the gross national product.

Bangkok was not the only port city with pretty, charming and intelligent ladies of the evening. While sailors' dalliances were an issue, generally speaking they were a temporary and not a long-term problem. Occasionally a young, inexperienced sailor would fall head over boots in love and want to marry a bargirl. The accompanying problems caused some real headaches and heartaches for all concerned.

In Bangkok I learned to never again over-indulge in alcohol. It's always a challenge for new junior officers aboard ship to maintain a good relationship with the chief petty officers. In the Navy, especially aboard ship, the chiefs run virtually everything. They have many years of experience in their fields and direct control over the enlisted men under them. While a junior officer outranks a chief petty officer, the chief can make or break the young officer's professional performance. Most of the time relations between junior officers and chief petty officers are excellent, and a smart junior officer does what he can to keep it that way. So, it was with that in mind that I accepted an invitation from a chief who didn't work directly for me to join him and a group of other chiefs for a drinking party at a favorite bar in Bangkok. The party started at 11 a.m. with Bloody Marys and continued non-stop for about 12 hours. I didn't get sick that night, but I paid the price with an upset system for at least a week afterwards. Given the amount of alcohol consumed I was lucky to have fared as well as I did but swore off ever doing it again, regardless.

By the 12th of July the *Buck* and her crew were ready to leave Bangkok and go back to work off the Vietnamese coast, this time to provide naval gunfire support (NGFS) to our troops ashore. We were ordered to proceed to Vung Ganh Rai in the III Corps area. (South Vietnam was divided into four Corps or military regions, I though IV, from north to south.) It would be the first but certainly not the last time we shot our guns at the Viet Cong (VC).

11

Naval Gunfire Support and the Rodent Incident

By July 15, we were proceeding up the Vung Ganh Rai channel, around 50 miles southeast of Saigon, where we eventually dropped anchor. We began a port and starboard watch rotation in order to be ready to fire our 5-inch guns 24 hours a day, seven days a week. It was a very busy time for our Gunnery Officer Lt. (j.g.) Mark Adderman. It also meant everyone had to be on watch for about twelve hours a day in addition to participating in refueling and resupply operations, calls to general quarters, and all the necessary routine work assignments. We didn't have to wait long before spotters were calling us to provide gunfire support.

My daily routine, typical for any line officer aboard ship, called for getting up at 6:00 a.m., going on watch on the bridge until 12:00 p.m., doing my regular work before returning to watch on the bridge at 6 p.m., and then going off watch at 12:00 a.m.—then repeat. Everyone lived with very little sleep. Some mornings it was next to impossible to wake up at 6:00 a.m. The messenger of the watch, whose worse than thankless job it was to provide wake-up calls, would sometimes have to throw water in my face to get me awake—and I wasn't the only one. The job of waking very tired men from a deep sleep could also be dangerous. Experienced messengers of the watch were well aware that men could suddenly lash out, punch or kick, acting out from a dream.

When firing the 5-inch guns we had team one and team two. I was on team one as "gun control officer," which sounds commanding but wasn't. Others had jobs on the bridge, in the Combat Information Center (CIC), in the Mk 37 Fire Control System director, etc. The Mk 37 fire control system was the key to the *Buck*'s success as a gunfire support ship. The accuracy of fire was excellent out to a dozen miles or more.

As gun control officer I stood on the bridge near the forward guns to make sure the guns were generally aimed in the right direction, listen to radio transmissions from the spotter, keep the captain apprised of what the spotter wanted, and perform related tasks. With the port and starboard watch rotation we could man all the necessary gunnery stations 24 hours a day and shoot four of the six five-inch guns at any time.

When we trained the gun mount past amidships as close to the wing of the bridge as it would train, and we raised the barrels to an elevation of about 45 degrees, the mouth of the barrel of the gun came within a couple of feet of the wing of the bridge. When the gun fired, a man standing on the wing of the bridge would literally bounce an inch or two in the air. Without ear protection the noise was literally deafening. I wore earphones but that didn't lower the decibel level by much. The noise could negatively affect your hearing not just shortly after the firing, but permanently. A few years ago, I had an audiologist ask me if I had ever experienced very loud noises as a young person. When I told him about my proximity to the 5-inch/38 gunfire, he said that undoubtedly that was the cause of my impaired hearing.

If we fired a broadside with all six guns, the firing was not just deafening but could literally move the ship sideways in the water. The extreme vibration from firing multiple guns at one time also wreaked havoc on the spaces in the interior of the ship, causing minor structural damage.

On the 16th of July we were anchored in the northwest corner of Vung Tau Bay at the convergence of several small rivers that were part of the Saigon River Delta. The much larger Mekong River Delta lay a little further south and east. The Viet Cong controlled a peninsula situated between two rivers about 1500 yards southeast of our position. A small town called Can Gio (Can Thanh on today's maps) sat on the peninsula's southeastern tip. A spotter working with us flew a small, slow, one-man Cessna O-1A, propeller-driven aircraft over the VC positions around Can Gio looking for bunkers, tunnels, supply dumps, and whatever other military targets he could find. He called us with the location of the target, and we fired on it until it was destroyed. At night we did harassment fire without a spotter into assigned sectors of the VC occupied territory. Every ten to fifteen minutes we would fire a round or two into one of the sectors to limit VC opportunities to move around freely.

On July 17th, we provided NGFS support for a U.S. Army assault designed to eliminate the VC from the Can Gio area. Several hundred or more U.S. troops moved in by boat and helicopter to secure the territory.

We also had visits from a number of U.S. Navy PCFs (Patrol Craft Fast) also known as swift boats. The 50-foot long twin diesel-engine vessels carried a crew of six, including a skipper, a boatswain mate, a radar and radio operator, an engineer and two gunners. Along with the PCFs came smaller 31-foot long PBRs (Patrol Boat Riverine). Twin 180 horsepower diesels powered the PBRs, manned by a crew of four. Usually the skipper was a First Class Petty Officer. Also on board were a gunner's mate, an engineman and a seaman. PBRs usually operated in pairs under the command of an officer who rode on one of the boats. The crews of these small boats loved to come aboard for a few hours for the creature comforts available; tops on their list was a hot meal. They all told us the same thing, how much they appreciated having the *Buck*'s big guns in their operating area because it made their jobs so much safer.

The PBR and PCF men told us that the shelling definitely had a negative effect on the VC's ability to operate. As previously mentioned, when the *New Jersey* (BB-62) did NGFS with her 16" guns the effect on the VC was remarkable, the VC would clear out as fast as they could go, well past the 23-mile range of the battle ship's guns. It was "shock and awe" before the phrase became part of our lexicon.

July 20 was a typical day of long hours and hard work. We began the day anchored just off Vung Ganh Rai providing gunfire support. At 0533 we ceased fire and by 0600 were underway for refueling from the USS *Ashtabula* (AO-51) and then rearming from the USS *Mazama* (AE-9). By early afternoon we had returned to our anchorage at Vung Ganh Rai where we soon commenced firing once more. Many of the same men who performed the demanding refueling and rearming operations manned the stations necessary for firing our guns. Someone might start the day helping load a 5-inch gun, then help weigh anchor, then handle or manage gear for refueling, then haul 55-pound shells down to the magazines, then help anchor the ship once more followed by helping load another 5-inch gun. In 90-degree temperatures with near 100 percent humidity and occasional rain showers it was not light, quiet, comfortable work.

By Monday, July 21, we were still on the gun line blasting away at VC positions. But the morning of the 21st (the 20th in the U.S.) brought us all a special experience, and it didn't have anything to do with guns. Lt. Dennie Miller and I had the watch on the bridge. Dennie asked our communications officer, Lt. (j.g.) Steve Arlett, to patch the American Forces Vietnam Network (AFVN) into a speaker on the bridge. They were carrying live the Apollo 11 landing on the moon. We were all spellbound listening to Commander Neil Armstrong get ready to step out of the module and slowly move down the ladder toward the surface of the moon. But just as Armstrong was about to set out we received a call for gunfire support and so we had to take down the broadcast. We had the guys in commo keep us abreast of how it was going, but we could not listen live to what was being done and said.

The successful landing and moon walk was a huge morale boost for everyone aboard ship; we were all proud of the remarkable achievement. We felt a part of it seeing the feat as an accomplishment by teams of hardworking and basically unrecognized individual Americans not unlike ourselves. I'm sure none of us will ever forget where we were and what we were doing when mankind first set foot on the moon.

From the 22nd to the 28th it was just a lot more of the same hard work. In addition to at least one refueling and one rearming mission we conducted naval gunfire support missions in III Corps places with unheard of names like Vung Ganh Rai, Luan Dat Do, Nui Tam Bo, Nui Ky Van, Mui Ho Lo and Mui Tan.

Gunfire wasn't the only action in the waters off South Vietnam. The warm, brackish coastal waters in the large delta region where we were are home to a great variety of wildlife, including large poisonous sea snakes. They can grow from a length of about four feet to as long as ten. Fortunately, these animals are reasonably passive creatures, but the sight of one in the water anywhere near you can get your attention. One type of snake we saw fairly often had intermittent black and white banding. When they're under a few inches of brackish seawater they look exactly like swimming skeletons. There were other nasty looking creatures as well.

One morning we sat at anchor waiting for a call from shore for gunfire support. As usual the air was warm and humid, the wind still and the water quiet under an overcast sky. Captain Mode sat uncharacteristically slumped in his captain's chair in the forward part of the bridge, just waiting for the call for a gunfire support assignment and another opportunity to shoot the hell out of the enemy. However, the day seemed to be turning into a slow mover and so in the absence of any action he decided to go to his cabin for a quick nap.

Dennie Miller, and I had the watch on the bridge. Miller was blessed with a quick wit and a dry sense of humor well suited to poking fun at Captain Mode's outbursts. But given Mode's propensity for explosive retribution, Miller did his best to keep his captain-humor well hidden behind the Captain's back, not that Mode probably wasn't well aware of Miller's comedic talent at his expense. On this day, as the hours dragged by in the tropical heat and humidity, boredom and fatigue began to take their toll on Miller and me. We needed something to keep us awake.

A note about the ability to sleep while standing: Before serving on the gun line and plane guard duty for weeks at a time, I never thought it was possible for a human being to fall asleep standing up. In fact, I proved to myself that it is indeed possible, especially during the 0400 to 0800 watch, usually around 5 a.m., when the sun is just starting to climb out of the sea. To try to stay awake I smoked, I drank coffee, I bit my lip, but nothing kept me from falling asleep, if only briefly. You wake up when you start to tip over. It is an odd feeling, not being able to stay awake; you feel the way you do immediately after you've been anesthetized for surgery. You literally can't stay awake no matter how hard you try. I hasten to add that, should there be a problem or emergency, the sleepiness disappears almost instantly.

In any case, just as Dennie and I were fighting to stay awake, a lookout reported something in the water off the starboard bow slowly moving towards us. Initial wariness that it could be some kind of saboteur attack—a VC tactic—melted away when I identified the approaching object as a water rat, one of the biggest I had ever seen. Coming from the New York City area, you get to be something of an authority in identifying such wildlife, and for sure it was a rat. With its huge bony tail trailing limply behind, the thing looked like an obese opossum in a grayish-brown fur coat. Miller immediately called down to the nearest sentry on the main deck, armed sentries were posted in case of attack from enemy swimmers; they also threw concussion grenades every now and then off the side of the ship just in case. Miller instructed the sentry to use a nearby mooring line to try and move the rat closer to the ship. Dennie wanted it for the captain.

Miller quickly explained his plan: As soon as the rat got a little closer to the ship, he would call the Captain out of his cabin. And, as we all knew, the Captain enjoyed shooting his .45, usually at nothing at all, and now he could have a target and we would have provided it for him! At the time, in the heat, humidity, boredom and fatigue, it seemed like a good idea.

But in the rat-target-organizing commotion, neither Dennie nor I heard or saw the door to the captain's cabin open. Nor in our focus on the fumbling efforts of the rat herding sentry on the main deck below did we see a somewhat bleary eyed figure slowly approaching us from behind. Then, just as Miller was providing our seaman sentry firm orders to get the rat as close to the ship as possible, Captain Mode suddenly realized his operations officer was encouraging the capture and placement of a large rat aboard his ship!

It was like the 4th of July revisited, rhetorical skyrockets were everywhere. Captain Mode gave us his best ever impression of an angry James Cagney. Sticking out his chin and his chest, pounding the air with his fists, jumping up and down and yelling at the top of his lungs, he let us know that no officer of his was ever to encourage a rodent of any kind, let alone a rat, to come aboard his ship! At this point there was little we could intelligently offer in the way of self-defense, so as punishment the Captain threw us off the bridge—if only temporarily, as there were too few watch standers as it was. In hindsight, we could understand how the Captain might have viewed our actions as suspect, but as far as I know he never learned of our real intent in trying to lure the poor creature close aboard. And for animal lovers everywhere, rest assured that the creature was allowed to resume its original course and rat-paddle off to wherever it was going before being lassoed by our sentry.

By July 28, the *Buck* had fired about 1,800 rounds of 5-inch ammunition at VC positions in our little corner of III Corps. We destroyed trenches, bunkers, foxholes, tunnels and camouflaged structures and buildings. By the end of the month, we were more than ready for a little rest and recuperation, but not before a quick visit to the I Corps area for a rendezvous with the USS *St. Paul* (CA-73), carrying Rear Admiral T.J. Rudden, Jr., commander of the Cruiser-Destroyer Group 7th Fleet. The Navy considered the ship's victory in the Ney Award food service competition to be of such importance as to warrant a personal presentation by the senior cruiser and destroyer officer in the 7th Fleet. So, at 0730 on July 30, the *St. Paul* transferred the admiral by high-line to the *Buck* so he could make the presentation face-to-face. He managed it in less than two hours, coffee and pleasantries included. At 0930 we high-lined him back to the *St. Paul*. By 1140 we had joined up with our task group and were en route to Subic Bay.

Following a week of rest and repairs in Subic, the *Buck* sailed for the ultimate 1969 WESTPAC rest and recuperation port, Hong Kong, arriving in that beautiful British-controlled city on August 8th for a six-day visit.

12

Hong Kong Mary,
the China Fleet Club, and
the Gulf of Tonkin Incident

Hong Kong Mary is a name familiar to sailors the world over. It seemed that no sooner had we moored to buoy 21 than Hong Kong Mary, or at least one of her surrogates, pulled their junk alongside the *Buck* to begin negotiations for painting the ship. Negotiations didn't take long. Mary's workers, mostly women, would paint the exterior of the ship for what was to us little in return. The ship would provide the paint and Mary's employees guaranteed to finish the job within the time frame of the ship's six-day visit.

Sailors often didn't give Mary cash; her fee usually came in the form of what Americans called "garbage." Excess food from the ship's galley got packed up and taken away for consumption by her workers or sold on the streets. But her most sought-after Navy trash was larger items made of reusable metal. Solid brass shell casings from expended 5-inch rounds ranked high up on her list of items of interest. Each shell casing was approximately a dozen pounds of solid brass. For a ship like the *Buck* fresh off the gun line, empty shell casings were not difficult to come by. Many casings ended up rolling off the side of the ship, so saving a few in anticipation of a visit to Hong Kong was not a problem.

Every ship's captain in the Navy wanted his ship to look clean and shipshape, and keeping it well painted was key. This was a never-ending job, with the constant saltwater exposure on metal decks, sides and exterior equipment. A few weeks at sea and the "running rust" could make any destroyer look almost as orange as it was gray. But the onerous jobs of preparation and painting could only be done in port and that was when every sailor wanted to be ashore on liberty.

Hong Kong Mary's fleet-wide reputation for excellent work delivered at low cost and on time kept her in business. Another big part of her success derived from her personality and unique social and business acumen.

In the late 1960s, running a thriving business of any kind in a city of eight million people demanded toughness, and managing a lucrative business on the waters of Hong Kong, Victoria Harbor, Aberdeen and accompanying tributaries in the dark shadow of communist China took something extraordinary. In 1969 some 800 million poor communist Chinese labored under the terror of Chairman Mao and his devastating Cultural Revolution, a movement that persecuted tens of millions of people while trying to purge any remnant of capitalism from the Chinese economy.

According to a *New York Times* article published in December 1968, Hong Kong Mary Soo (few knew her last name) was barely 4'7" tall. While tough as iron underneath, Mary used a demure smile, modest demeanor and appropriately deferential manner to win over the Navy's most demanding boatswain's mates and ship's officers. She also spoke English like a teacher in a tough school, able to counter any verbal assault. She handled the people who worked for her in the same low key but no-nonsense way.

The *New York Times* article says her real name was Chan Kam, born around 1910 on an Aberdeen junk, and that as a child she went by the name Soo Mei. She began her career by selling food and drink from her sampan to sailors on visiting ships. They gave her the name Mary Soo, later shortened by most to just Mary.

Some sailors wondered why the U.S. Navy would provide a Chinese with reusable metals when that metal could be quickly and easily turned into arms and ammunition for use against the American military. After all, there was no end-user agreement with Mary. There seems to be no clear-cut answer to that question. The *New York Times* article pointed out that not only did U.S. Navy ship captains allow Mary to service their ships, Mary enjoyed official approval to do so. She held a letter of recommendation from 7th Fleet Headquarters describing her as "most competent and trustworthy" and authorizing her to clean and paint the "exterior hull, wardroom, galley and the CPO's quarters of US Navy ships, to remove their garbage and maintain a soft-drink concession on their decks."

Maybe a successful background check led 7th Fleet Headquarters to write what they apparently did. As the *Times* mentioned, in 1968 Hong Kong Mary Soo had plans to visit New York City and visit a niece living there.

12. The Gulf of Tonkin Incident

One of the main attractions for the crew of the *Buck* in Hong Kong in 1969 was the famous, old China Fleet Club. On March 21, 1934 the British had formally opened their China Fleet Club, located near the harbor on Gloucester Road across from Kowloon on Hong Kong Island. One of the Club's draws even from its earliest days was its location on the edge of Hong Kong's Wanchai District still known for its wild night life and, of course, the dens of iniquity wherein the world's oldest profession was practiced. Richard Mason's 1957 novel entitled *The World of Suzie Wong*—and later the movie of the same name—did much to make the district's traditional culture famous worldwide.

In 1954, the U.S. Navy asked to become part of the Club so American personnel on liberty or rest & recreation (R&R) visits in Hong Kong could enjoy the benefits. In time the U.S. Navy took over the main building's third floor. The 1960s with the war in Vietnam brought a tremendous increase in American military visitors, the crew of the *Buck* included.

In the shops of the Club the crew spent money like the proverbial drunken sailors, which, indeed, some were. It was where I purchased a top-of-the-line Singer sewing machine for Elaine. Few, if any, of the crew left without buying some kind of technology of the day—especially fancy stereo equipment—at the Club's very low prices. And the tailors were kept busy with orders for dress suits, monogrammed shirts and all manner of personally fitted attire offered at rock bottom prices. Some of the guys came back with dress suits in colors and design that probably would have been impossible to even find in the States except possibly in New Orleans during Mardi Gras season.

The Club prospered to the point where a new, bigger Club could be opened. So the old building was demolished, and in May 1985 the Governor of Hong Kong opened the 25-story Fleet House on the same site as the old China Fleet Club, the Club occupying the first nine floors of the structure. However, all good things must eventually come to an end, and so it was with the Club. It closed its doors for good in November 1992.

By August 14, 1969, *Buck* was underway once again, this time for a projected 35 straight days at sea. Our destination was Yankee Station. Between the 16th and the 28th we remained on Yankee Station jumping back and forth between plane guard assignments for two carriers, the *Bon Homme Richard* or the *Oriskany*.

After two weeks of snuggling up to the back end of Yankee Station carriers we welcomed a change of venue. Early on the 30th we received orders to proceed to the South Search and Rescue (SAR) Station, aka South SAR. South SAR was about five nautical miles east of Ngoc Lam, North Vietnam, just north of the 19th parallel (approximately 19N 106E). It was on the west side of a horizontal line between the middle of China's Hainan Island and the North Vietnamese Coast. For comparison purposes, Yankee Station was further south and about 90 miles off the North Vietnamese coast. By 0930 that same day the *Buck* had relieved the USS *Wiltsie* (DD-716) and become part of a two-ship task group with the USS *Biddle* (DLG-34).

The primary purpose in maintaining two destroyers at South SAR was to retrieve pilots whose planes managed to make it at least as far as the Gulf after being hit by North Vietnamese anti-aircraft fire. Electronic Countermeasures (ECM) and monitoring North Vietnamese and Chinese electronic transmissions was another responsibility. Maintaining the U.S. Navy's right of passage in international waters in the Gulf was yet a third mission and refueling helicopters on sensitive missions over the north yet another. As DASH officer my job in this instance was to talk to the pilots from the DASH control station as they approached from astern. They always sounded appreciative we were there.

Two destroyers also normally worked the North Search and Rescue Station (a.k.a. North SAR) located at (20N 107E). Their jobs were similar to those of the destroyers on South SAR, but the North SAR was closer to both Hanoi and mainland China.

Five years earlier our location in the Gulf had made the headlines. The Gulf of Tonkin Incident, a major turning point of the war, began on August 2, 1964, when three Soviet-built North Vietnamese P-4 torpedo boats approached the USS *Maddox* (DD-731). The North Vietnamese responded to warning shots from the *Maddox* with torpedo and machine gun fire that caused no significant harm while the *Maddox* badly damaged one of the North Vietnamese boats.

In the aftermath of the August 2 exchange of fire the Navy sent the USS *Turner Joy* (DD-951) to join the *Maddox* while raids backed by U.S. forces took place against two North Vietnamese shore positions. On August 4, North Vietnamese torpedo boats appeared to be preparing to attack the *Maddox* and *Turner Joy* as they steamed in the area of the first attack. During low light conditions, rough weather and high seas, the two destroyers picked up radar and electronic intercept information indicating an imminent attack. For a period of about four hours the destroyers fired on radar and possible visual targets taking evasive action to avoid damage from their attackers. The destroyer crews believed they had sunk two of the attacking torpedo boats.

The U.S. Naval task group commander in the Gulf immediately reported to Washington the attack by the North Vietnamese. However, subsequent to his report a check of the battle area revealed no wreckage or other evidence of the loss of any North Vietnamese craft. Within hours of his initial report the task group commander revised his statement of what he believed had happened. He said that in the early afternoon of August 4, "freak weather effects" on the ships' surface search radar (AN/SPS-10) had made an attack now seem unlikely, and that no one on either ship could say he had visually identified a North Vietnamese patrol boat. The commander suggested a more in-depth analysis be completed before any action was taken.

However, the task group commander's revised analysis arrived too late. President Johnson used the August 2 and August 4 incidents as reasons to escalate the U.S. role in the war and, as they say, the rest is history.

For years after the August 1964 incidents an international debate raged as to what actually had happened to the *Maddox* and *Turner Joy* on that August 4. While many Americans believed the two ships had come under attack even when no physical evidence of the attack was found, a growing body of knowledgeable people thought the attack unlikely. Much discussion within the Navy focused on the radar echoes the ships had picked up purportedly indicating patrol craft approaching. Most of the time the Navy's surface search radar, especially to trained and experienced radar operators, provided reliable data. The suggestion that both destroyers received similarly incorrect radar echo data over a prolonged period was surprising and inconsistent with a great body of experience. However, U.S. Navy personnel with experience monitoring radar in the northern Gulf had found radar returns with puzzling anomalies. While flocks of birds, the tops of high waves, large sea mammals, or other natural activity can sometimes display on the radar screen as a ship or low flying aircraft, such anomalies are unusual. Many military and technology experts inside and outside the Navy thought the multitude of radar contacts in the northern Gulf could not have come from such natural anomalies, but something else.

In late August and early September, within weeks of the time of year the *Maddox* and *Turner Joy* perceived themselves to be under attack, the *Buck* patrolled very close to the same area. I was eager to see for myself what kind of surface search radar reception we would experience. Having spent many hours over the past year staring at a surface search radar screen I knew what to look for and probably what the radar echoes represented.

During our patrol the seas and winds were mostly calm, the humidity high, sea and surface temperatures quite warm and with no precipitation. Yet the *Buck*'s surface search radar also occasionally displayed false echoes of what could be interpreted as ship contacts traveling on a realistic course and speed. I came away convinced that it would have been possible for the crews of the *Maddox* and *Turner Joy* to interpret the radar returns as patrol craft if they had received the same or similar returns as the *Buck*. Also, the *Maddox* and *Turner Joy* had the added difficulty of reading their radar returns in high seas and bad weather in what they knew to be a reasonably high threat environment. Finally, one has to wonder what kind of electronic warfare the Soviets and their North Vietnamese hosts or the nearby Chinese might have used to affect surface search radar displays.

It seemed that no sooner had we gotten on our SAR station patrol than we were interrupted by something more powerful than any bomb, gun or missile. From before our arrival on station we had been following the progress of Typhoon Doris. By August 30 it had tracked on a near-due westerly course through the South China Sea aimed to pass just south of Hainan Island and into the southerly part of North Vietnam. By Sunday the 31st the storm was headed straight toward our position. It was time to head out to sea to a safer place. The monstrous seas close to the center of the storm not only could damage the ship but also make accomplishing anything virtually impossible. That evening and into the next day we suffered through high seas and wind but managed to avoid the full force of the storm.

By the night of September 1, the effects of tropical storm Doris had mostly passed, and we were on our way back toward our south SAR Station post with plans to remain there for at least another week. On the 5th the USS *Long Beach* (CGN-9), another magnificent warship with its powerful weaponry and distinctive bridge design, replaced the *Biddle*. Commissioned in September 1961, the 720-foot long cruiser was the first nuclear powered surface warship in the world and the first large combatant in the U.S. Navy with its main battery consisting entirely of guided missiles.

13

A Possible Kraken
and Okinawa Legacy

Through the ages sailors have been superstitious. Contributing to their often-unfounded fears is the reality that the sea can be uncontrollable, unpredictable and fearsome. One of the oldest superstitions is that of the legendary *kraken* first recorded in the Norse sagas. The Vikings described the *kraken* as a giant octopus-like creature said to dwell in the depths of the sea, capable of grabbing warriors from the decks of ships and dragging them under never to be seen again. The great American author and whaling ship crewman Herman Melville in his novel *Moby-Dick* writes about the *Pequod*'s encounter with "The great live Squid, which, they say, few whale-ships ever beheld, and returned to their ports to tell of it."

Another well-known maritime superstition, immortalized in Coleridge's "The Rime of the Ancient Mariner," holds that it is beyond bad luck for a sailor to kill an albatross.

> And I had done a hellish thing,
> And it would work 'em woe:
> For all averred, I had killed the bird
> That made the breeze to blow.
> Ah wretch! said they, the bird to slay,
> That made the breeze to blow!
>
> Ah! well a-day! what evil looks
> Had I from old and young!
> Instead of the cross, the Albatross
> About my neck was hung.

Some of these superstitions have their origins in long, physically demanding and dangerous days at sea. The Norse in open longships sailed the North Atlantic in bitter cold. During the Great Age of Exploration, men sailed where few had gone before. Often enough these ships were lost at sea for unknown reasons. Mariners on the long-haul sailing ships of the 18th and 19th century also experienced phenomena that gave rise to nautical legend and superstition. Thus sailors on the *Buck*, having spent long periods of time under equally demanding conditions, were probably primed to believe such stories.

One quiet Sunday evening the DASH crew had gone to the Sunday evening movie. Before they left, they closed the watertight door entry to the hangar but left the main hangar door half open. The first man to return to the hangar from the movie opened the watertight door and froze in his tracks. In the near-total darkness some twenty feet in front of him stood what appeared to be a giant creature with two large glowing eyes flanked by two pointed horns. The sailor jumped back outside and slammed the door shut, his heart pounding. When the other men showed up each in turn peeked in the door and slammed it shut just as quickly as the first man. What could it be? Our leading petty officer, EN1 Fred Homer, always the bravest of the group, volunteered to enter the hangar and turn on the lights so they could at least see what it was confronting them.

Eyewitness testimony said that as soon as Homer hit the lights the thing turned and, with huge, furiously flapping wings and large clawed feet, made for the main hangar door. Homer had wisely hit the deck near the watertight door, just in case whatever it was decided to attack. To everyone's great relief the thing soared out the main hangar door, over the flight deck and disappeared into the darkness.

In an after-action discussion, the crew decided the creature had to be some kind of a large bird that settled on a rotor of one of the two DASH birds for a rest during a long flight at sea. But what manner of bird had such a fearsome appearance no one knew. In the near total darkness, they had only been able to see the big eyes, horn-like features on its head, the large wings and the fearsome clawed feet.

Researching it later, I thought it might be an eagle-owl that inhabits areas of Southeast Asia. A mature eagle-owl is more than two feet in length with the ninth longest wings of any living owl. The ear-tufts on each side of the owl's head are conspicuous, looking like horns and measuring up to three inches in length. Finally, the owl's feet and talons are especially large, heavy, and powerful for the size of the bird.

The owl-creature incident taught us how sailors' real-life experiences could lead to superstition and stories of the supernatural. Our owl wasn't as big or deadly as the *kraken*, but we could all understand how in an earlier time sailors might have perpetuated the story of a winged monster with the big glowing red eyes.

13. A Possible Kraken and Okinawa Legacy

We completed our SAR assignment on the 9th of September, returning briefly for more plane guard work on Yankee Station before making our way northeast through the South China Sea past Taiwan headed for Okinawa on our way to the U.S. Naval Base at Sasebo, Japan. Sasebo sits about thirty miles northwest of Nagasaki in western Japan. On September 18, we reached Sasebo, marking our 35th straight day at sea, including a fair amount of that time in rough weather thanks to the western Pacific typhoon season. Everyone was relieved to finally have a break in the tedious yet demanding at sea routine and be able to set foot once again on dry land.

Setting foot on dry land after many days underway, there exists a human malady that occurs after a long time at sea. Identified centuries ago by European seafarers, *Mal de debarquement,* or "illness of disembarkation," is the odd feeling you get after leaving a ship after a long time at sea. Some scientists believe that over time a part of your brain adjusts your mind and body to the motion of the ship. When you go ashore, your mind and body are still making the adjustments they had aboard ship and so you feel as though the pier, like your ship, is rolling beneath you. It normally takes a little while for you to adjust and feel normal again.

Sasebo was the final stop for three of the *Buck*'s officers, ASW Officer Skip Leeson, CIC Officer Joe Johnson and the Damage Control Assistant (DCA) Jim Kosica. They were all finishing their service and flying home. Even with replacements the ship would be missing some valuable expertise. I was surprised to learn that absent a replacement for Kosica, Captain Mode had decided to make me the new DCA, at least temporarily. I had taken a week-long course in damage control procedures at the Naval Technical Training Center (NTTC) on Treasure Island. NAVSTA Treasure Island closed in 1997. The manmade island of less than one square mile in San Francisco Bay is now a California Historical Landmark with diverse uses. Normally the DCA would take a ten-week course in the duties and responsibilities of the position that include firefighting, structural repair, control of the ship's stability, list and trim, watertight integrity, and compartment testing. I had little of the necessary training, but probably more than any other officer aboard, so I got assigned the job. I had to rely almost completely on the advice and guidance of my chief petty officer.

On September 28, the *Buck* put to sea again, this time operating about 200 miles south of Sasebo in a place known as the Okinawa

Operating area. Once again we were part of a carrier task group, this one composed of the USS *Oriskany* (CVA-34), USS *Mahan* (DLG-11), USS *Mason* (DD-852), USS *Rupertus* (DD-851) and the USS *Orleck* (DD-886). On Sunday the 5th of October we detached from the others and headed for Buckner Bay, Okinawa, for a six-hour stop to refuel. Visiting Buckner Bay meant seeing the location of an important moment in American history, a moment now unknown or forgotten.

Okinawa, the smallest of the five main islands of modern Japan, has a rich history going back many hundreds of years. In 1852 Commodore Matthew Perry mapped the island purportedly naming its bay Perry Bay. The name did not stick; the Japanese and most of the rest of the world continued to call it Nakagusuku Bay. In 1879 Japan annexed the Ryukyu archipelago including Okinawa, and so the Japanese name remained.

World War II made the name Okinawa familiar to many Americans. On April 1, 1945, U.S. forces launched the largest amphibious attack in the entire Pacific Theater against the Japanese forces on Okinawa. We tend to think of Pacific island invasions as terribly bloody but at least reasonably short-lived battles, but not this one. For 83 days, from April 1 to June 22, American soldiers on Okinawa experienced the bloodiest ground battle of the entire war in the Pacific. During the battle, the U.S. lost 12,510 troops while the Japanese lost an estimated— and amazing—95,000 soldiers. Approximately 150,000 civilians were also killed. These terrible figures do not include the wounded and those who later died from their wounds.

Today many people remember the Battle of Iwo Jima, fought from February 19 to March 26, 1945, and not the larger, longer and by far more costly in terms of American lives, Battle of Okinawa. They probably do so because of the dramatic and now iconic photo and the Washington, D.C., memorial statue of the six marines raising a U.S. flag atop Iwo Jima's Mount Suribachi. The 36-day Iwo Jima conflict resulted in the loss of 6,800 brave Americans compared to the 12,510 on Okinawa. Also, Iwo Jima is 855 miles east of Okinawa and proved not to be of the strategic importance of Okinawa.

Following the conclusion of the Battle of Okinawa U.S. troops began to refer to Nakagusuku Bay as "Buckner Bay." They did so in memory of Lieutenant General Simon Bolivar Buckner, Jr., U.S. Army, who had been commander of the U.S. invasion force. Buckner was killed by enemy artillery fire on June 18, only four days before the end of the lengthy and bloody battle. With the island captured, the Navy established a permanent base on Buckner Bay to support U.S. Naval forces. For many of us it was an honor just to be there.

On October 19, in heavy seas the *Buck* began the trek back home to San Diego.

There is little to compare to returning to your wife after nearly seven months of deployment. As bad as you feel on the day you leave, your emotions are the opposite—even stronger—on your return. It may actually be what the man meant when he told me Navy deployments probably save more marriages than they ruin. I once took his words lightly, but now I've come to think he meant separation gives everyone

Mid-to-late October 1969, on the signal bridge of the *Buck* while steaming in heavy seas in proximity to the USS *Bonne Homme Richard* (CVA-31) while on the return voyage to San Diego (author's collection).

the opportunity to learn what is most important and the strength to remember it. On the morning of the 29th of October, in bright sunshine, the *Buck* pulled alongside Pier 2 at the 32nd Street Naval Station welcomed by a small Navy band and a large contingent of friends, wives and children. It had been a long six and half months for all of us.

In a mid–October 1969 message to the Commander of the 7th Fleet, the Commander of the 7th's Cruiser-Destroyer Group nominated the *Buck* for ship of the year. The nomination states the following:

1. *Buck* (DD-761) is nominated for subject award (Ship of the Year).

2. During her deployment to the Seventh Fleet which commenced in April *Buck* has performed every task that Seventh Fleet destroyers are normally called on to perform. Each task assigned has been performed in an outstanding manner.

3. During the months April to June *Buck* logged nearly 85 hours of DASH flight time. In June alone almost 42 hours were flown, a tremendous achievement under present operating conditions.

4. In fifteen days on the gunline providing Naval Gunfire Support for allied forces ashore, *Buck* accounted for 31 bunkers destroyed, 30 bunkers damaged, six structures destroyed, 10 caves closed, six secondary explosions and three enemy KIA. In addition she fired numerous unobserved missions into known enemy base areas. Her gunline activity led to high praise from the senior advisor in the RSSZ (Rung Sat Special Zone was the name for the Can Gio mangrove forest near Vung Tau) for the outstanding accuracy and responsiveness displayed. The gunline commander reported her NGFS activities to be outstanding.

5. During support operations *Buck* has served as defensive escort for search and rescue and anti-air warfare ships and as rescue destroyer for carrier operations. These duties led to repeated laudatory comments from her superiors for the seamanship and professional skill displayed in ship handling and for her overall outstanding performance. Ashtabula (AO-51, a fleet oiler of 664 feet in length used heavily during the war) reported *Buck*'s performance as the smartest of any PacFlt destroyer.

6. *Buck* arrived in WestPac C-1 in training/readiness (There were five unit resource status category ratings from C1 to C5 with C1 meaning fully capable of performing her assigned wartime missions with respect to personnel, supplies, equipment, equipment status, and training) and has remained at that level throughout her deployment. She has met all operational commitments during

the deployment and has remained C-2 or above in all categories of readiness during her entire deployment with the Seventh Fleet.

7. *Buck* won the CRUDESPAC Ney Memorial Award and placed second in the Navy wide Ney Memorial program for small messes afloat. Inspection for the Navy wide award was conducted while *Buck* was deployed in Southeast Asia.

8. Overall *Buck* has been an outstanding ship in all respects and is recommended for ship of the year award.

14

Wardroom Changes
and Another Friend Lost

On November 10, 1969, only two weeks after the *Buck*'s return from Westpac, Commander Dale W. Duncan replaced Commander Paul J. Mode as the commanding officer. Commander Mode was awarded a Bronze Star for his performance aboard *Buck*.

Captain Duncan did not approach managing a ship in the manner of Paul J. Mode. The two men had different personalities and different management styles. Under Captain Mode the *Buck*'s wardroom was a cohesive unit. The 15 or so officers all got along well, united in bonds formed by shared concern at angering or disappointing the often intimidating Captain Mode. They enjoyed a camaraderie derived in part from universal duress. Under the management of a far less autocratic Captain Duncan, the wardroom became a less cohesive unit. While the Duncan wardroom had a number of officers new to the ship, the difference in personnel could not account for a clear change in the camaraderie. There were no fistfights—at least not right away—but neither was there an underlying spirit of unity. Without Mode, there was no martinet, no one to force teamwork from 15 officers all driven by the same desire for self-preservation.

Under Captain Duncan I got relieved as the DCA and felt honored to be given the job of 1st Lieutenant, the officer in charge of deck division, aka 1st Division. I took over from Lt. Mike Sobyra, a friend who had managed the division very well.

First Division is the home of the boatswain's mates. Rich with naval tradition, the work of boatswain's mates dates to the time men first went to sea. Deck division is responsible for mooring and anchoring the ship, the ship's maintenance and upkeep, handling the ship's tackle and rigging, conducting underway replenishments, maintaining and operating the ship's boat, manning various positions on the bridge while underway, and announcing any and all the events of the day at sea.

Aboard the *Buck*, 1st division consisted of some 35 hardworking, durable, unspoiled young men. Many were undereducated, from small towns in rural areas in the south, used to hard work and getting little in return. Most of the young men in 1st Division were undesignated seamen, meaning they had not been selected for a rating with special skills like sonarman, gunnersmate, torpedoman, etc.

On the *Buck* the men of 1st Division shared one berthing compartment in the forward part of the ship, a space that might charitably be described as cramped. The men slept in columns three deep on a stretched canvas, aluminum-framed rack, without curtains or privacy of any kind. Each had one small locker in which to store their uniforms and personal items.

Life for 1st Division's junior enlisted men aboard this late World War II design warship wasn't easy. There was no room for "snowflakes," no safe spaces for the easily offended, and no trigger warnings—unless you count warnings from the Chief Boatswain's Mate about your performance or behavior. On fortunately rare occasion there was such a thing as strictly unofficial, off the record "get-togethers" with senior boatswain's mates in the bosn's locker (a relatively small compartment in the forward part of the ship used to store equipment and supplies belonging to the deck division). A seaman with an attitude who decided he wasn't going to behave in accordance with the rules got invited to meet privately with the senior boatswain's mates in the boatswain's locker. The rated boatswain's mates could be remarkably persuasive, the sailor almost always a changed man after the meeting. Discipline such as this, used very sparingly and without malice, saved men from making bigger mistakes and usually made life better for all 1st Division's men.

Although it didn't so state on any written job description, one of the responsibilities of the 1st Lieutenant was to try to keep his men from getting into trouble. Trouble could take almost any form, from missing ship's movement (not showing up before the ship left port), to financial difficulties, drug use, fighting, and significant domestic problems. Deck division on any Navy ship is usually known for having more troublemakers than any of the ship's other divisions. Its inexperienced, younger, and less well-educated sailors were often still teenagers, the Navy their first experience away from home. Adjustment problems were to be expected.

First Division personnel appear more frequently at Captain's Mast than do those from other divisions. Captain's Mast is non-judicial punishment authorized by the Uniform Code of Military Justice, allowing the captain to administratively discipline sailors under his command for offenses that do not rise to the level of a court martial. Aboard the *Buck*, Captain's Mast was a formal procedure that took place in the DASH hangar, with participants at attention in dress uniform, the captain behind a podium. Fines and reduction in rank could be levied against offenders. Being restricted to the ship for a period of days or weeks was not an unusual punishment. Sometimes restricting a man to the ship for some relatively minor infraction could be more trouble than it was worth. On more than one occasion a restricted man's wife had come down to the ship and made a scene, demanding that her husband be allowed to go home.

One punishable incident involving a few of the *Buck*'s 1st Division men happened when the ship was moored to a pier in the Long Beach Naval Shipyard getting some repair work done. At around 2 a.m. an agitated messenger of the watch reported that an admiral was on the quarterdeck demanding to know what had happened to his car. No one had any idea what the admiral was talking about but an angry admiral on your gangway at 2 a.m. was a matter recognized by all as a situation requiring priority attention.

A quick investigation revealed that the admiral was upset because someone had painted black racing stripe trim on his brand-new light blue and cream-colored Cadillac. The admiral had parked his four-door DeVille at the end of the pier to attend a social function. When he and his wife returned, they found their beautiful new car had been redecorated. The admiral said he understood men from the *Buck* had done the work. The admiral wanted to know what was going to be done to restore his vehicle to its pristine condition.

Further investigation revealed that, for whatever reason, around midnight a number of 1st Division's men, most with a few beers under their belts, had decided the pastel blue and cream-colored car would look much better with some shiny black contrast. So they went to the boatswain's locker, got some black spar varnish (it is hard to find a black paint more difficult to remove—it's what the Navy uses on anchor chains and the like) and some paint brushes and within no time had that Cadillac looking just like an L.A. street racer. They didn't even try to hide from passersby who they were or where they were from. Finished with their work, they packed up their paint and brushes and retired for the night. However, shortly after their 2:30 a.m. reveille, they quickly agreed that if the admiral and his wife preferred the original, more sedate look, they would fix it without delay, a sentiment strongly encouraged by *Buck* management.

14. Wardroom Changes and Another Friend Lost

So, from about 3 a.m. until late the next day, the entire deck division of the USS *Buck* worked feverishly on getting every hint of black spar varnish removed from the admiral's car and restoring the pastel colors to what they had been the night before. I could never understand why the admiral didn't insist on some form of punishment for the dummies who had done the painting, but once the car had been restored that was pretty much the end of it. Kudos to the admiral.

* * *

It was during this first six-and-a-half-month deployment to Westpac that I learned to drive the ship and qualified as an Officer of the Deck (OOD) underway. An OOD underway is certified in writing by the ship's captain as fully capable of driving the ship in all situations. An OOD effectively commands the ship for the captain, giving all orders related to the operation of the vessel. The 376-foot long ship is a complex amalgamation of hundreds of men and machines. The long vessel responds differently in a myriad of at-sea conditions and situations. To become a qualified OOD requires time, experience and a certain amount of natural ability. Usually a destroyer such as the *Buck* will have no more than four qualified OODs at any one time with those officers at the rank of Lieutenant or lieutenant junior grade (Lt. j.g.).

Underway a watch crew including the OOD usually stands a four-hour watch. These include the "20 to 24" (2000 to 2400), "the mid watch" (2400 to 0400), "the 4 to 8" (0400 to 0800), the "8 to 12" (0800 to 1200), and the "12 to 16" (1200–1600). Two-hour watches are the "first dog watch" (1600 to 1800) and the "second dog watch" (1800 to 2000). Dog watches make for an odd number of watches in a ship's day allowing sailors to rotate through the sequence.

There are many centuries-old explanations as to why it is called the "dog watch." My favorite is the term is derived from Sirius, the "Dog Star," because Sirius can be the first star to be seen at night.

Directly underneath the OOD in every bridge watch is the Junior Officer of the Deck (JOOD) who is learning to become a qualified OOD. On a destroyer JOODs are usually ensigns and junior Lt. (j.g.'s). All watch standing comes in addition to the officer's regular work.

When a destroyer such as the *Buck* is in port, the OOD is something very different. In port the OOD is a junior officer or senior petty officer who stands watch on the quarterdeck. Watch periods are of the same duration as bridge watches. The quarterdeck is not an actual place or even fixed location on any ship. It is basically an undefined space wherever the end of the gangway meets the ship. In dress uniform, the OOD serves in both an administrative and ceremonial capacity, from managing the receipt of goods and services to welcoming visiting officials and dignitaries aboard ship. Whenever the commanding officer of the ship comes aboard, the watch on the quarterdeck announces it over the 1MC (the ship's public address system) by saying, "*Buck* arriving." Similarly, whenever the C.O. leaves the ship the quarterdeck announces, "*Buck* departing." Among other things the announcement serves to make everyone aboard ship aware of who is in charge.

When an officer has what is referred to as "the duty," he must spend the night or the weekend on the ship. Most of the time officers had the duty every fourth night—sometimes every third night—and every fourth (or third) weekend. Sometimes, albeit rarely, duty could even be "port and starboard" meaning every other night/weekend.

On weekends officers' wives were allowed to join their husbands in the wardroom for dinner and that was always a nice occasion. The steward on duty would make a restaurant quality dinner for two that was formally served by the duty steward dressed in a waiter's white jacket. The wardroom table was set for two with a white tablecloth and silverware, the food excellently prepared and delicious. Following dinner the officer could show a reasonably current movie on the wardroom movie projector, changing the film reels and adjusting the machine as necessary. After the movie the wife would go home.

As mentioned earlier, our food preparation and Supply Division in general was first rate. When I joined the Buck, the Supply Officer was Lt. Keith Swayne who came from a well-known family in the food industry in California. Keith's nickname was "Pork Chop," not because of any predilection on his part for pigs' feet or ham hocks, but because the Supply Corps oak leaf uniform insignia resembles a pork chop. Throughout the Navy supply officers were affectionately referred to as pork chop. Keith, as the supply officer, had nothing to do with driving the ship, firing the guns, or making the propellers turn, but without his work the ship could not function. He managed all aspects of the ship's food service, laundry, the ship's store, disbursing, consumables, and spare parts. He was the one who paid people, and it was he who was directly accountable for all expenditures of government money. Aside from paying us, we all thought the best thing he—or more properly his men—did was making fresh bread. Standing the 0400 to 0800 watch on the bridge was made bearable by the smell of the bread wafting up from the galley, just out of the oven. We often sent the messenger of the watch down to the mess decks to get some fresh out of the oven. When Keith left the Navy, he returned to his family business, serving for many years as President of the Case Swayne Company of Corona, California. In 2019 he was named Orange County, California, philanthropist of the year.

* * *

In mid–February 1970 came the news of yet another tragedy. A close friend, 23-year-old Captain John Michael Gibbons ("Mike" to his high school friends and "John" to his Army buddies) U.S. Army, had been killed in action in South Vietnam. Mike was a high school classmate close to both Elaine and me. He was in many of Elaine's and my high school classes, a football teammate of mine, and an Oswego State University classmate of Elaine's.

We learned that on Thursday, February 12, Mike was Aircraft Commander of a Dolphin UH-1H flying troops into a "hot" landing zone, one that was under enemy fire. After successfully dropping his troops into the "hot zone" he was lifting his helicopter off the ground to leave the area when the aircraft suddenly came under ground fire. Rounds from a single AK-47 came through the underside of the aircraft, hitting him and killing him almost instantly. Somehow his co-pilot was able to take control and fly the helicopter out of the fire zone and back to their base while the others in the aircrew did everything they could to try to save Mike.

According to *www.174ahc.org/174ahc3.php#CPTGibbons*, WO1 John Bailey, a close friend of Captain Gibbons in the 174th Assault Helicopter Company made the following comments:

> His co-pilot was Warrant Officer 1 (WO1) Robinson. "Gibby" was A/C flying left seat. It was a two-ship movement of troops from one location to another. "Gibby" was Platoon Leader and he was also Flight Leader this day. They were "climbing out" of the area. The C/E spotted a military-age male standing out in the open. The man seemed to have produced an AK-47 from under his clothing. The C/E said the man just "swept up" toward the aircraft on full automatic. One of the rounds hit Gibbons in the left side under his armpit and three other rounds hit behind his left ear of his helmet. Gibbons slumped forward and his right foot went forward and the aircraft went out of trim & drifting towards the other ship. Robinson grabbed the flight controls. Two (or more) rounds had come through the radio console & his cyclic disabling his radio. His C/E and Door Gunner left their stations to pull Gibbons back into cargo and apply some first aid. They managed to make it back to the 11th Brigade Medevac area. Either the C/E or the Gunner had to make the radio transmissions to Duc Pho Tower. By the time that they got the aircraft down, "Gibby" had died due to loss of blood and the nature of his wounds.

From Vietnam to the Arctic Circle

When he died Mike was a member of the 174th Assault Helicopter Company, 14th Aviation Battalion, 23rd Infantry (the Americal) Division of the United States Army. The 174th flew various models of the UH-1 "Huey" helicopter. From 1966 until 1971 the unit saw a lot of combat action in the rice paddies and mountains in the northern half of South Vietnam.

Among Mike's many ribbons and awards was the Bronze Star, with "second and third awards for heroism." Mike's valor in the field reminded me of another quote from G.K. Chesterton, "Courage is almost a contradiction in terms. It means a strong desire to live taking the form of readiness to die." Indeed, Mike did his job, willingly assuming the substantial risk of making the ultimate sacrifice. One of his many friends commented that Mike stood for every attribute one can think of contained in the words "All American."

Years after Mike's death, Islip Town Councilman Christopher D. Bodkin found a way to recognize the immeasurable sacrifice of John Michael Gibbons. Bodkin was able to facilitate the naming of a new street in Mike's honor in his hometown of Sayville. I think Bodkin realized that no soldier is truly dead and gone when people still say his name.

15

Back to Vietnam

The first half of 1970 found the *Buck* in the waters off San Diego conducting training and participating in a variety of relatively small exercises. On the 1st of February the ship began the Navy's formal triennial INSURV Inspection, designed to determine the suitability of the ship for future active service. The inspection determined the ship was in remarkably good condition and fit for at least one more year of service. The finding was a little surprising. Compare the *Buck* to a twenty-four-year-old car. How many cars still on the road at that age are in "remarkably good condition" and might be expected to perform well for at least another year? And the *Buck* survived as well as it did in a corrosive, open ocean environment! In great measure she lasted the way she did because of the professionalism and hard work of the men who sailed her all those years.

One small assignment in the first half of 1970 turned out to be more memorable than the others. We were ordered to conduct a burial at sea.

The day of the service for the cremated remains of a former sailor dawned overcast with a good wind and a fairly heavy sea. The trip out to a location a few miles offshore was through moderately rough seas.

The ceremony accompanying a burial at sea is as old as seafaring itself. Various traditions and procedures have come and gone but a solemnity befitting the occasion has always been present and so it was on this day.

When the appointed hour arrived for the brief ceremony, those not on watch assembled on the aft deck in dress uniform. Conducting the service was not easy as the stern of the ship wallowed heavily in a following sea. Everyone, including the honor guard of seven riflemen, had a difficult time maintaining their balance.

The chaplain delivered the final words and the riflemen fired the customary three-volley salute as the box of ashes was opened and thrown to the winds. It was a dignified performance signifying the end of mortal life and the promise of the hereafter.

From Vietnam to the Arctic Circle

No family members are allowed to be present for the burial, but it is customary for the captain of the ship to send a letter to the family following the execution of the service, something I'm sure Captain Duncan did. Today the Navy still conducts burials at sea, but they are limited to active-duty members of the uniformed services, retirees and veterans who were honorably discharged, U.S. civilian marine personnel of the Military Sealift Command and their dependents.

What followed the service reinforced everyone's awareness of his own mortality, and how at sea the unexpected can happen in an instant.

As the service closed, the seven riflemen, weapons on their shoulders, marched off the aft deck and into the ship through a passageway just below and forward of the torpedo magazine and DASH hangar. Suddenly from inside the passageway a rifle shot rang out. No one knew what had happened. Had someone been shot?

We soon learned that at least one of the honor guard riflemen had been using live ammunition. In emptying his rifle, he somehow accidentally fired a round left in the chamber. The bullet did not strike anyone, but it went through the overhead and into the torpedo magazine where, thank God, it came to rest without striking a torpedo. We understood that our torpedo warhead explosives are very stable and difficult to detonate without the proper firing sequence, so probably nothing would have happened even if the round had hit the explosive. But no one believed that firing a round into hundreds of pounds of high explosives was a safe practice. Once again, we learned that life at sea can be dangerous and inevitably it is so because of human error. We were all thankful this mistake did not turn into something far worse.

Later in the spring of 1970, Ingrid "Irene" Kiesling, Elaine's mother, came to San Diego for a visit, so we took her aboard the *Buck* for dinner when I had the duty. She loved it. I took her on a tour of the ship and when she got to the bridge she looked around and said, "Oh, this is right where Robert Mitchum stood on the bridge of the *Haynes*!"

Ingrid was referring to the 1957 movie, *The Enemy Below*, one of the finest war films ever made about the battle of wits between a German submarine captain and his American destroyer escort pursuer. The movie starred Robert Mitchum as the captain of the American DE, the USS *Haynes* (DE-181), and Curt Jurgens as the captain of the German submarine. Ironically, only about six months earlier, as previously described, the *Buck* had been playing cat and mouse with an unknown submarine and its captain off the South Korean coast.

It is instructive to briefly recap the movie because it conveys a lot about the mindset of many Americans at the time of Ingrid's visit, coming off World War II and the Korean War and going into the war in Vietnam. Almost 50 years after Vietnam many Americans probably have a different view of combat with foreign enemies. To recap:

At the conclusion of the film the German captain succeeds in torpedoing Mitchum's destroyer escort (DE). However, the American isn't about to give up and conjures up one final plan. Before ordering his crew to abandon ship, Mitchum instructs them to set fires on the deck to give the Germans the impression the ship is more damaged than it really is. Mitchum's bet is that when the German captain sees the DE in flames, he will surface and try to finish off the Americans with his deck gun instead of using up another precious torpedo. The trick works, and when the German submarine surfaces, Mitchum orders his gunners to open fire, disabling the sub. He orders his engine room to increase to full speed and then abandon ship before steering his sinking ship towards the U-boat. Seeing what's about to happen, the German orders his crew to rig the sub's detonators and abandon ship. Mitchum's DE rams the U-boat slicing it almost in two.

Mitchum, the only one left aboard ship, is about to jump when he sees the German captain in the conning tower of his U-boat, his severely wounded executive officer at his side. With obvious respect, the German captain salutes his American counterpart who, in similar fashion, returns the salute. Mitchum then does the totally unexpected, tossing a line to the submarine and pulling the two Germans on board. Mitchum then tells the German captain they must abandon ship and leave his dying second-in-command to his fate. But the German captain chooses death over disloyalty and refuses to leave his dying shipmate.

The film ends with members of both the German and the American crews climbing on board the DE, helping the three men into a lifeboat. They just barely manage to get clear of the sinking wrecks before the detonators on the sub explode. Everyone, including the two German officers, is rescued by another American warship. The film ends with the German executive officer's body being buried at sea with the American crew respectfully observing the burial.

The real-life inspiration for *The Enemy Below* was the USS *Straub* (DE-181). She served primarily in the Atlantic during World War II providing anti-submarine escort service for convoys. In late spring 1944 the *Straub* recovered the commanding officer, executive officer and 18 crewmen of a German sub sunk by other units.

* * *

From Vietnam to the Arctic Circle

On July 27, 1970, at the age of 24, the *Buck* deployed to WESTPAC for the final time. In company with the *Lynde McCormick* (DDG-8), the *Perkins* (DD-877), and the *Wiltsie* (DD-814) we headed for Pearl Harbor, approximately 2,600 miles away, and always the first stop for any Navy ship on a Pacific crossing.

We arrived in Pearl on August 1, but with an engine problem that would keep us there for almost a week while the other ships made their way west. By August 7, we were back underway, steaming for the western Pacific, a cruise that seemed interminable. Day after day the cerulean blue water passed under our keel with nothing on the horizon except more water. Anyone who has crossed the Pacific comes away amazed at just how much ocean there is. Standing on the bridge, I was mesmerized as the endless deep blue sea slipped past in the humid air of the South Seas. For anyone standing on the fantail in the evening, the phosphorescence produced by the disturbed plankton in the ship's wake provided a spectacular natural light show.

Approaching Midway Island on August 10, I was fortunate enough to catch an unusual sight. I watched an albatross following in the *Buck*'s wake soar slowly and effortlessly over the tops of the waves, as though it were surfing on its wing tips. This remarkable bird can use its more than 10-foot, glider-like wingspan to fly at speeds as high as 67 miles per hour. They are also able to travel incredible distances—up to 10,000 miles—without pause. Immortalized in Coleridge's poem, the remarkable seabird may be seen as an omen of good fortune or bad if you harm it. I definitely saw it as a good sign.

We stopped for a six-hour refueling at Midway Island before setting course and speed for an August 17 arrival in Guam for another quick refueling. By August 21, the quiet ocean crossing was over at last and we were moored to a pier in Subic Bay. On August 24, four weeks after leaving San Diego, the *Buck* got underway headed for a Naval Gunfire Support (NGFS) mission in an area just north of Vung Tau in South Vietnam's III Corps.

On August 26, the *Buck* was at anchor just north of Vung Tau waiting for the start of Operation "Massey Harris." The objective of "Massey Harris" was to locate and destroy Viet Cong (VC) food crops growing in the Binh Chau area as well as destroy the rice caches hidden in the jungle meant for use either by the VC (militia forces from South Vietnam) or the Viet Minh (soldiers from North Vietnam). It was also an attempt to deny any rice deliveries to the Viet Cong in Phước Tuy Province just north of Vung Tau. Rice was the primary food for the enemy, which meant that a significant enemy presence required large amounts of it. An army marches on its stomach (the phrase first attributed to Napoleon), so denying the enemy its primary food source was important. Massey Harris was to run from August 29 to September 20, conducted by ANZAC (Australian, New Zealand and American infantry) forces.

Over the next fifteen days the *Buck* fired her guns almost non-stop, firing over three thousand rounds of 5-inch ammo. Halfway through the operation the *Buck* got relieved by the *Bausell* (DD-845) and headed back to Subic Bay for repairs, replenishment and a little down time. It was a needed opportunity for the crew to get off the ship and do something with their time besides shoot 5-inch/38 guns, rearm, refuel, stand watch, eat and, seemingly once in a great while, sleep.

Never ending gunfire support missions, plane guard duty and underway replenishment operations kept everyone on their toes all the time. And when men are constantly performing at that tempo—all work except for eating and minimal sleep—sometimes for four to five weeks at a time, psychological pressures build. The boredom, cramped quarters, heat and humidity, and the potential for danger or deadly mistake at any time naturally affected people. And working the gun line, often with round-the-clock firing of the ship's 5-inch/38s, meant the gun crews working the magazines, ammunition hoists and guns had little respite. There were no TVs, radios, cell phones, email or other diversions from the stresses and strains of constantly moving ammunition weighing in excess of 50 pounds.

What happened on the USS *Lloyd Thomas* (DD-764) on September 11, 1970, highlighted the dangers involved. On that September day the *Thomas* was working the gun line off South Vietnam providing gunfire support to the troops ashore. Suddenly there was an in-bore explosion in her forward 5-inch gun mount. The horrific blast killed three men and injured ten others. The *Thomas* immediately sailed to Subic Bay. According to Terry Miller writing in *Tin Can Sailors*, the July–August–September 2017 edition, the investigation afterwards found the accident apparently was not the result of a hot shell "cooking off" (the shell exploding prematurely due to heat in the gun), but rather a result of defective ammunition.

The *Buck* arrived in Subic Bay not long after the *Thomas* had undergone her temporary repairs. Left on the pier was the shell of the topside portion of the *Thomas*'s 5-inch gun mount. The inside of the mount was a scene of terrible devastation. The men who had been inside obviously never knew what hit them.

Having seen the gun mount, a few in Subic Bay repeated a warning story about an extremely dangerous game some gun crews were rumored, and I stress rumored, to play. The rumor held that in their boredom and fatigue, some dared others to strike the bottom of a shell casing with a hammer or a mallet. The rumor did not suggest that the explosion onboard the *Thomas* occurred as a result of such a "game of dare," rather it seemed to take the form of a cautionary tale about the need for eternal vigilance aboard ship.

16

Subic Bay and Olongapo

The *Buck* moored to a pier in Subic Bay on Saturday the 12th of September, nineteen days after getting underway from the same piers. The break in our intense gunfire support routine meant everyone would try to relax usually by going out and drinking a few beers either at one of the clubs on base and/or in the adjacent Philippine town of Olongapo. Getting a little buzz on with a buddy or two before heading back to the ship to sleep it off was the most popular way to forget the recent past and escape to a better place.

Subic Bay Naval Station, one of the largest military installations ever operated by the U.S. overseas, was actually only a small part of the beautiful harbor that is Subic Bay. The bay sits just off the South China Sea in the southwestern part of Luzon, the largest and most populated island in the Philippines. The natural deep-water harbor is about 50 miles northwest of the capital Manila, the two separated from one another by the Bataan Peninsula. The Peninsula was the site of much of the infamous Bataan Death March. In April 1942 the Imperial Japanese Army force-marched approximately 76,000 prisoners of war—approximately 66,000 Filipinos and 10,000 Americans—some 66 miles through the jungle from the coastal southern tip of the Bataan Peninsula to Camp O'Donnell in the mountains just north of Mount Pinatubo. Along the way thousands of prisoners died terrible deaths from disease, physical abuse, and unprovoked murder. On June 15, 1991, Mount Pinatubo became infamous for producing the world's largest volcanic eruption in the past 100 years. Ash from the event severely damaged the Subic Bay Naval Station.

Geographically, the Subic Bay Naval Station encompassed 262 square miles, an area comparable to the city-state of Singapore at 279 square miles. In 1967 the average number of ships visiting the base per month was well over 200 and rising. While the carriers docked in Subic Bay Naval Station, their planes stayed next door at Naval Air Station (NAS) Cubi Point. NAS Cubi Point, located on a small peninsula southwest of the Naval Station, served as the primary maintenance, repair and supply center for the approximately 400 carrier-based aircraft of the Seventh Fleet. When a couple of carriers and their supporting destroyers were in port at the same time, the number of visiting sailors was huge. Each carrier had a complement of approximately 5,000 men.

The base offered sailors a number of different possibilities for escaping the tedium of shipboard life, which included liberal amounts of inexpensive alcohol and cigarettes—cigarettes sold for only $2.50 per carton. At 25 cents a pack, just about everyone smoked. The enlisted men's club, the chiefs' club and the officers' club all stayed open long hours and served any alcoholic beverage you wanted, in unlimited quantities, and at very low prices.

Often guys would spend their off-hours drinking with their buddies at their on-base club and then walk into Olongapo for another drink or two at one of the hundreds of clubs. Occasionally the Navy would address the problem of excess or binge alcohol consumption through notices and bulletins but never to the point where any serious restrictions or controls were imposed. For a fair number of career Navy men, excess alcohol consumption over prolonged periods led to the problems one might expect. One chief petty officer in a moment of candor told me what had happened to him. When he was on shore duty and drinking heavily every night, he woke up one morning and literally couldn't move. It scared him so much he decided to change his ways right then and there. That was how he ended up aboard the *Buck*. Supported by his family, he requested sea duty on a deployed ship to avoid the everyday temptation of readily available alcohol.

Chain-smoking was not unusual—no one seemed to realize the health risks. To be fair, in the late 1960s public awareness that smoking could be hazardous to your health was in its nascent stages. It wasn't until 1965 when the federal government mandated that cigarette packs carry a warning on them saying "Caution: Cigarette Smoking May Be Hazardous to Your Health" that people started to worry about tobacco related health problems.

One officer aboard literally lit one cigarette from another from the time he got up until he went to bed. He even smoked during meals taking puffs between bites. The Navy never addressed excessive cigarette consumption at all, except indirectly. Periodically the Navy would decide that its sailors were not sufficiently physically fit and would reinstitute an "annual" PT test to measure their inadequacies. The idea was that the test itself would encourage sailors to engage in more and better physical conditioning over the long term. A few did their best on the test, but many cheated, and there was no follow-up program to encourage progress. In addition, on a relatively small ship like a destroyer, there wasn't enough free space or time to allow for much of a workout. Thus, while the Navy's intentions were to be applauded, the mind-set for most sailors after the annual test appeared to be anything but more exercise.

Sailors were not allowed to smoke in certain situations, such as during refueling, reloading ammunition or General Quarters. Sometimes when there was no smoking allowed for more than an hour or so, some people went nuts; they couldn't wait for the "smoking lamp" to be lit again. At night on the bridge, in a combat situation or during "darken ship," when no light was to be showing, smoking was forbidden because of the light given off by the cigarette. Officers on watch who couldn't leave the bridge often snuck a smoke anyway.

And speaking of excesses, if you were an unattached young guy and had just completed a month or more on a destroyer in the war zone, Olongapo would be the town you might design in your dreams. As mentioned, Sin-city bordered Subic Naval Base, a virtual extension of the base. Its bars and brothels, unpaved streets and honky-tonk saloons lay just outside the main gate on the other side of the aptly nicknamed "Sh*t River." On the maps the "Sh*t River," named for the raw sewage dumped into it, was inadequately labeled a drainage channel. A cement pedestrian bridge crossed the rancid ditch between the Base and Olongapo. No matter the time of day, Filipino youngsters in makeshift boats called for sailors passing on the bridge over their heads to toss coins in the water. No coin was too small for them to dive into the sickening muck to retrieve.

Today we worry about the conditions migrant children face at our facilities on the southern border. As far as I know, at the time no one, I'm embarrassed to admit myself included, worried at all about these Filipino kids risking all manner of disease right outside the gates of one of our major military bases.

Once over the bridge, down Magsaysay Drive, the neon lights of myriad bars and clubs offered the sailors the time of their lives. Live country and western and pop music seemed to be everywhere. Unpaved roads—a few got paved as the years wore on—were crowded with raucously decorated jitneys—jeepneys, some say. Jitneys were basically tricked out old Jeeps in outlandish colors, with garish chrome and brass trim and the occasional water buffalo horns or similar totem of male prowess. The young male drivers were inevitably as crazy as their machines, and for a sufficient tip could be enticed to speed to some favorite bar, unencumbered by concern for pedestrians or car traffic rules of any kind.

Food vendors were everywhere hawking barbecued meat on a stick, meat they insisted was chicken or beef, but which bore little resemblance to either. We called it monkey meat, which was optimistic, but whatever it was it could seem irresistible to an always hungry and semi-inebriated sailor. More than one sailor ended up in sickbay with stomach and intestinal difficulties. But for the true aficionado of Olongapo street food, nothing could beat a baloot—a fertilized chicken or duck egg buried in the ground for two to three weeks, then dug up and served at room temperature. Even Olongapo cuisine connoisseurs—-eaters-of-just-about-anything—always accompanied their baloot with at least one San Miguel beer, and usually many more, both before and after consumption of the specialty.

Rizal Avenue, another main drag, hosted just about every kind of "fun" facility imaginable. Scantily clad young ladies beckoned to sailors from the smoke-filled lobbies of the bars, taverns, hotels and roadhouses. They probably weren't actually all that beautiful in daylight, but at night and after drinks with one's buddies, sailors seemed to think they looked pretty good. Many of the bars advertised "live entertainment," a short phrase that could mean just about anything. For men who have spent months far from home, senior officers included, the nightlife temptations were difficult to completely resist.

But Olongapo wasn't some kind of Disneyland for sailors. There were plenty of fights, and areas of town where sailors weren't supposed to go because of the dangers to life and limb. There was an enforced nighttime curfew with unruly sailors carted off to the local jail. The Shore Patrol was always busy. I witnessed a machete—the weapon of choice—pulled on a sailor once, but fortunately differences got resolved before things got too out of hand.

On the 19th of September we said good-bye to Olongapo and Subic Bay Naval Station and headed north for Taiwan. By the morning of the 21st we were moored to buoys 21 and 22 in the always-frenetic Kaohsiung Harbor.

17

Saving John Wayne
and the Fight

One junior enlisted guy who had worked for me did an outstanding job. He knew his job inside and out, never failed to make things work, shared his knowledge, and generally made shipboard life better for those with and for whom he worked. A big, rugged guy in the John Wayne image (I'll call him John Wayne), he was well respected by everyone. In one port I found the opportunity to repay the man's remarkable professionalism in an admittedly unusual kind of way.

John kept it secret that he preferred men to women. Remember that in the late 1960s being gay in the military or just about anywhere in American society was strictly forbidden. In some states the police could, and did, arrest gays under sodomy laws. On June 28, 1969, in always-liberal New York City, the police conducted their now infamous raid of the Stonewall Inn, a gay club located in Greenwich Village. In the summer, squads of police in Suffolk County, New York, traveled by boat nearly five miles across the Great South Bay to the beach community of Cherry Grove to arrest "the queers" for unlawful conduct. So, if you were gay in the military, you made damn sure you kept it to yourself.

In Kaohsiung, one reasonably large hotel served as a popular venue for sailors looking for food, drink, and companionship. I happened to be in the bar when one of our sailors came in and told me John Wayne was in some kind of trouble on the fifth floor.

I went up in one of the tiny elevators and when the door opened, there in the hallway stood John and a young local guy. The two were just standing there shouting angrily at one another. John told me the guy wanted more money, and he wasn't about to pay anything more. "All right," I said, "get in the elevator quick and let's just get out of here." So John got in, but the angry local managed to jump in as well. The argument immediately resumed, only more heated than before. When John

117

told the guy in no uncertain terms he wasn't going to pay, the local pulled a switchblade.

A very small elevator is not a good place to engage in a knife fight. This maxim is especially true when you're not the one with the knife. Having been stabbed once before in my life, I wasn't of a mind to repeat the experience.

So, what to do? I asked the local how much John Wayne owed him. He said fifty bucks. Very fortunately, I happened to have $50 in my pocket. So, I gave the man the money, the elevator door opened on the lobby, the local flicked his knife closed, and everyone went about their business as though nothing had happened.

John did not return my fifty dollars, and we never spoke of the incident again. I don't think John knew what to say. He had probably wanted to tear the considerably smaller local man limb from limb, but realized that had he done so his career could well be over. He also knew I wouldn't say anything to anyone about what had happened. In the end, I think he decided to accept the $50 as a gift and just leave it alone.

On the 25th of September, after four days in Kaohsiung, we found ourselves once again headed south for a few more days at the pier in Subic Bay. Most everyone had seen more than enough of Subic Bay and Olongapo and found little left to keep themselves occupied. Without the constant drumbeat of demanding work, people had time to do things they probably would not otherwise do.

Sometimes alcohol-fueled venting led to behavior even by officers that was out of character and would not have happened under normal circumstances. One of my superior officers (I'll call him Rocky Balboa) and I were illustrative of what could happen.

One evening we decided to forego the usual visit to the Subic Bay officers' club in favor of a visit to the Cubi Point Naval Air Station officers' club. As mentioned earlier, Cubi Point NAS adjoined the Subic Bay naval station and was no more than a short cab ride from the ship.

The two of us bellied up to the bar along with many other officers and spent a couple of hours downing whatever the special was on that particular night. Around 10 p.m. we decided it was time to head back to the ship.

During the cab ride back, Rocky and I got into a disagreement. I don't even remember what it was about. Both of us being somewhat aggressive, stubborn and reasonably athletic, we decided to settle things with a fistfight. We told the Filipino cab driver to forget about taking us back to the ship and instead take us to one of the empty piers. The driver, who had been listening to what we had been saying, was happy to comply. Guys love to watch other guys fistfight and there was also a chance to make some extra money by letting some of his friends know there was to be a private fistfight between two American officers.

We got out of the cab on the well-lit pier and proceeded to take off our outer shirts and watches, placing them on a nearby stack of lumber. Unfortunately for me, Rocky neglected to take off his emblem-faced ring. And so it began, much like any boxing match, with the two of us circling and then jabbing. Before long we were slugging each other like the other was a punching bag. Even now I have to admit, connecting with a solid right to Rocky's chin was a great feeling.

Whether it was the cab driver notifying his buddies, or dockworkers just stumbling on the scene, before long there were approximately thirty or so Filipino workers perched on the stacks of lumber, loudly cheering us on in their local Tagalog, and actively wagering on who might win.

At first, with a slightly longer reach, I was able to punch Rocky's head practically at will giving him a nasty swelling over his left eye, a long cut on his left ear and other nicks and dents. Remember, this was bare knuckle so anything that landed on the head tended to leave a mark or worse. After a few more minutes of banging away we decided to take a short break to remove ripped T-shirts before starting in on round 2.

Tired of being pummeled without landing a serious blow himself, Rocky decided maybe he should try grabbing me into a clinch and punching from in close. The change in strategy worked. I was soon getting the worst of it. Body blows to my mid-section definitely had an effect. Toward the end of the second round, he threw me to the ground and then, from his position on top, landed a heavy right to my head. The ring on his finger caught me just above the right eye opening an inch long cut which began to bleed profusely.

Fortunately for both of us, just as round three was getting underway, the Shore Patrol (SP) sirens started to wail in the background and within moments two SP trucks with four enlisted shore patrol arrived on the scene. Frankly, at that point I was happy to see them, but by this time Rocky was really into it. After all, he was winning. He told the SPs to back off, go home, and let the fight continue. The SPs handled it well. They talked to us at some length, giving Rocky time to settle down enough to accept the fight was over and it was time to return to the ship.

The SPs let us gather our shirts and belongings, or what was left of them, from the nearby stack of wood. My prized gold watch, given to me by Elaine a couple of years before, had gone missing. It was my good luck piece, my connection with home, and an object of great personal value. There was no getting it back, no sense in even looking around. And because I was bleeding so much from the cut over my eye, the SPs insisted we hurry along. In one of their trucks, they ferried me to the base dispensary to get sewn up. Unfortunately, it was not the end of the incident.

I later learned from friends that after we separated Rocky's temper flared anew. I did not witness it, but my friends said that once back aboard ship Rocky began stomping around, swearing he was going to beat the hell out of me as soon as he could find me. The same friends told me it was the C.O. himself who intervened and got Rocky to calm down. While all this was going on I was getting the cut over my eye stitched up by one of the doctors at the base infirmary who then released me to return to the *Buck*. By that time, it was the wee hours of the morning. When I finally got back aboard ship things were quiet in officers quarters and I went straight to bed, blissfully unaware of Rocky's continued anger and threats.

The next morning all was quiet. But the fight was the talk of the ship for both officers and crew. In addition to the rarity of a fistfight between officers, the physical appearance of both Rocky and me, with stitches, cuts, black eyes, swollen noses, scraped knuckles and the like, added color to the rampant gossip on how it all went down. Also, many who worked with both of us wondered how this apparently new dynamic between the two of us might affect them personally.

First thing that morning, the Captain called Rocky and me into the wardroom for a private meeting. He began by asking us to explain to him what had happened, which we did. Both of us in a matter-of-fact, straightforward manner, without any display of personal rancor, described the events as they had unfolded. Both of us said that in hindsight the incident was unfortunate but just something each of us felt he had to do. Our fistfight after a couple of drinks did not hold any deep significance, or mean the two of us could not continue to work together in the future. The Captain, who seemed satisfied and relieved dismissed both of us with the stern warning that he'd better not see even a hint of any more of this kind of behavior or he would be forced to take action we would not like.

What I did not know at the time of our morning meeting with the Captain was how Rocky apparently had carried on after the SPs returned him to the ship. My friends told me later that the Captain must have had a talk with Rocky that night, telling him his behavior and his threats were not acceptable. At some point the Captain probably also told him that, as the senior officer of the two of us, it was his responsibility not to let differences between junior officers escalate into a physical fight. Finally, Rocky probably also got instructions to reestablish a collegial relationship with me and to make sure nothing like that ever happened again.

Whatever the C.O. told him, it worked. The two of us found no reason to quarrel, remaining cooperative shipmates. One brief incident told me the Captain had made it clear to Rocky that there were to be no further incidents. At a dinner a week or so later at the officers' club, one of my junior officer colleagues who was close to Rocky started to taunt me about how he could easily beat me in a fight. Rocky immediately cut him off telling the guy he was not to start anything, or else.

18

Project 100,000
and Typhoon Joan

The reception I got from my 1st Division men at "Quarters" that first morning after the fight came as a surprise. "Quarters" is a brief semi-formal meeting each division officer has every workday morning around 7:30 with the enlisted men who work for him. The 30 or so sailors of *Buck*'s deck division met on the fos'cle. The process called for the men to be called to attention as I came to the head of the formation. I would then give the order "At ease" and proceed to brief the assembly on schedules, planned activities, work to be done, etc. Often warnings about behavior ashore would be included, direct reminders not to get drunk, to avoid ladies of the evening, not to get in fights, etc.

As mentioned previously, the men in 1st division do hard, dirty, physical work chipping paint, painting the ship, caring for the lines, anchors, ship's boats, and handling the mooring lines. Men who hadn't demonstrated the ability to excel as electricians, propulsion experts, communicators, sonar technicians or other technical specialists were assigned to 1st division.

In the late 1960s, a new, navy-wide program increased the separation between sailors in deck division and those in other divisions. In 1966, then Defense Secretary Robert McNamara and his staff began a program to recruit and train men who normally would not qualify to serve in the military at all, calling it Project 100,000. The program sought to provide training and opportunity to thousands of the uneducated and poor, many of them from the rural South, while helping to staff the military. The men were classified as "New Standards Men."

Despite promises to the contrary, the men who were recruited or enlisted under this program did not receive the opportunities for training that other, "regular" recruits and draftees received after the completion of basic training, because they were judged incapable of handling the work. A number of them could barely read and write, and so after

122

graduation from basic training they were sent directly to ships in the fleet. Once in the fleet, many if not most went directly to 1st division. This led to morale problems among some of the program recruits, and the *Buck* was not immune.

While Mr. McNamara insisted that during their 4-year enlistment these men would be trained to enter into virtually all fields, they were not, and this led to frustration on the part of many. Furthermore, they were denied promotions, and the resultant better pay and benefits because they could not compete with the better-educated and better-trained sailors. I tried to help some of them by spending hours at a small table in the cramped 1st Division berthing compartment tutoring and reviewing old navy tests, trying to help them prepare for advancement exams. Both sides of the table learned a lot from this. I found it one of the more personally rewarding things I had done. I learned firsthand that while some of these guys were bright and motivated enough to get ahead, they clearly had been held back by their circumstances. McNamara's program was great in theory, but in practice the Navy lacked the time and the resources to educate these men to become more productive or in some cases even excel.

Morale and promotion problems aside, when these men went ashore in a port city such as Olongapo, they were often some of the first to get drunk and get into fights. In fact, at the Friday morning meeting on the foc'sle, I routinely included a stern warning about the dangers and problems associated with having too much to drink and fighting. And on more than a couple of occasions, Monday's meeting was a survey of the walking wounded: men with bandaged eyes and arms in slings, etc.

When I came out in front of my men on that morning after the fight with my black eye, bandages, bruises and scraped knuckles, I was surprised to be met with big smiles and *sotto voce* acclamation—the response of a group of men who suddenly learn their leader really is one of them. I was both proud of and humbled by their reaction. I've always felt thankful to the Navy for providing me with that unexpected reward.

Project 100,000 came to an end in December 1971, generally considered to be a failed initiative. In many ways it was not. It gave a lot of underprivileged men the pride of service, the experience of earning their own way, and seeing what life was like outside their hometown. Unfortunately, declaring the program a failure provided those who are against universal service an argument for why a universal draft would be too expensive and unworkable. I'm convinced the real expense is in the loss our country suffers from not having more of its citizens understand what it means, and what it's like, to serve their country.

*   *   *

On October 2, we were underway once more, this time back to South SAR (Search and Rescue) Station where we replaced the USS *Fox* (DLG-33). We steamed in company with the cruiser USS *Chicago* (CG-11).

It was the time of year in the South China Sea when it is a good idea to pay attention to forecasts of major storm development. In fact, the 1970 tropical storm season in the Western Pacific was an especially busy one. By early October there was already above average tropical storm activity. By the end of the calendar year the Western Pacific would have suffered through 24 tropical storms, of which 12 reached typhoon intensity and seven became super typhoons.

On October 10, a tropical disturbance east of the Philippines, a long way from our position in the Gulf, organized into Tropical Storm Joan. By the 11th, Joan had reached typhoon status and from late on the 11th to early on the 13th she had intensified to a 175-mph super typhoon. Moving west at a rapid rate the storm struck southeastern Luzon as the second strongest typhoon ever to hit the Philippines.

On October 14, a diminished Joan entered the South China Sea at minimal typhoon status, but once again over warm water, she re-intensified to a 115-mph typhoon. The storm also grew much larger with an area of tropical storm-force winds fanning out to a 250-mile radius from its center. The diameter of its eye also grew to an unbelievable 80 miles, far larger than an average typhoon. By October 15, Joan covered almost the entire northern South China Sea threatening to approach the Gulf of Tonkin. With the massive storm headed in our direction we were forced to spend several days in rough weather doing storm evasion and away from our post at South SAR Station.

The western Pacific was beautiful with its gentle breezes, warm tropical air and billowing clouds. The vibrant colors of the spectacular sunsets on a calm sea with mountainous thunderclouds in the distance simply don't exist anywhere else I've ever been. But when it stormed, the sea could scare even the most experienced sailors.

Getting caught in a typhoon, or even the edges of a typhoon as happened to us, meant many hours of holding on for life and limb. On the *Buck*, green water punched out several of the windshields on the bridge.

18. Project 100,000 and Typhoon Joan

We were literally going through some of the huge waves. At noon, the darkness from the heavy cloud cover, the driving rain and the spray from the breaking wave tops lowered visibility to no more than a hundred yards. Fortunately, being on the edges of the storm prevented us from suffering too much damage.

We watched the storm waves come at us in sets, with about every seventh wave bigger than the others. If you wanted to turn the ship to reverse course, it was good to begin the turn just after the largest wave in the set. For almost any ship, minimizing the potential for rolling over in such weather requires keeping the waves near head on, or almost directly astern. The Chief Engineer has to make sure the ship has the proper ballasting. Three American destroyers—the *Hull*, the *Monaghan* and the *Spence*—capsized in a bad storm in December 1944 because they were low on fuel and had not taken on ballast. With little fuel and no ballast their center of gravity was too high, making them unstable in the bad conditions.

In a strong Western Pacific typhoon, the tops of the waves can rise higher than the destroyer's mast. The very biggest waves in a major typhoon, measured from crest to trough, can approach measured world record heights of 100 feet, as high as a ten-story building. Such high seas can tear off weapons and equipment welded in place on a ship's deck. Sky and sea can seem to become one. The ship pounds and rolls violently to the point where it seems it could get swallowed up whole.

Sailors can suffer broken bones and other impact injuries from being tossed around inside the ship in the unpredictable violence of the seas. The simple act of walking down one of the ship's internal passageways becomes difficult. The deck can be a bulkhead one instant and back to being a deck the next. On one occasion I was standing on the port side of the bridge and lost my grip on the bulkhead. I flew through the open door of the pilothouse, out the open door on the other side and finally came to an abrupt stop on the opposite side of the bridge. Fortunately, along the way I was able to break my fall enough to keep from being injured.

Life aboard ship in a storm is a good deal different than it is normally. For one thing, no work can get done because sailors have to use all four limbs to stay upright. There can be no food service for obvious reasons. Men who are not on watch try to stay in their racks but sleeping is difficult because of the violent motion of the ship. Many sailors found it impossible to remain in their racks unless they tied themselves in. I tied myself in on more than one occasion.

125

From Vietnam to the Arctic Circle

We weren't the only ship that had to weather this massive storm. In fact, we had it much easier than one of our sister destroyers.

On October 14 the USS *Agerholm* (DD-826) had been detached from the Gulf of Tonkin for independent transit through the South China Sea to Hong Kong, her crew looking forward to some down time in that beautiful port city. Unfortunately, the *Agerholm* was unable to outrun Typhoon Joan. For almost two full days she had to battle some of the worst of the storm. At one point the destroyer is believed to have come within 60 miles of Joan's center, fighting extremely high winds and seas conservatively estimated to be at least 40 feet. But the crew managed to bring her through.

After the storm, on board the *Buck*, rumors of terrible times aboard the *Agerholm* got passed around. I stress rumors because I never heard any of the information from original sources; however, from our own experiences the stories sounded plausible. One story held that for a lengthy period of time the crew had no idea of the ship's location and there was concern about nearby islands, shoals and reefs. The South China Sea is full of small islands, skerries and reefs including the Paracel Islands, lying generally to the east of Yankee Station, and unnamed skerries and shoals generally to the south of Hong Kong. The story was that the only operational navigation device working aboard the *Agerholm* in the height of the storm besides the Mk 1 eyeball was the fathometer, and at one point it registered a very shallow depth indicating the ship may have passed over a land mass.

By October 16, Typhoon Joan had made landfall on eastern Hainan Island and ceased to threaten the survival of ships at sea. The *Agerholm* had survived, and we had returned to our South SAR Station duties. By October 28 we were on our way to Bangkok for three very welcome days of R&R.

Underway again on November 4, this time we were called on to provide Naval Gunfire Support (NGFS) in South Vietnam's II and III military regions. Our 5-inch gunfire supported ground operations by the First Australian Task Force and the 1st Air Cavalry Division.

The First Australian Task Force (1 ATF), consisting of New Zealand as well as Australian army units, had been in South Vietnam since 1966. They were responsible for the Vung Tau area where *Buck* had provided so much gunfire support in the past. In November the 1 ATF began its withdrawal from South Vietnam because of the move toward "Vietnamization" of the war effort. Vietnamization was President Richard Nixon's plan announced in June 1969 to reduce American and allied involvement in the Vietnam War by transferring all military responsibilities to the South Vietnamese.

One year later, by December 1971, the 1ATF were gone completely and the South Vietnamese were once again in charge in the Vung Tau region. Communist forces soon took over the area we had worked so hard to protect. During their time supporting the war effort the Australians lost 478 killed and more than 3,000 wounded. New Zealand had 37 killed and 187 wounded.

For its part the 1st Air Cavalry Division had spent much of its time in South Vietnam in the Central Highlands. But by November 1970 the Division worked primarily defensive actions while allied military units withdrew from South Vietnam.

The 1st Air Cavalry and the 1st Australian Task Force had fought tirelessly against surging communist forces. The *Buck*'s guns provided intense gunfire support for operations by both of these units. The command leadership of both organizations said they greatly appreciated the *Buck*'s responsiveness. For the second year in a row the *Buck* earned the nickname "Fastest Gun in the West" from appreciative Allied ground forces.

By mid–November we were again on our way to Subic Bay for repairs, upkeep and a little relaxation. No sooner were we in Subic than Tropical Storm Patsy forced us back to sea to evade potential storm damage. In and out of Subic for the next three weeks, by December 11 we were on our way north for Yokosuka, Japan and Christmas in the Tokyo area. Everyone looked forward to a little peace and quiet away from the intensity of non-stop operations in Southeast Asia.

19

Homeward Bound

After a fabulous farewell party, I left the *Buck* in Yokosuka in mid–December 1970 and got a flight home to San Diego from Tokyo's Haneda Airport via San Francisco International. I had orders in hand to report to the USS *Chehalis* (PG-94) in January 1971 replacing Lt. Pete Long as the ship's Executive Officer. The *Chehalis* was home ported in San Diego; however, we were to learn soon enough she wasn't going to stay there.

For almost two years Elaine and I had little contact with people outside military circles. I spent most of that time aboard ship, while Elaine had lived in the basically conservative and pro-military city of San Diego that entire time. Thus, neither of us was really aware of the depth and strength of the anti-war sentiment. We had no experience with the burgeoning anti-military attitude of many Americans, particularly among younger people and especially in more liberal areas of the country with large populations of college and university students. Communication, especially in the news arena, was much different in 1970 than it is today. There was no email, no social media, no cable channels, and an often very slow snail mail system. We were soon to become more aware of the virulent anti-military/anti-war sentiment that was gaining momentum.

We decided to return to Sayville to visit family and friends over the Christmas holiday expecting a happy welcome if not a proud and joyous reception. While the parents were indeed pleased to see us, little was said or asked about the war, or our ideas, comments or opinions. Of course, that is one of the first lessons of military or overseas life in general—don't expect your family to have much interest in where you've been, what you've seen, or what you've done. In the vernacular of the less well educated in the local high school, "It ain't gonna happen, Babe." Still, the disinterest came as something of a disappointment.

However, disinterest is one thing and angry opposition another. I had one younger sibling in college in the northeast who had absorbed a great deal about the baby-killing warmongers who served in the U.S. military in Vietnam. One evening after my parents had gone to bed, this sister decided it was time to voice protest at older brother's participation in the evil war. Somewhat surprised, I nonetheless fired back igniting a loud disagreement. The noise awoke my parents with my mother coming downstairs to put a firm end to the discussion. My mother essentially sided with my sister, telling me not to spoil the holiday with my arrogant lectures. Their pointed stance against my serving in Vietnam came as a somewhat demoralizing surprise.

Their reaction served to open our eyes as to how the military was perceived at that time. I had matriculated at Brown University from 1964 to 1968 and toward the end of that period got used to being unwelcome on campus in uniform, but that was at a liberal university, not at home. My father had been a decorated navy pilot in World War II and the family was mostly conservative in political outlook, but those factors didn't seem to weigh heavily in deciding the morality of service in Vietnam.

With the family it seemed time to retreat. The subject of the war and the military did not come up again during our visit, but Elaine and I returned to San Diego wiser about how people perceived this terrible war, and the military people like me who believed we were serving our country.

20

Patrol Gunboats

Near the end of my tour on board the *Buck* I spoke several times with my detailer, a lieutenant at the Bureau of Naval Personnel (known by the acronym BUPERS), who was responsible for placing me in my next assignment. The Navy tries to place you in a position you want, but of course the needs of the service come first, and the Navy needed young officers in Vietnam.

At first the lieutenant strongly encouraged me to take one of the many assignments open in Vietnam, "in-country" as it was described. I countered that I'd spent the better part of two years there, or getting ready to go there, and would like something a little different. He suggested the Navy's destroyer school in Newport, Rhode Island, where, after six months of training, I would return to the destroyer fleet as a department head. I demurred saying I'd like to remain on sea duty for the next couple of years, but preferred to experience something other than a destroyer. Finally, he offered me the job of executive officer, or second-in-command, of the USS *Chehalis* (PG-94) home ported in San Diego. I jumped at the chance.

Along with a great job, the opportunity to keep our home in San Diego was just what Elaine and I wanted. We had grown to love the place and the people, living in a small beach front apartment on Ocean Front Walk. The local restaurants were small but four-star, the beachgoers always entertaining, and the weather mild and warm most of the time. Elaine had a good job teaching elementary school at the Francis W. Parker School in Mission Hills. Between the two of us we had made a lot of friends and didn't want to leave.

One friend, our next-door neighbor, a military psychiatrist named Socrates Pappas, became a lifelong dear friend. Soc grew up in a close-knit Greek family in Arkansas. A brilliant man with a gift for self-deprecating humor, he never failed to entertain by his wit. Soc could deliver his message or offer his sage advice on any difficult subject using instructive allegories derived from years of professional

20. Patrol Gunboats

USS *Chehalis* (PG-94) underway in heavy seas (U.S. Navy).

experience. Elaine and I agree we've had very few friends as intelligent, perceptive and caring as Dr. Socrates Pappas.

In brief, we were thrilled to get another tour in San Diego and more time with all our friends; it was perfect for both of us. But the military has a way of changing your plans without much notice and so it would be for us.

I reported aboard the *Chehalis* docked at the gunboat pier at San Diego's 32nd Street Naval Station on a rainy morning in early January 1971. I relieved Lt. Pete Long as the ship's Executive Officer. Pete, who was a Naval Academy graduate, would go on to make Rear Admiral, which was no surprise. He was a dynamic officer up to any challenge. Pete actually proved to me once again what a small world it is. In the late fall of 1999, my son John and Pete met at a U.S. Naval War College reception in Newport, Rhode Island. Pete was commanding officer of the War College and John was attending the Surface Warfare Officer course following his commissioning earlier that year.

The commanding officer of the *Chehalis* was a young, up and coming lieutenant by the name of Ralph K. Martin. Command of a U.S. Navy warship as a lieutenant came to only a very few of the navy's best junior officers, and Ralph was among them.

Ralph's outward appearance and demeanor were deceiving. He was fair skinned, very thin, with a clean-shaven head. He was soft-spoken, quick to smile and courteous to the point of being deferential. But Ralph was a first-rate manager proficient at getting the most out of each of his men. Everyone liked and respected him. He recognized and used the talents in others, and everyone benefited. He was a confident officer and talented ship handler, meaning he could get his ship safely and smoothly in and out of most any spot, a capability appreciated by sailors. His men trusted him. He was also aggressive with senior officers, getting officers of flag rank to take notice of him and his ship. He took a number of admirals out for brief demonstration cruises, explained how *Ashville* class gunboats like *Chehalis* might be used effectively in different situations, and generally provided them with practical exposure to a level of the Navy they didn't often get to see.

Ralph had a beautiful ship to show off to the brass. The *Chehalis* was almost brand new, launched on June 8, 1968, and commissioned on November 8, 1969. She was named in honor of a small city in Lewis County in Washington State with a population of less than 10,000. The city had adopted the name *Chehalis* in 1879 after the Chehalis, or Tsihalis, a group of indigenous people from western Washington State. Fittingly, the ship's insignia bears the head of a Native American superimposed over an anchor, with the ship's name and the motto "More than Our Share." Not long after commissioning, *Chehalis* visited its namesake city where officers and crew enjoyed the warm reception and hospitality of the local folks. The men were treated to such a good time that they were still talking about when I reported aboard *Chehalis*.

PG-94 was actually the second U.S. Navy ship to carry the name. The first *Chehalis* was a gasoline tanker placed in service toward the end of World War II. On 7 October 1949, as she lay alongside the pier in American Samoa, one of her gasoline tanks exploded, killing six of the 75-man crew. She quickly caught fire, capsized, and sank, eventually slipping into deep water. I mention it because older veterans still remember the first *Chehalis* and sometimes think it's the first *Chehalis* I'm talking about.

PG-94 like her sister ships carried a full complement of only 25 including four officers and four chief petty officers. Having such a small crew meant everyone got to know everyone else, which was good for morale and good for the ship's overall performance. No one wanted to be the one who didn't do his job and in the process let down his shipmates.

Speaking of shipmates, not long after I reported aboard *Chehalis*, we had a surprise guest come aboard. My former commanding officer on the *Buck*, Commander Dale Duncan, came for an unofficial call to see the *Chehalis* and have a cup of coffee with us in the wardroom. He paid me a compliment that I value more now than I did when he said it. He said he had not understood before I left the *Buck* in December how much I was contributing to the smooth functioning of his ship, and he wanted to thank me personally for it. He did not further explain, and I did not ask. I never saw or talked to him again but still think of him to this day.

The *Chehalis* was a remarkable ship with an overall length of 165 feet and a beam of only 24 feet. Everyone said *Chehalis*'s shape more closely resembled that of a canoe than a warship. The hull was made of aluminum and her superstructure from fiberglass molded over an aluminum frame, making her very light, with a displacement of only about 250 tons fully loaded. Had she been made of steel her displacement might have approached 300 tons or more. Compare that to the displacement of the battleship USS *New Jersey* (BB-62), at approximately 60,000 tons fully loaded. *Chehalis* also drew only nine and a half feet of water, enabling her to move quickly through waters much too shallow for a ship like a destroyer with a sixteen-foot draft.

Chehalis' weaponry consisted of a single 3-inch/50 caliber Mk34 rapid fire gun mounted on the bow, one Bofors 40 mm gun mounted on the stern, four .50 cal. machine guns that could be mounted two to a side and miscellaneous small arms including M16s, M60 machine guns and grenade launchers. *Chehalis*' weapons officer was Lt. (j.g.) Mike Younker, another Naval Academy graduate. Mike also wore a second hat as the ship's supply officer. Well-liked by everyone, Mike did a great job handling two very different departments. He earned the Navy Achievement Medal for his outstanding work aboard the *Chehalis*.

With her General Electric LM-1500 marine gas turbine running, using her controllable pitch propellers, *Chehalis* was like a cigarette boat, able to go from standing still to 40 knots in only 60 seconds! She could also come to a complete stop within little more than her own length from 40 knots. No other class of ship could come anywhere close to that. The seats on the bridge even came with seatbelts. However, we did not make such drastic changes in speed. The potential for

A model of the *Chehalis*. Weapons systems included the Mk 63 Gun Fire Control System that controlled the 40-millimeter gun mount aft and the rapid fire 3-inch/50 caliber gun mount on the bow. She also carried two .50 caliber machine guns—one port and one starboard amidships on the second deck—as well as a stock of M16s, M60 machine guns, and M79 grenade launchers (author's collection).

mechanical failures and other problems was too great. Think what would happen if you stopped your car in its own length from a speed of almost 50 miles per hour.

The power plant that drove the *Ashville* class was new and different, much of it cutting-edge technology. The Combined Diesel or Gas (CODOG) turbine propulsion system consisted of twin Cummins diesel engines for speeds under about 15 knots and one GE LM-1500 marine gas turbine engine for speeds above that. The engines were hooked up through reduction gears to two large reversible pitch propellers. The LM-1500, capable of generating as much as 15,000 shaft horsepower, was basically the same as the J-79 engine powering an F-4 Phantom fighter aircraft. The *Ashville* class ships were pioneering, the first U.S. Navy warships to employ gas turbine propulsion. To me, it seemed the smooth, whirring sound of a powerful jet engine driving a ship rapidly through the sea was near miraculous. One day in calm waters, when we had *Chehalis* at close to top speed, I stood in the bow, leaning over the edge. Only a few feet above the water, I felt like we were flying over the surface of the sea.

With new mechanical systems glitches can be commonplace, but not here, although I was a little surprised at a problem with the metal composition of the controllable pitch propellers. The Navy had no metal alloy from which the propeller blades could be made to keep them from wearing out! There was no problem when the propellers were hooked up to the diesels. However, when the propellers were coupled to the LM-1500 and the ship was at very slow speeds or stopped, the edges of the propeller blades would spin through the water so fast that tiny air bubbles formed on the outer edge of the blades. Over a relatively brief period of time these tiny bubbles could literally boil the metal away causing the propellers to become nothing more than stubs. The cost to replace a set of propellers was significant. The Navy's solution was to use the gas turbine only for speeds above 12–14 knots and the diesels for slower speeds. I had assumed the Navy had found a solution to the metal alloy problem for high-speed propellers from work on the nuclear submarine program and possibly other advanced systems, but they had not.

Lt. James Tuller was the Chief Engineer. He and I were classmates at Brown. We couldn't believe we ended up on the same small ship together. Jim knew his stuff and would eventually replace me as the executive officer when I left the ship. Tuller's exceptional men, led by Engineman Chief Simmons, had special training in maintaining the advanced plant and kept everything running smoothly. EN3 Gene Van Orden was typical of Simmons' crew. One day I asked him what part of his job made him feel like he was truly contributing to the ship's mission. He said that every time he went on watch at sea and used his expertise, he knew he was making a contribution.

* * *

In the early 1960s following the Cuban Missile Crisis the Navy decided to build a littoral combat vessel for use in the Caribbean and so designed the *Ashville* class gunboat. However, by the late 1960s and their introduction to the fleet, a significant requirement for such a ship in the Caribbean no longer existed. So, what to do with a dozen or so ships no longer needed for close to home coastal operations?

Some suggested using the ships as mini-destroyers for assignments such as plane guarding and naval gunfire support. However, the gunboats' lack of seaworthiness and endurance, particularly in rough seas, made them unsuitable for long periods of work with the carriers. When it came to naval gunfire support, destroyers had vastly more firepower—six 5-inch guns versus one 3-inch. Also gunboats had no anti-submarine warfare capability whereas destroyers had multiple ASW detection and weapons systems. Finally, destroyers were for the most part made of steel, offering a vastly superior defense against attack as opposed to the gunboats' aluminum and fiberglass construction. While gunboats could do some of what a destroyer could do, and a few things a destroyer could not, they were not mini-destroyers. They were good at what they were designed for, as littoral combat ships for missions such as observation, interdiction, and surveillance where they could use their speed, maneuverability and shallow draft to advantage.

In the mid–1960s the Soviet Navy formed the 5th Squadron, a.k.a. the Soviet Mediterranean Fleet, with plans to increase the numbers of ships. By 1970 the U.S. Navy assessed the 5th Squadron as powerful enough, especially in the eastern Mediterranean, to pose a serious threat to the 6th Fleet. Thus, in 1970 the Navy decided to use several of the *Ashville* class boats to help counter this growing Soviet naval threat. The idea was to use the gunboats to shadow the Soviet missile boats that had been shadowing and harassing the larger 6th Fleet ships.

In late 1970 the Navy formed Patrol Division 21 (PatDiv 21) in Naples, Italy with two ships, the USS *Surprise* (PG-97) and the USS *Defiance* (PG-95). Not long thereafter we heard rumor the *Chehalis* would be reassigned to Naples to join them, but two other surface-to-surface missile equipped gunboats got the nod instead. In late 1972 the USS *Antelope* (PG-86) and the USS *Ready* (PG-87) joined PatDiv 21, bringing its strength to four ships. In August 1973 the USS *Grand Rapids* (PG-98) and the USS *Douglas* (PG-100) replaced the *Surprise* and the *Defiance*, both of which were transferred to the Turks. Pat Div 21 continued Mediterranean operations until 1977 when all the ships returned to Little Creek.

In the late 1960s small, fast, shallow draft ships were also needed in Vietnam. The Navy had begun Operation Market Time in 1965 using U.S. and Vietnamese ships to seal off the 1,000 miles of South Vietnamese coastline from North Vietnamese infiltration of troops, weapons, and supplies. For this task the Navy formed the Coastal Surveillance Force made up of destroyers, Coast Guard cutters, and swift boats (Patrol Craft Fast or PCFs). The effort paid dividends almost immediately putting a big crimp in the North Vietnamese maritime resupply activities.

The Navy decided *Ashville* class gunboats might use their capabilities effectively in Market Time ops where their speed, maneuverability, armament and shallow draft appeared to fit the job requirements perfectly. On April 30, 1967, the USS *Gallup* (PG-85) became the first PG to enter the war zone. The *Ashville* (PG-84) was not far behind arriving in Cam Ranh Bay on May 7. The USS *Antelope* (PG-86) and the USS *Ready* (PG-87) home ported in Guam were also added to the mix before their eventual reassignment to the 6th Fleet. In early 1968 the USS *Crockett* (PG-88) entered the war zone joining Operation Market Time.

By 1967 the Navy had begun to focus its resources not just along the coast but also inside the coastline; i.e., in the numerous rivers and channels running into the interior of the country, especially in the far south. The Viet Cong (VC) and the North Vietnamese Army (NVA) were having great success using these inland waterways as logistical pipelines and they needed to be stopped.

In September 1968, Rear Admiral Elmo Russell (Bud) Zumwalt, Jr., became Commander of Naval Forces Vietnam including the Coastal Surveillance Force, the River Patrol Force, and the Army-Navy Mobile Riverine Force. By late 1968 he had created the Southeast Asia Lake Ocean River Delta Strategy (Operation Sealords) to deal with extensive VC and NVA activities in the Mekong Delta in the southern part of South Vietnam. The Sealords strategy mirrored the very successful Operation Market Time concept. Patrol gunboats would play an important combat role.

June 1969 brought Operation Sea Float or Seafloat for short. Seafloat was a Mobile Advanced Tactical Support Base (MATSB), but the base was built in the middle of the Song Cau Lon (Song Cau River) in the Mekong Delta region, a VC stronghold. Constructed of a number of pontoon barges tied together and anchored in the river, Seafloat became the main operating base for U.S. and South Vietnamese naval forces for the region. With a staff of approximately 40 Navy personnel, Seafloat supported a powerhouse of swift boat and riverine units, two helos, Navy SEAL (Sea Air Land) teams, Navy Under Water Demolition (UDT) teams, and a variety of support craft. But Seafloat was a dangerous place to be, a sitting duck in the middle of the river. It was a frequent target for VC attacks using a multitude of weapons. Seafloat support operations probably most tested the mettle of the patrol gunboat crews assigned to duty in Vietnam.

In September 1969 the VC ambushed the *Crockett*. The enemy fired four rockets, two of which caused no damage. The third rocket exploded when it hit a lifeline near the 3-inch/50 gun mount wounding two crewmen one of whom had to be medevaced. The fourth rocket blew up the control box for the 3-inch gun mount. On May 4, 1970, the VC attacked the *Antelope* from the north bank of the Cua Lon, causing a 5-inch hole in her main deck, apparently from a lobbed satchel charge. Fortunately, no one was injured in the assault.

The morning of August 11, 1971, saw the most devastating attack. The VC ambushed the *Canon* from both sides of the Song Cua river. She got hit with eight B-40 rockets as well as automatic weapons fire causing extensive damage to the entire superstructure including the bridge. Despite the devastating assault, the crew fought back with all it had. Of the crew of 24, 14 were wounded including the commanding officer Lieutenant Commander David Robinson who was later cited for his heroism. Of the 14 wounded, 5 had to be medevaced. Because of their valiant response a number of the crew received awards including the Navy Cross, three Silver Stars and five Bronze Stars as well as numerous Purple Hearts for their heroism.

Scuttlebutt among gunboat riders with whom I spoke in late 1971 was that the *Canon* crew believed they were lucky anyone survived the attack, that the aluminum hull and composite superstructure had withstood the gunfire about as well as *papier-mâché*. Everything passed right through, in one side and out the other without even slowing. Likewise, the superstructure proved just as porous if not more so, adding to the problems by giving off noxious gases where it caught fire. Purportedly the only semi-safe place on the ship during the attack was between the two big Cummins diesel engines, which stopped dead anything that hit them. The above information was secondhand, even third-hand testimony, but taken from people who knew gunboats very well.

The people on the gunboats who did not serve in Vietnam took pride in the performance of the men who did. To a man they hoped they would act as courageously in such combat situations, especially as bravely as those who served aboard the *Canon*.

As mentioned earlier, in June 1969 newly elected President Richard Nixon had announced his new strategy of Vietnamization. The plan was to reduce American involvement in the war by transferring, over time, all military responsibilities to the South Vietnamese. That transfer included naval forces. By 1971 all aspects of Sealords had been turned over. Patrol gunboat missions continued for a time but had begun to taper with the new policy of handing over all responsibilities to the Republic of Vietnam Navy.

21

East Coast Here We Come

The *Chehalis* wasn't headed for Vietnam; in fact, the opposite direction. Only a few months after I reported aboard, we got orders to change homeports to Little Creek, Virginia. The departure date was set for June. We barely had time to notify landlords, give notice to Francis Parker School that Elaine would not be returning, and prepare for moving to the Norfolk, Virginia, area. In company with the USS *Beacon*, USS *Green Bay*, and the USS *Boulder* (LST-1190) *Chehalis* departed San Diego on June 21 headed for Acapulco.

The waters between San Diego and Acapulco were near dead calm. The off-duty crew liked to stand on deck and watch the abundant sea life—sharks, giant sea turtles and myriad species of fish. In all the seas I've traveled before and since, I saw that this expanse of water was by far the most crowded with life.

Acapulco is one of Mexico's oldest and most beautiful beach resorts. From the 1950s to the early 1970s the town was a popular getaway for wealthy Americans, particularly big Hollywood stars such as Elizabeth Taylor, Frank Sinatra and Marilyn Monroe. By the late 1960s American tourism had led to a building boom for luxury resort hotels, particularly in the hills on the south side of Acapulco Bay. There was no gang and drug violence in the town to discourage tourists or investors. Some of us decided to enjoy the relatively cheap luxury accommodations and got rooms at one of the best hotels in the south side of the bay in the Diamante section. Each room had its own small, heart shaped pool with a fantastic view overlooking Acapulco Bay.

Leaving the beautiful natural harbor, we sailed south toward the Bay of Panama for our transit through the canal. At that time the Panama Canal was still U.S. Government-owned and operated with a sizeable U.S. military presence in the area, including the Headquarters of the Southern Command. All the U.S. military services were well represented. The Panamanian economy prospered in great measure because of all the U.S. dollars available from the strong U.S. presence. Panama

City, located right on the water on the Pacific side, also benefited from the multitude of sailors on all the international ships passing through. Prostitution was legal, and so the nightlife could be particularly wild with many bars and restaurants and several large well-known brothels to capture sailors' attention.

The trip through the canal was a memorable experience for everyone; the complex system of locks that enabled passage was a manmade wonder to behold. I was amazed that such a remarkable feat of engineering had opened for business as far back as 1914, and the technology of that period still operated perfectly.

I was also surprised to see large crocodiles sunning themselves on the banks of the canal. Once through, we anchored in Lake Gatun—a freshwater lake manmade between 1907 and 1913 and a big part of the canal. Despite the threat from sizeable hostile creatures, everyone went swimming, just to say they had done so. Crocodiles are supposed to remain fairly close to the shallows, but just to be on the safe side, a couple of sailors stood watch with loaded weapons.

From there we sailed to Cartagena, Colombia, one of the oldest cities in the Americas, founded by the Spanish on June 1, 1533. In Colombia political unrest was ongoing, but visiting Americans did not feel threatened. It was not until almost ten years later, beginning in the early 1980s, that the country came under attack from the violent drug cartels: the Medellín Cartel under Pablo Escobar and the Cali Cartel.

Most of the time ashore we spent happily tracking down deals on the beautiful indigenous emerald gemstones. From there it was time for the final leg of the trip, north to Chesapeake Bay and the ship's new homeport at the U.S. Naval Amphibious Base, Little Creek, Virginia. The Amphibious Base is located about five miles due east of U.S. Naval Station, Norfolk.

On the trip north we passed the scenic coastline of the Carolinas. On the bridge one of our senior enlisted men, I'll call him Jed Clampett, mentioned in his thick Southern drawl that we were looking at the place he calls home. Jed was easy to tease and so one of the guys said it was more likely he lived in a drying shed on somebody else's tobacco farm. No, he said, actually he owned a fair portion of the coast we were sailing past. Everyone laughed, his claim was so outlandish we all assumed he was kidding and thought no more of it. A couple of months later we had a ship's inspection, and Captain Martin noticed in Jed's locker a bunch of un-cancelled checks for significant sums of money. Jed said the money came from businesses he owned. He explained that when he was younger he befriended an old man, visiting him for years, doing chores for him and calling on him when he was old and sick when no one else did. When the man died a few years ago, he left him his entire estate. The man lived very frugally but it turned out he was actually worth a great deal of money and owned a number of very profitable businesses around the country and a number of acres of shore front property.

Jed went on to explain that he loved his job in the Navy and contributing to his country. He thought he could sort out what to do with the businesses and the money once he finished his Navy service.

On July 10, 1971, the *Chehalis*, the *Beacon* and the *Green Bay* arrived at the Naval Amphibious Base Little Creek to become part of the recently formed Coastal River Squadron 2 (CosRivRon 2). Commander John Connelly, COMCOSRIVRON 2 and his staff welcomed us. The large amphib base is a stone's throw from the mammoth Naval Station Norfolk, the world's largest naval station at more than 6,200 acres. Naval Station Norfolk, which came into being at the start of World War I, employs more than 67,000 people, both military and civilian. Norfolk Naval Station has no less than 14 piers holding carriers, destroyers, frigates, cruisers, amphibious assault ships, submarines, tenders and a myriad of other U.S. Navy ships. It has command staffs and structures, large aviation facilities, storehouses, fuel and oil storage depots, housing and recreation areas, a submarine base, and much more.

As we settled into the Hampton Roads area, Elaine prepared to begin a sixth-grade teaching assignment in Norfolk. When she accepted the position the Norfolk Education Department explained that the elementary school to which she would be assigned was an "inner city" school meaning that most of the children were from poor families in Norfolk. She found that many of the children could not have been more underprivileged; some obviously did not get enough to eat, some endured parents with enormous personal problems, there were near-constant fights, and none of the children had any money for anything extra.

It proved to be a tough assignment with more than thirty children in the class, many of whom were special needs cases. There was no air-conditioning, the windows were barred and covered with wire mesh, the kids and teachers were instructed to make sure to leave the neighborhood before dark, and there were infestations of cockroaches and water bugs.

Despite the problems, Elaine managed to build rapport with all of the children, even the toughest of the boys, and was often touched by their actions toward her. At Christmas one of the boys wanted to get her a gift, but he had no money to do so. One day after lunch he came back into the classroom and wishing her a Merry Christmas handed her an unwrapped package of cutlery, the price tag still on the item.

In the late summer and fall of 1971 the *Chehalis* and her sister ships were in and out of port but with no long periods at sea or plans for deployment. From Friday the 13th to Monday the 16th of August we visited Newport, Rhode Island, and then from the 16th to the 19th participated with the *Beacon* (PG-99) in a small exercise called Operation Beaver Tail. The exercise in Narragansett Bay was designed to demonstrate the effectiveness of gunboats at patrolling the bay, quickly intercepting intruding enemy vessels. Indicating that the Navy was still trying to figure out the best role for these *Ashville* class gunboats, we even planted sonobuoys in the bay providing us with an ASW capability, albeit a very limited one.

From September 19 to October 3, we were part of another exercise with PG-99 called Operation Escort Tiger. We sailed in the waters north of Roosevelt Roads Naval Station (commonly referred to as "Roosey Roads," pronounced Rosy Roads) in North Eastern Puerto Rico and the Vieques Naval Training Range Island (VNTR) on Vieques Island about five miles from Roosey Roads. An historical note: In 1919, as Assistant Secretary of the Navy, future U.S. President Franklin D. Roosevelt visited the area that became Roosevelt Roads Naval Station and thought it ideal for a for a military base. In 1940 he ordered the base to be built.

Because of the bombing range, I always thought of Vieques as the San Clemente Island of the east coast. The big difference was that no one actually lived on San Clemente. The Navy's use of Vieques for bombing practice became increasingly unpopular with the Puerto Rican population and the last straw came in 1999 when a civilian employed as a security guard died from an errant bomb dropped during a routine exercise. Residents and outside activists protested until the Clinton Administration eventually agreed to cease all live bombing at Vieques.

We participated in one major fleet exercise, READEX 2–71. *Chehalis* was ordered to locate a carrier attack group sailing toward Florida from somewhere in the South-eastern Atlantic. Once located, we were to track the group's movement. Our expectation was that finding a carrier and its accompanying ships would not be that difficult, but we were wrong. After just a day or two of fruitless searching we decided that the Atlantic Ocean is much bigger than you'd think, and that there was no way one small ship like *Chehalis* could find a carrier and her escorts without a lot of good luck.

One interesting part of our fruitless search for the carrier group was a sail into the Sargasso Sea. It is a huge area in the mid–Atlantic, the only sea in the world with no land boundaries. Rather, its borders are four major ocean currents, the Gulf Stream, the North Atlantic Current, the Canary Current and the North Atlantic Equatorial Current. We found the water inside the boundaries to be without a ripple from any breeze and a beautiful blue in color, but clogged with an endless morass of Sargassum seaweed. It seemed an oddly still and quiet place. It is easy to understand how early sailors whose ships got becalmed in it thought they might never escape.

Chehalis also got assigned "show the flag" port visits to locations with large populations but shallow harbors where larger ships could not go. The weekend of August 20–23 we visited historic Salem, Massachusetts, settled in 1626 and home to the House of the Seven Gables and the famous Salem witch trials of 1692. Salem's scenic harbor, on Massachusetts Bay, was just barely deep enough near the shore to permit us to dock at the main pier.

We spent four days, October 22–26, tied up to the quayside at the U.S. Naval Academy. From Little Creek the Academy is a straight sail north up the Chesapeake Bay to the mouth of the Severn River. I was invited to lunch in the academy's King Hall named for Fleet Admiral Ernest King who was the Chief of Naval Operations and Commander in Chief of the U.S. Fleet during World War II. The facility is large enough to permit the entire Brigade of over 4,000 midshipmen to sit at one time to eat breakfast, lunch and dinner. As an officer and a guest, I sat at the head of one of the tables and answered a number of questions about my service. It was a memorable event. I thought it would be wonderful if more Americans could experience a meal such as that with the Middies. It is impressive to see so many patriotic young people in one place at one time training to become our future military leaders.

In the late summer and fall of 1971 *Chehalis* also had a number of inspections measuring our competence and proficiency in virtually every aspect of the ship's operation, from engineering to operations, gunnery and supply.

For the year 1971 the USS *Chehalis* performed exceptionally well. The ship achieved the Command Excellence White "E" award for gunnery, the Green "E" for communications, the Red "E" for engineering, the Blue "E" for supply, and the Green "E" for operations. The criterion for a command excellence "E" award was the overall superior readiness of that department within the command to carry out its assigned tasks. The award is based on a year-long evaluation incorporating the department's performance during training exercises, inspections, and tactical readiness evaluations. In addition, *Chehalis* was a first runner-up in the 1971 COMPHIBLANT (Commander Amphibious Forces Atlantic Fleet) Captain Edward F. Ney Awards competition for best small mess afloat. *Chehalis* also received a grade of outstanding in the Command Inspection and was commended by COMPHIBLANT for the achievement.

The ship performed so well in communications thanks in great measure to Radioman 1st class (RM1) Del Clouser. In addition to being responsible for all the ship's communication gear and message traffic, Clouser helped manage all the classified material. On paper I was the classified publications control officer, but it was RM1 Clouser who ensured the documents were properly secure and accounted for. As a result, we received perfect grades on all our inspections. The Navy takes classified material very seriously recognizing that any error or possible compromise has the potential to cause serious harm. The storage, transportation, and inventory of classified items, from communications codes to tactical publications, must be done with meticulous attention to accuracy and detail. Experiencing the Navy's strict attention to protecting classified information makes what has happened over the recent past within the upper echelons of the Federal Government even more shocking.

When it came to operations YN2 (Yeoman 2nd Class) Dale W. Armstrong brought home the gold, or in this case the green. Armstrong, or "Armo" to most aboard ship, kept the ship's scheduling and administrative affairs in perfect order despite the fact that his office was shuffled like a deck of cards every time we went to sea. Armo's office was in the most forward inhabited compartment on the ship. Whenever we hit any sea head on, the bow would rise and then crash down against the sea, bouncing papers and equipment into the air as though the office was in a San Andreas Fault earthquake. In fact, the force of the blow between sea and ship was so tooth rattling that the Navy used force impact technology to make sure it was within tolerance. There was no way to secure everything; Armo just had to clean up after we got into calm seas or back to port. Armo had a great sense of humor. He was a man who could laugh at himself, one of the people that made long hours on a small ship more bearable for everyone else.

Ralph told me the only time he wasn't certain the ship would hold together was coming out of San Francisco Bay. Under certain conditions there are largely invisible, long-period, deep swells that roll in from the Pacific. The locals call them Sneaker waves. Ralph said that one time they sailed under the Golden Gate Bridge at high speed not seeing or expecting these large swells. They hit one and the ship almost went airborne, flying off the top of the huge swell and crashing down in the trough. He said it literally shook up everything including the crew.

Right after Christmas C.O. Ralph Martin got orders to leave the ship almost immediately. He had been scheduled to leave that June but now had to leave by no later than mid–January for a position in the White House. His replacement, Lieutenant Dennis Crosby, had been selected for command but could not report to the *Chehalis* before the end of February at the earliest. The ship needed a C.O. for at least six weeks and Ralph asked me if I'd take the job. Of course, I said yes and the Navy agreed. So, on January 14, 1972, in a formal change of command ceremony in Little Creek, Virginia, at the age of 25, I followed Ralph as the commanding officer of the USS *Chehalis* (PG-94). Over the coming weeks the ship performed well. I really did not want to give up the job, but in late February I had to turn over command to Lt. Crosby as had been the original plan.

While I was C.O., the ship sailed to the naval base at Newport, Rhode Island, to take aboard a team of engineers and technicians who were working on a variety of naval-warfare related research programs. One of the many experiments involved testing a newly designed stabilizer. Stabilizers are the fins mounted on the hull of the ship below the waterline to reduce roll. To perform the test, they had to get the *Chehalis* to roll as far as possible without, of course, capsizing. In fact, one of the reasons the *Chehalis* had been selected for this assignment was because a gunboat hull, shaped much like a canoe, could roll even in a light sea. Gunboat riders often experienced rolls of as much as 45 degrees, a roll angle that would concern sailors on larger ships.

The day of the roll test was very cold with a strong breeze out of the north. Getting the ship to roll was no problem. We simply headed east or west at a slow speed in the trough of the north-south wind and wave action.

We did not know what the maximum safe roll would be, so whenever I judged the ship had reached its maximum safe limit, I would alter course and speed, and the experiment would end. We had no formula or data available to determine a maximum safe roll; it had to be done on "feel" and experience. There is documentation stating that destroyers

The author standing in front of the rapid fire 3-inch/50 caliber gun mount on the bow of the USS *Chehalis* (PG-94) docked at San Diego's 32nd Street Naval Station in the spring of 1971 (courtesy Elaine Kiesling Whitehouse).

caught in a typhoon in World War II survived rolls in excess of seventy degrees, but they were extremely close to capsizing. A couple of times we took the *Chehalis* past 55 degrees, the maximum roll I had ever experienced. She finally rolled to around 60 degrees or a little over, a point that I thought was enough. Any further and she might not come back, so the experiment ended. I don't recall the reading on the inclinometer, but I clearly remember thinking we're not going there again, at least on purpose. It was a strange feeling to purposely allow our ship to get into an *in extremis* situation. All your instincts work against it.

On Tuesday February 22, 1972, Lt. Dennis Crosby took command of the *Chehalis* in a formal change of command ceremony on the gunboat pier in Little Creek. Dennis was coming from a tour in Vietnam as an aide to Rear Admiral Phillip S. McManus. He was authorized to wear the Bronze Star with Combat V and the Vietnamese Cross of Gallantry with Palm Unit Citation among other decorations. The Vietnamese Cross of Gallantry was awarded to military personnel, civilians, and Armed Forces units and organizations for deeds of valor or heroic conduct while in combat.

Almost immediately after the change of command the ship got orders to deploy for an indefinite period to Naval Station Guantanamo Bay, aka Gitmo, the abbreviation long ago adopted by the military. Dating to 1903, Gitmo is the oldest overseas U.S. Naval Base. It is also the only U.S. naval station existing in a country that does not have diplomatic relations with the U.S. The long-term lease under which the U.S. holds the property was obtained from the Cuban government following the U.S. victory in the Spanish American War in 1898.

We received our deployment orders on Friday, February 25, saying we had to leave for Cuba at 0800 on Monday the 28th. We had no scheduled return date. This meant we had the weekend to prepare to leave home and family indefinitely.

Such is life for families in the military. If you're a spouse you'd better be prepared to function on your own at a moment's notice. It is especially tough on families with children; the kids do not benefit from a father's sudden and prolonged disappearance. As sailors sometimes complain, it never works in reverse, where you're deployed and all of a sudden you get orders to return home for an extended period of normal life. For us the burden fell to Elaine to once again immediately adjust to life on her own.

I've often thought there should be a military medal or at least some form of recognition for being the spouse of a deployed soldier, sailor, airman or marine. Spouses serve the military by enabling the military member to leave his home and family on a moment's notice for many months at a time.

22

Guantanamo Bay

Ten years before our arrival in Guantanamo Bay the world had come the closest it has ever come to all-out nuclear war. That confrontation had taken place because of Soviet aggression in Cuba. Indeed, Cuba had remained an underpublicized hotspot of the Cold War. *Chehalis* went to Cuba to help ensure such aggression would not reappear and bring about another confrontation.

To briefly recap the tumultuous decade leading up to our deployment:

In April 1961, a CIA-trained force of Cuban exiles invaded southern Cuba at the Bay of Pigs (*Bahía de Cochinos*) on the southern coast of Cuba. The attack failed miserably and proved a significant diplomatic embarrassment to President John F. Kennedy and the U.S. Government. However, despite that failed attempt and the international embarrassment it caused, in late 1961 and 1962 the U.S. continued to try to derail and overthrow the Castro regime. Specifically, U.S. policy makers backed stepped-up raids by U.S. supported anti–Castro guerrillas on the island of Cuba. While open hostilities between the U.S. and Cuba did not exist, the Cubans believed armed raids into Cuba had the backing of the U.S. Government. Given what they believed was a strong possibility of another U.S. supported military attack, the Castro regime asked Soviet Premier Nikita Khrushchev for support. Khrushchev welcomed the opportunity to provide Cuba with military assistance, not so much to save Cuba but to impede U.S. interests.

In 1962, strategic military advantage lay with the United States. Soviet missiles could strike any target within Europe but not reach the U.S., while American missiles could strike anywhere inside the Soviet Union. In April 1962, Khrushchev decided he could even things up by placing intermediate range missiles inside Cuba. Most of the U.S. would then be within range of Soviet nuclear weapons.

So Castro had something Khrushchev wanted and Khrushchev had something Castro wanted and thus Soviet missiles came to Cuba.

22. Guantanamo Bay

In mid–1962 the Soviet Union began secretly constructing its missile installations in Cuba.

By mid–October 1962, the U.S. had reconnaissance photos proving the Soviets were building offensive missile sites on Cuba. On October 22 President Kennedy publicly announced the discovery of the installations and that he had ordered a naval blockade to stop the delivery of any more Soviet offensive weaponry. In addition, Kennedy demanded Khrushchev remove from Cuba all its offensive weaponry already in place.

Tensions built quickly. On or about October 24, the President raised the DEFCON (Defense Condition) of the Strategic Air Command (SAC) to DEFCON 2 meaning that SAC was on alert to engage the enemy. On a scale of 1 to 5 DEFCON 2 was the highest DEFCON ever ordered since the program's inception in 1959. The only other time in history the DEFCON has been that high was on January 15, 1991, when the Joint Chiefs of Staff declared DEFCON 2 for the entire U.S. military in the opening phase of Operation Desert Storm in the Persian Gulf War.

On the 26th of October 1962 the U.S. Government received a letter from Khrushchev proposing the removal of the Soviet missiles if the U.S. guaranteed not to invade Cuba. On October 28, Khrushchev announced that he would dismantle the missile installations and return the weapons to the Soviet Union with the understanding that the United States would not invade Cuba.

After two weeks of being at the brink of nuclear war, tensions began to ease. President Kennedy and Chairman Khrushchev negotiated a detailed agreement that included the primary concern for each side: The U.S. promised not to invade Cuba and the Soviets promised to remove all offensive weaponry from Cuba.

However, despite the Kennedy-Khrushchev agreement the situation in Cuba remained tense. U.S. covert support for anti–Castro exile forces continued and according to some reports included using selected Cuban exiles to conduct sabotage operations not attributable to the United States or the Cuban exile community. For his part Castro vehemently wanted the U.S. out of Guantanamo Bay and looked for every opportunity to help bring that about. For their part the Soviets appeared to be abiding by the understanding reached between the two leaders not to put offensive weapons into Cuba, but that did not mean they weren't continually looking for an opening to hurt the U.S. and strengthen their strategic position in the island nation. One such Soviet move was to posit that the Kennedy-Khrushchev agreement did not necessarily apply to Soviet naval forces.

In 1969 and 1970 Soviet warships had been discovered visiting Cienfuegos Bay on the southern coast of Cuba. They had been detected installing equipment to support Soviet nuclear submarines at the Cienfuegos Bay base. According to George Quester, writing in the April 1971 journal *Foreign Affairs,* by late September through early October 1970 the Soviet naval threat had become such that President Nixon let the Soviets know that the Kennedy-Khrushchev agreement included Soviet naval forces and that any violation would be viewed with the utmost seriousness.

Despite the warning, Soviet naval ship visits continued. In February 1971, a nuclear-powered November class submarine visited Cuba accompanied by a Kresta-I guided missile cruiser and a submarine tender. The submarine was serviced at the Cienfuegos installation. Similarly, in May 1971 a submarine tender serviced an Echo II SSGN at the port in the Bay of Nipe (*Bahia de Nipe*) on the northeastern coast. A year later, a Golf II SSB—with three nuclear ballistic missiles—entered Nipe accompanied by a destroyer and submarine tender. Thus, despite the Kennedy-Khrushchev agreement and Nixon's follow-up warning, Soviet offensive weapons had returned to Cuba in the form of submarine-borne strategic missiles.

Chehalis left Little Creek on schedule on February 28, 1972, heading south for Gitmo with a brief visit to the seaport of Port Everglades in Fort Lauderdale. The trip from Little Creek to Fort Lauderdale was uneventful except that just after we passed Cape Hatteras the Loran (Long range) navigation gear broke down. We were out of range of land for the surface search radar, so between Cape Hatteras and Florida we depended on a DRT or dead reckoning track—an estimate of the ship's location based on elapsed time and estimated speed over ground. Today with GPS and other navigational tools such "flying blind" would be unheard of. We arrived in Fort Lauderdale on March 3, our highly experienced Quartermaster Chief Roy Mills sticking with the tedious plotting and keeping us safely on course.

Members of Fort Lauderdale's exclusive Coral Ridge Yacht Club invited a few of us for lunch at their clubhouse. We were impressed not only with the club and the great food but the kindness and respect the members showed us. The way we were treated was a morale booster. Our March 3 visit came after years of pictures and stories on TV and in newspapers and magazines about the atrocities of the war in Vietnam, often stressing errors and mistakes by some in the American military. The *New York Times* had recently published the *Pentagon Papers*, officially titled *Report of the Office of the Secretary of Defense Vietnam Task Force*. The lengthy trial of Second Lieutenant William Calley, Jr., for his conduct in the horrific My Lai Massacre was still fresh in everyone's mind. It was often difficult for members of the military to find the kind of support we got from people at the Coral Ridge Yacht Club.

Heading southeast toward the Windward Passage, we traversed the western side of the Bermuda Triangle without noticing anything unusual. The area has gotten so much publicity that it's impossible to sail through without questioning anything even in the slightest bit unusual. If nothing else, we all enjoyed the show put on by the flying fish. They would leap from the water and soar above the waves for distances of up to forty to fifty feet. A couple of times we had to collect several that had landed on deck. All went well and by March 6 we were tied up to a small pier on the east side of the harbor near the entrance to Guantanamo Bay. The crew of the USS *Green Bay* (PG-101) welcomed us. The *Green Bay* had left Little Creek on January 3. Like us, she did not have a date for returning home.

Our assignment was both open-ended and classified meaning we couldn't talk to anyone about why we expected be gone for a long time or what we were doing. In brief, the job required the ship to periodically put to sea for a few days to a week and otherwise sit in port in a ready-to-get-underway status. Occasionally we would be told to proceed immediately to sea.

When we put to sea it was always in the general area of the Windward Passage. Located between the islands of Cuba and Hispaniola, the Windward Passage is a relatively narrow strait only 50 miles wide. On one occasion we went barreling out into the strait and found ourselves overtaking a U.S. Navy cruiser. The skipper of the cruiser demanded to know who we were and what our intentions were. Fortunately, it got sorted out quickly enough and we went our separate ways.

Not long after arriving at Gitmo the ship received a classified message detailing our rules of engagement (ROE). In brief, ROE are meant to be what the name implies; i.e., they detail the circumstances under which the ship was authorized to engage a hostile or potentially hostile force. It provides instruction on when, where, how, and against whom force may be used. The idea of providing such guidance is sound in principal but in practice not so much.

The ROE message the *Chehalis* received was a couple of pages of small print. It consisted of legalese that only a maritime lawyer could competently interpret. It seemed to us, even after several close readings, that the key questions of who, what, when and where do we shoot were very much open to interpretation. We concluded the ROE message was telling us that we should use common sense and our own best judgment, and that the rules legalese was not much more than an exercise in backside covering in the event there was a problem.

Of course, the entire crew was well aware of the potential risks the ship faced. I once asked EN3 Gene Van Orden if there was a particular performance or action by the ship that made him feel like he was truly serving his country. His answer would probably be the answer of most of the crew. He said the special operations *Chehalis* conducted out of Gitmo made him feel that way.

At first, we spent a good deal of time in a waiting status tied up to the pier. Other than our standard shipboard work routine there was little to do but sit there, whiling away the hours in the tropic sun and steamy Cuban heat. At Gitmo we had one armed forces radio station, one armed forces TV station and no telephone. A mail plane came in twice a week. RM1 Del Clouser happened to be a ham radio operator, and thanks to him we did get to speak via ham radio a couple of times with our wives, but the connection was very public and thus we were limited in what we could say. We didn't have an information and entertainment blackout but received nowhere near what the average American was used to at home. With so much going on in the world between developments in Vietnam, Nixon's opening to the Chinese, and Nixon's summit with the Soviets we all greatly missed real time access to newspapers and TV news stories.

A crew standout was our cook, "Pappy," a Southerner and something of a character. Everyone enjoyed kibitzing with Pappy, who always had an entertaining and original comment on practically any subject. But his most outstanding trait was his talent as a chef. We all looked forward to his meals, especially his fried chicken—I've never had better. When he was making his fried chicken guys would sneak down into the galley in pairs, one to distract Pappy and the other to make off with a couple of pieces before Pappy knew what was up—or at least so he acted.

We were fortunate to have access to an outstanding officers' club with its almost brand-new private rooms, tennis courts and, of course, bar and restaurant. There was nothing else to do after hours other than read a book, work out, play cards, write home, play softball, shoot hoops or go to the club. We saw and interacted with the same people, day in and day out. We used to make ourselves feel better, or guilty I'm not sure which, by reminding one another of what it must be like to be a prisoner in the Hanoi Hilton, real name the Hoa Lo Prison.

Despite the beautiful weather and scenic surroundings, Gitmo felt like a weird sort of place. The total absence of children, pets, unofficial cars and non-military people gave it a sterile, "twilight zone" feeling. There were almost no women except for a few clerical employees and the wives of the few senior officers permanently stationed there.

The base also had some Cuban workers. Official U.S. Government representations employ local workers in almost all countries in which there exists an official presence. The rationale for this is cost: it's cheaper to employ local workers than to bring in Americans. The flip side of that is security. It is expected that Cuban national workers would provide the Cuban intelligence services with information.

In February 1964, when Castro cut off the base's water supply, President Lyndon Johnson took the opportunity to fire most Cuban workers. Eventually Jamaican and Filipino guest workers were brought in to take their place. Some Cubans remained. These Cuban workers even had their own small semi-clandestine sandwich shop in the hills. One of the guys had heard that the sandwiches were good, so one evening a couple of us decided to go see what it was all about. We weren't welcomed with open arms, but neither were we shown the door. And our source had been correct, the "Cuban" sandwich of toasted bread, ham, cheese, mayonnaise, pickle, lettuce and tomato was pretty good.

Gitmo also had a golf course. The course had some lovely views and long fairways, but in 1964 when Castro turned off the water supply to the base there was no water to spare to water the course. Only a few dead tufts of grass and brown patches existed where once there had been fairways and greens. Despite the poor condition of the course a few of us tried to play a round. The ball took some amazing bounces off some of the exposed sand, gravel and rocks. The occasional downhill drive would go on forever bouncing down the fairway. I had one 400-yard tee shot that flew about 250 yards in the air covering the remaining 150 yards by ricocheting off the rocks. Most late afternoons and weekends Dennis and I played tennis for hours on end and then downed martinis and dinner in the O Club before doing the same thing the next day.

The immediate area around the officers' club had been green grass but it quickly turned into more of a field-like terrain. The field was home to a large feral cat colony. At night the more aggressive animals would move into the patio areas of the club and hunt the giant tropical bugs attracted to the club's outdoor lights. The cats would put on a show scavenging for any available scraps, raiding the garbage cans and leaping for the lights in pursuit of the bigger bugs. The cats we saw seemed remarkably healthy.

We understood from base employees that the cats came from families that had to evacuate on extremely short notice during the 1962 Cuban Missile Crisis who had been forced to leave their pets behind. Surely that group of felines was added to over the years by pets that also did not return to the U.S. for whatever reason. In any case, the feral cat population was huge.

One Saturday night, just as the officers' club was closing, Dennis got a phone call from the watch officer on the ship saying we had to get underway immediately. We raced back to the ship just in time to get on the bridge and order the lines brought in. Dennis ordered me to take the conn and get the ship underway and out of the harbor. It was the one and only time I ever sailed a ship under the influence of alcohol. All went well, but I knew I wasn't at my best. Most of these quick deployments to the open ocean ended as abruptly as they began with orders to cease and desist and return to port. Such was the case in this instance. No sooner did we get into the open ocean just south of the Windward Passage than we turned around and headed back to port.

Days in Gitmo turned to weeks and weeks turned to months with no word of any relieving ship. I recall thinking that it was fortunate we had the quality of personnel we did. The navy had done a good job in selecting people for duty on *Ashville* class gunboats. The crew was so small that there was rarely more than one man in each work specialty. That man had to have a high level of competence in his job and be able to contribute in other areas as well.

One thing that broke up the routine, at least for a little while, was a request to Captain Crosby from a reporter from the *New York Times* for an interview about what the *Chehalis* was doing in Gitmo. Dennis and I met with him in a room at the officers' club and were as forthcoming as allowed about our presence there. The reporter must have used our information for background to a bigger story, because as far as I know none of what we had to say ever got published.

For a needed change of pace, the ship occasionally got permission to briefly visit ports close to Gitmo. On two occasions we visited Port-au-Prince, Haiti. We also spent time in Ocho Rios in Jamaica, and Great Inagua Island in the Windward Passage.

22. Guantanamo Bay

Ocho Rios over the weekend of April 22 was our first liberty port and a beautiful change of pace. At that point we had been in Gitmo for more than six weeks and definitely needed a change of scenery. Picturesque Ocho Rios sits right on the coast in the middle of the north side of Jamaica.

Jamaica originally belonged to the Taino Indians who settled there around 1,000 BCE. In May 1494, during his second voyage to the Americas, Christopher Columbus claimed the island for Spain. In 1503–1504, Columbus and his crew spent an entire year marooned in St. Ann's Bay just to the west of Ocho Rios. We could feel his pain. In 1655 the British took over the island replacing Spanish rule. Independence from the British did not come until 1962. Regardless of who claimed the island, Ocho Rios changed little over the centuries remaining a remote fishing village until the early 1960s when modernization and tourism began to take hold.

Dennis and I paid a courtesy call on the local police chief who was kind enough to give us a tour of the area. Of course, he knew just where to go to impress us with the tropical island's natural beauty. We saw magnificent waterfalls cascading into ponds in dense green foliage leading down to white sandy shores and crystal-clear ocean.

We also visited the nearby Playboy Club on Bunny Bay (not the bay's original name) and the Jamaica Hilton. The end of April is the height of tourist season in Jamaica, so nothing was cheap. We skipped the big hotels and got rooms at a place called the Silver Seas, also very nice but not as elaborate or well-known as the first two hotels. In recent years Jamaica, like so many Caribbean islands, has suffered a crime problem, but when we were there, we found none of that.

Port-au-Prince, our second port visit, also proved fascinating but for different reasons. On the last weekend of April 1972, from a distance, the natural harbor area surrounded by lush green hills was a beautiful sight. We moored to the main pier jutting out into the harbor, a place with a lot of commercial activity, so it was busy with workers. The workers were the lucky ones. Many if not most of the Haitian people lived in dire poverty.

At first it seemed odd to us that despite the extreme poverty the streets were empty of litter or garbage of any kind. We were told that it was so because many of the people were so poor that they would try to salvage anything, even scraps of paper. Leaving the pier area and walking down the streets of the inner city we saw that many of the buildings were dilapidated. People used the street for a toilet and defecated openly on the side of the road. Others languished nearby, sick or otherwise in very poor physical condition. To American citizens of 1972, the sights were shocking.

When we arrived in Haiti longtime ruthless dictator Francois ("Papa Doc") Duvalier had passed away only one week before. The Navy timed our visit to show the flag. Papa Doc's 19-year-old son Jean-Claude "Baby Doc" Duvalier was in the process of assuming the mantle of leadership. Haitians with whom we spoke, including a local Port au Prince newspaperman, told us people were somewhat hopeful things finally would get better. Papa Doc had used his secret death squad, the infamous *Tonton Macoute*, to extort businessmen and kill anyone even suspected of opposing his regime.

After taking over as the country's leader, "Baby Doc" initially introduced some minor changes to his father's iron fisted rule, but nothing like what the Haitians had hoped. Unfortunately, things did not improve much at all, and "Baby Doc" was eventually overthrown in 1986.

For dinner we took a taxi up a main road to the four-star Hotel Montana, a popular tourist resort for Americans and diplomats. It was located in the Petion-Ville suburb of Port au Prince in the hills just to the east. The beautiful evening views of the port city from the patio of the luxury hotel were almost enough to make one forget the poverty of the city. At night, sipping a drink by the pool, the sounds of drums could be heard echoing in the darkened hills further to the east. Someone told us the deep rumbling sounds came from voodoo ceremonies out in the countryside. The sounds were not of a joyous or celebratory nature, rather they seemed to provide an ominous backdrop to the scenes of poverty we had witnessed earlier in the town. I remember thinking that if ever I were to feel like a wealthy colonialist this was it. There I sat, sipping drinks, enjoying fine food in a luxurious hotel overlooking one of the world's poorest capitals while native drums pounded ominously in the distance. I couldn't get the image of colonial rule out of my mind.

In 2010 a devastating earthquake collapsed the main building of the Hotel Montana. Built in 1946, it had remained a popular tourist resort visited by a large number of well-known guests bringing needed capital into the country. The 7.0 magnitude quake centered only 16 miles from downtown Port au Prince killed an estimated 100,000 to 160,000 Haitians and left many buildings in Port au Prince uninhabitable.

Our third "liberty port" was Great Inagua Island, the second largest island in the Bahamas at almost 600 square miles. It sits only 55 miles from the eastern end of Cuba with a population of less than 1,000.

The island is home to the Morton Salt Company's main sea salt production facility; the great salt evaporation flats produce around a million tons of sea salt a year. On May 6, the *Chehalis* moored to the old wooden pier used by the Morton salt freighter that came to haul away tons of salt about twice a year.

The depth of the ocean water for most of the length of the pier was approximately 35 feet, but the water was so crystal clear that it looked to be only inches deep. I had never before or since seen such crystal-clear water. We stood on the deck and were dazzled by the amazing display of colorful sea life swimming at various depths. Big, mean-looking barracuda with their long sharp teeth were the dominant species.

The salt flats were huge and home to some remarkable creatures. The most noticeable were the brilliant pink West Indian flamingos that seemed to be everywhere we looked. The population is said to approach 80,000 birds. The other creatures that captured everyone's attention were not so highly visible. Surrounding the vast salt flats are several relatively narrow channels used to bring in the seawater from the ocean to flood the flats. Large pumps supply the seawater for these channels. Baby fish are accidentally also pumped into the channels where some of them survive and grow. The result is that the channels are over-stocked with barracuda. Throw a pebble anywhere into the channel and it's instantaneously attacked—the barracuda were like swarming piranha. Everyone who witnessed the action gave the channels a very wide berth.

A trip into Matthew Town for lunch with the commissioner of the island and the Morton salt company rep provided the opportunity to see beautifully colored parrots in their natural habitat. I saw a number of the fantastically colored birds called Scarlet Macaws, 30 inches long with long pointed tails. The feathers are mostly brilliant red with tail feathers of light blue and the wing feathers a mix of yellow and gold. We also saw green and orange Bahama parrots and a wide variety of other exotic birds.

Lunch was delicious and centered on meat from the queen conch. Queen conchs are indigenous to the Bahamas and easily taken from the sea floor. They are actually a giant sea snail. Many of the most popular dishes for the few hundred people in Matthew Town include conch fritters, chowder, salads, etc. The big pink colored shell is also valued for its beauty.

A visit to a place like Great Inagua with its proximity to Cuba serves the purpose of "showing the American flag" to the local population. *Chehalis* made an excellent impression on the locals who rarely if ever see an American warship, at least up close. The island people also enjoyed hosting a lunch for an appreciative crew, making friends and showing off their native food and culture.

In mid–May we totaled up our sea time and found that we had been at sea for about four of the previous five weeks—27 of the previous 35 days.

The first weekend in June we again visited Port au Prince and essentially repeated our initial visit. The place was a kind of *Beauty and the Beast*; the land was naturally beautiful, but the political situation horrendous.

The last few weeks of June I spent in preparation for getting on a plane back to Norfolk, my tour at an end. I was eager to once again see Elaine and visit with friends in Little Creek and back home in New York before taking on my next and decidedly different assignment.

23

The Loss of a Best Friend

In June 1972 my required four years of active duty were up and I was free to leave the active duty navy. However, my Bureau of Personnel detailer wanted me to accept a new position he thought would be interesting, exciting, personally rewarding and something different from what I had been doing. He offered me the opportunity to become the first U.S. Navy exchange officer with the Royal Norwegian Navy.

My detailer reminded me that the U.S. Navy Chief of Naval Operations, Admiral "Bud" Zumwalt Jr., had established personnel exchange programs as an important part of the Navy's future. Per his directive of 29 October 1971 (Z-gram 100), the Admiral wanted exchange officer programs with all the navies in the North Atlantic Treaty Organization (NATO). He saw the goal as strengthening NATO through a better understanding of the operations of one another's naval forces. The program was also an opportunity to enhance international relationships while broadening the experience of younger personnel. If I accepted the assignment, the plan was for me to become a fully integrated member of the Norwegian Navy for two years while a Norwegian officer would serve in the U.S. Navy for two years.

A number of things helped convince me to say yes to the offer. Mastering a modern foreign language was something I had always wanted to do. Serving as a Norwegian naval officer seemed like a goal I could achieve (although I was in for a few surprises). I still hadn't done all I wanted to in the U.S. military, and this was an opportunity to do more. I took pride in considering that I could become the first U.S. naval officer ever to serve in the Royal Norwegian Navy whose origin goes back more than a thousand years. The prospect of leaving the service to settle down as a businessman or similar did not seem appropriate given my many years of expensive training and priceless experience.

Elaine and I both liked adventure. In this assignment we would work with Norwegians who were on the front lines with the Soviet

Union, an increasingly dangerous enemy of the U.S. in a Cold War the U.S. had to win.

Our entire lives we had lived in the shadow of the Cold War. The words "Cold War" actually came into use almost immediately after World War II. British novelist Eric Arthur Blair (aka George Orwell) first used the term in October 1945 in his essay entitled *You and the Atom Bomb.* In 1947 American journalist Walter Lippmann popularized the term when he made it the title of a series of essays. The Cold War existed from the descent of the "Iron Curtain" Winston Churchill described in his speech in 1946, to the Cuban Missile crisis of 1962, to the eventual downfall of the Soviet Union in 1991. The completely unexpected Soviet launch of Sputnik, the first satellite in space, on October 4, 1957, further heightened Cold War tensions. The launch started the "space race," which became an extension of the Cold War and the "arms race."

As time marched on the threat of nuclear destruction only seemed to get worse. In 1956 we heard Soviet First Secretary Nikita Khrushchev say, "Whether you like it or not, history is on our side. We will bury you!" In October 1962 we had witnessed firsthand the result of Soviet aggression in Cuba. In the late 1960s and early 1970s we had seen how the Soviet Union intervened in Vietnam to kill our soldiers, sailors and airmen. Somehow America had to defeat the Soviet aggression and stop the potential for Soviet elimination of the West.

Most junior officers, myself included, held Admiral Zumwalt in high regard. When he took over as Chief of Naval Operations in 1970, morale within the fleet was not very good because of aging ships, long deployments, and unnecessarily strict regulations on everything from discipline to hairstyles. Many officers and enlisted men sought to leave the Navy not only because of the long periods away from home but also because of a rigid navy culture that had not kept up with changing civilian mores.

Admiral Zumwalt instituted necessary but often controversial change with a series of new directives nicknamed "Z-grams," which were official naval orders sent directly to the fleet. Many of Zumwalt's Z-grams focused on improving the lives of navy men and their families through improved leave policies, spousal travel, drug and rehabilitation programs, and the like. I really liked Z-gram 31 of 23 September 1970 establishing a junior officer ship-handling competition whose winners would be able to pick their next duty assignment, and Z-gram 64 of 3 December 1970 that encouraged commanding officers to increase the opportunities for junior officers to practice ship handling. But the most important Z-gram to me was Z-gram 100 establishing the new personnel exchange program. If Admiral Zumwalt and his Navy wanted someone like me to be an exchange officer, it seemed I should accept.

By the end of June, I had said goodbye to the *Chehalis* in Guantanamo and was on a flight back to Norfolk. Once again it was a wonderful homecoming with so much to plan and prepare for. It was time to use up some annual leave, pack up our meager belongings for another move, and squeeze out what time we could to visit family and friends in our hometown of Sayville. That summer of 1972 we were happy to have some time together away from the constant demands of a ship and energized with the prospects of a new and unique assignment in Northern Europe.

But by mid–August the trauma of the war in Vietnam came back to us once again in a very personal way. On August 13, as we came through the door to the family home in Sayville, my mother greeted us with terrible news. She immediately blurted out that Merrill Masin, my best friend in high school and the best man at our wedding, had been killed on August 12 in Vietnam. His funeral would be on August 24 at St. Ann's Church in Sayville followed by internment in St. Ann's Cemetery. We were crushed by the news.

The weeks following notice of Merrill's death were spent in mourning, trying to help the Masin family cope with their grief. According to the official reports about an hour before sunrise on August 12, 1972, Captain Merrill H. Masin, USAF, attached to the 776th Tactical Airlift Squadron, was in a Lockheed C-130 Hercules taking off from Soc Trang Airport in South Vietnam. As Merrill's plane began to lift off the ground it was hit by enemy small arms fire and crashed. Of the crew of eight on board seven were killed with Merrill among the dead. Twenty-three of the thirty-six passengers on board were also killed.

Merrill had been on his second tour in Southeast Asia. Newspaper accounts recounted that he had spent a year there as a fighter pilot before returning to the U.S. for training as a transport pilot. On completion of his transport training, he volunteered for duty in Taiwan flying C-130s. He was due to return to the U.S. in December and complete his military service on March 29, 1974.

Everyone knew the terrible loss of Merrill to be even more tragic because he was the only child in the Masin family with the prospect of continuing the family name. His older brother, Graham, had suffered all his life from cerebral palsy. Merrill was engaged to be married to a lovely girl who was, of course, devastated.

From Vietnam to the Arctic Circle

The eleven days leading up to Merrill's funeral proved emotionally very difficult. In addition to our friendship with Merrill we had been close to all of the Masins. In fact, it had been Merrill's mother, Lorraine, who told me that I should invite Elaine to the high school junior prom—our first date. Everyone in the town knew the Masins as icons of the best of small-town America. Lorraine Masin was a licensed practical nurse who for twenty years worked in the emergency room at Bay Shore's Southside Hospital. Merrill's father Howard was the longtime town mailman. The official number on the crest of his postman's hat was the number 1. And in addition to all the work they did caring for Graham, they were foster parents to five children. They were also leaders of the Community Ambulance Company, leaders of the local sailing association, longtime active parishioners in St. Ann's Church and participants in numerous other local groups and associations.

When a devastating loss such as this takes place, people who are hurt by it often don't react in expected ways. Two things happened that I did not expect. First, Merrill's other best friend and also a good friend of ours, Chuck Raynor, owned and operated the local funeral home handling Merrill's burial. Chuck felt as bad as Elaine and I did but suffered the extra burden of being responsible for handling the body and the arrangements. Even with years of experience, Chuck told me he found dealing with Merrill's preparations extremely difficult.

The thing that always bothered Elaine and me was that after the burial and into the future neither one of us could bring ourselves to have much contact with the Masins. I went back once to sit with them not long after Merrill's funeral and that was it, I could not bring myself to go back again. Of course, I was away for years with the Navy but even after that and after the passing of Lorraine I found I could not force myself to spend time with Merrill's dad, a man whom I had been close to most of my life. To this day I remain disappointed in and angry with myself for my failing. As the song from *Les Miserables* goes, "There is a grief that can't be spoken." It can't be spoken because there are no words, only devastating emotion that never really goes away, even in time.

Many years after Merrill's death when I occasionally bumped into Merrill's dad on the street our brief exchanges told me he understood, at least I hope that was what he was telling me. I think he felt the same way I did, there is nothing more to say or do, ever, at least not in this world.

In the years following Merrill's death many local people helped Howard, Lorraine and Graham get by as best they could. The Air Force facilitated the transport of Sukki, a dog Merrill had adopted in Taiwan,

Sayville's monument to Vietnam War hero Merrill Howard Masin. Merrill's family home is located about 200 yards to the left of the stone, close to Browns River seen in the background. The small island on the other side of the river where he used to play as a child now bears his name (courtesy Elaine Kiesling Whitehouse).

back to Sayville for adoption by the Masin family. Merrill's friend, lawyer Bill Garbarino, took over the legal burdens. Local humanitarians Don and Judy Hester provided a great deal of personal and administrative care, especially for Howard, up to and after his death.

More than two decades after Merrill's death, longtime personal friend and former Islip Town Councilman Christopher Bodkin initiated an official request of Suffolk County to name a small island in Merrill's honor. In November 1998 Suffolk County named the island in Brown's River near the Masin home Captain Merrill H. Masin Island. A stone monument in his honor was placed on River Road overlooking the island. It still seems not enough.

24

Getting to Norway

Before beginning my tour of duty as the U.S. Navy's exchange officer with the Royal Norwegian Navy, I was assigned to a nine-month intensive Norwegian language program at the U.S. State Department's Foreign Services Institute located in Roslyn, Virginia, just across the Potomac from the Capitol. I started the course in early September, finishing in late May with departure for Norway set for June of 1973.

We found a nice apartment not far from Roslyn in a new high-rise building in Falls Church. As soon as we moved in, I started school.

I had no idea what to expect in this full-time language study program. It had been a while since I spent eight hours a day in a classroom with two hours of homework every night.

I had seven classmates, all of whom were equally new to intense modern language study. They included U.S. Air Force Major Roger Friese, a lawyer from the Judge Advocate General (JAG) Corps, U.S. Army Captain Robert Kaiser from the Army Special Forces and five sergeants also from the U.S. Army Special Forces. All the Special Forces guys had recently come back from Vietnam.

The class had two native Norwegian instructors, Fru (Miss) Eva Sweeting and Fru Ann Storm. They were in the same small classroom with us for eight hours a day, five days a week. They had their hands full. The language aptitude for the eight students ranged from very good to not very good, so the instructors had to work extra hard to try to keep everyone on the same page.

Intensive language training has its own stresses. We were eight experienced military men from three different service branches, with different backgrounds and capabilities, cooped up in a small classroom for a big chunk of the day. The two instructors, no-nonsense Norwegian women, did a good job in keeping it all together. Truth be told, despite the unusual stresses and all our differences, no one had any substantive disagreement with anyone else. Certainly, that reflected a great deal of stability and maturity on the part of all involved.

From Vietnam to the Arctic Circle

At the end of the nine months, we were tested using the U.S. government's Interagency Language Roundtable scale to measure our abilities to communicate in Norwegian. The government's scale grades proficiency from 0–5 with 0+, 1+, 2+, 3+, or 4+ assigned when proficiency exceeds one skill level but does not meet the criteria for the next level. A 0 indicates no proficiency, a 1 means very basic skills, a 2 describes someone just able to get by in everyday situations. A 3-level student is able to participate effectively in most conversations. A 4 means the person can participate in any conversation with a high degree of fluency and precision of vocabulary. A 5 score describes an educated native speaker.

Grades were assigned for reading comprehension, speaking, and listening comprehension. My final exams in May showed my Norwegian at about a 2+ to 3 in each of the three categories, good enough to be ranked first in the class. When I finished my two years with the Norwegian Navy, I was retested and my ability in all categories had moved up to a 4+.

Americans tend to not learn foreign languages because they don't need to speak foreign languages. Spanish has become something of a "need-to-know" language for Americans, but there are few if any others. Most educated Norwegians have fluency in three, four or five languages, not to mention the sister languages of Swedish and Danish. This is so primarily because Europe is made up of small countries in close proximity. Norwegians are more or less constantly exposed to other European languages through business dealings, vacations, sports events, music, educational institutions, etc. They almost can't avoid learning them. For us, it would be as though New Jersey spoke one language, Connecticut another and Massachusetts yet another. Educated people here would speak those other languages.

In Norway, English usually tops on everyone's second language list, except Norwegian doctors, for whom German is first because many of them train in Germany. It's often hard to practice Norwegian with Norwegian friends and colleagues because they quickly switch to English when the conversation drags.

Other considerations in learning to speak a language fluently are the various dialects, accents, education of the speaker, slang, profanity, expletives and everyday phrases that are illogical when directly translated—"it's raining cats and dogs" doesn't make any sense in Norwegian. There are also words and phrases that are nearly impossible to translate. For example, the nomadic Samisk people, or Lapps as they are known in the U.S., have many words to describe reindeer. Likewise, the Norwegians have many words for different kinds of snow. Some languages such as Norwegian also have two competing languages, Nynorsk (New Norwegian) and Gammal Norsk (Old Norwegian) both of which can be competently used by most any Norwegian.

I learned that to be able to speak a foreign language competently it is necessary to use it more or less constantly. The bridge of a Norwegian warship was a great place to learn Norwegian thoroughly because there could be no lapsing into English with the helmsman, lee helmsman, lookout, etc. You had to know immediately what to say and what was being said in return.

In June 1973 we packed up our meager belongings once again and left for Norway, arriving in Oslo on Friday, June 22, just in time for the big Midsummer's Eve holiday weekend. In Norway, Midsummer's Eve, the longest day of the year, is known as *Sankthansaften* (St. John's eve).

Originally a pagan festival and then a Christian celebration, today the holiday is secular, more like the original pagan festival. Until approximately 1840, Norwegians marked the Christian celebration with visits to their *stavkirkene. Stavkirkene* are medieval churches built of wooden staves or posts. The early Norwegians built an estimated 2,000 of them. Of the 28 that remain today, most were built between 1150 and 1350, which means that the oldest of these wooden structures were built only about 150 years after Leif Ericson established his L'Anse aux Meadows settlement in North America, 300 years before Columbus sailed to the New World. These venerable churches are memorials to almost a thousand years of Norwegian civilization. A visit to one is a lifetime memory.

The magic of midsummer is the theme of much of the Midsummer Eve celebration with large bonfires representing the sun visible everywhere. The bonfires are the central point of the partying by all age groups with grilled meat, shrimp, smoked salmon, *kransekake* (ring cake) and *rømmegrøt* (Norwegian porridge) the specialty foods of the day. It is supposed to be Norway's biggest holiday festival of the year after Christmas, but I think their National Day on May 17 is easily the equal of Midsummer Eve. Norwegians are extremely proud of their country and their heritage and celebrate it accordingly. The enthusiasm with which the Norwegians celebrate Midsummer's Eve is also understandable given the limited warm weather in the average Norwegian summer. One year we were there the temperature managed to reach 70 degrees on only 7 days all summer!

From Vietnam to the Arctic Circle

The Norwegians, at least those with whom we associated, also liked and respected America. They did not like strong criticism of the United States, particularly by Americans. More than once we saw American entertainers, apparently used to youthful American audiences, met with silence when they insulted the U.S. with anti–American jokes or comments. Insulting one's own country in front of foreigners seems a uniquely American trait and, at least in our experience, not well received.

Lunch in the hotel dining room gave us a hint of what would be happening to our waistlines over the next couple of years. I ordered a steak and French fries. The steak, while excellent, was the size of what an American restaurant might call an appetizer, with the number of accompanying French fries countable on one hand. It was a delicious but tiny meal. Serving portions for virtually everything came in at about one half of comparable American fare.

Portion size aside, both Elaine and I came to really enjoy Scandinavian food. In my experience, wild Norwegian salmon taken right out of the fjord with its high levels of proteins, vitamins and fatty acids is incomparable to any other variety of Atlantic or Pacific salmon.In Norway the fish markets are numerous, offering seafood caught that day. The *fisketorvet* (fish market) in Bergen is a major tourist attraction, and rightly so, with its open market offering every kind of local seafood taken from local boats at the nearby piers. Or you can head for the piers and buy delicious fresh cooked shrimp very inexpensively right off the shrimp boats after they tie up in the harbor.

After our lunch and once back in our room we got a call from Norwegian Navy Lieutenant Trygve Andreassen who was a good friend of Ralph Martin, the U.S. Navy Lt. I replaced on the *Chehalis*. Ralph had sent Trygve a letter of introduction, and so Trygve felt obliged to meet us and take us out for dinner. Trygve worked at the Norwegian Military Headquarters just outside Oslo known as the Norwegian Pentagon. He spoke fluent American English from having had a tour in the U.S. and was a big help explaining things to us on our first day in Norway.

Trygve asked if we enjoyed skiing, a Norwegian national pastime. We answered honestly, saying we had done a little downhill skiing in high school but nothing since. He said he thought we'd probably get a chance to get back to it, quickly adding that he'd tell us something of an open secret about himself. He is one of only a few people in all of Norway who hates skiing. He said his dislike of the sport was not a social plus, sort of akin to hating football in South Bend, Indiana, or golf in Florida. Trygve was right, it would be virtually impossible to get through two years in Norway without becoming at least a passable cross-country skier. There's actually more to the sport than it would seem, especially learning to go uphill.

On Monday I reported to the U.S. Naval Attaché's Office at the American Embassy on Drammensveien, directly across from the Royal Palace. We met with the Naval Attaché Captain David De Cook and everyone else in the attaché's office, including Chief Warrant Officer Jerry Tingle, who in the future would prove to be very useful contact. One of this officer's collateral duties was to arrange for individuals attached to the office to purchase tax-free cigarettes and liquor. In Norway, that perk made a huge difference financially. Norway taxed both liquor and cigarettes at an extremely high rate. In Norway good liquor and American cigarettes were so valuable they were used as an alternative form of currency. You could get a lot in return for a bottle of Johnny Walker Red or a carton of Marlboros.

We saw many examples like this of how Norway's socialist laws had unintended and unacknowledged consequences. In the Norwegian barter system people would go far out of their way to trade services rather than have traceable receipts. The Norwegian naval officers complained to me that as government employees they were among the lowest paid workers in the country. The government knew exactly how much money they made in income, so they had to pay the exorbitant income taxes on every kroner they earned.

In 1973, in a Norwegian government-owned and operated liquor store called a *vinmonopol*, a 750 ML bottle of Johnny Walker Red Label cost the kroner equivalent of well over $40.00. The Norwegian idea behind such prices was to reduce the public's alcohol consumption through punitive taxation. The price manipulation actually accomplished this; at least for the public's consumption of commercially produced alcohol. It did not, however, curtail the Norwegians' alcohol consumption. Much like Prohibition in the 1920s and early 1930s in the U.S., the Norwegian effort fostered a huge, and strictly illegal, cottage industry of homemade alcohol. The Norwegians called their moonshine *hjembrendt* (literally translated, "home-burned"). *Hjembrendt* was terrible stuff that killed a number of Norwegians every year from explosions and fires in the distilling process and also from methyl and ethyl alcohol poisoning. However, that didn't stop anyone from distilling their moonshine. Everyone did it, even the police and justices in the courts. Every Norwegian grocery store featured a section dedicated to "flavoring ingredients" and brewing equipment specifically designed for the production of everything from bathtub gin to kitchen sink scotch. The laws against making *hjembrendt* may have been on the books, but they were never enforced, even when someone died as a direct result of imbibing home-burned hooch. Most of it was not pleasant stuff to drink. Even if it didn't kill you outright, in my experience, the product offered the consumer the opportunity for a memorable hangover.

Almost any intelligent, self-respecting adult Norwegian assigned considerable value to a commercially produced bottle of booze. In fact, they even valued the glass bottle because they could refill the empty with their own homemade stuff, thereby impressing guests with proof of a recently consumed bottle of genuine gin or scotch. We soon learned to put any empty Gordon's gin bottles or Johnny Walker bottles on the top of our garbage can. That way a neighbor could take home the bottle prize without having to work too hard. The glass bottle would live on for many years, filled and refilled countless times with the neighbor's best *hjembrendt*. It was amusing to see labels on booze bottles occasionally worn to the point of illegibility.

* * *

A brief orientation at the embassy was followed by an official introductory visit to the Norwegian Navy headquarters within the Norwegian "Pentagon" or military headquarters. There I learned I would be assigned to the KNM *Trondheim* (F-302). KNM is the abbreviation for *Kongelig Norske Marinen* or, in English, the Royal Norwegian Navy, and is used the way we use USS (United States Ship). The *Trondheim* was one of the five Norwegian frigates home-ported at Haakonsvern, the main Norwegian naval base and largest naval base in the Nordic region located about five miles southwest of Bergen. In addition to the frigates the Norwegian Navy had 14 diesel-electric subs, 38 fast attack craft, 10 minesweepers and 7 landing craft and assorted other vessels. Eventually I would see duty on most of the other kinds of ships in the Norwegian fleet.

The *Trondheim* was an Oslo-class frigate of about 316 feet in length, with a beam of 36 feet, and a draft of 18 feet. The Norwegians built five Oslo Class ships in Horten, Norway based on the design of the U.S. Navy's Dealey-class destroyer escort. The Oslo class design incorporated a higher freeboard in the forward part of the ship to better suit the often-difficult Norwegian sea conditions. The U.S. funded half the cost of the frigates' construction under the Mutual Defense Assistance Program.

24. Getting to Norway

Commissioned in 1966, the *Trondheim* was twin screw with a top speed of around 25 knots. The crew included 120 officers and men. Well-armed, she had one twin 3-inch gun mount, one Sea Sparrow SAM (Surface to Air Missile) launcher with eight missiles, and six Norwegian built Penguin SSMs (Surface to Surface Missile). However, her primary mission was anti-submarine warfare, especially anti–Soviet submarine warfare. She carried one Terne anti-submarine rocket system and two Mk 32 triple torpedo tubes.

The Soviet subs sailed close by and sometimes in Norwegian waters where, using the walls of the fjords, they could determine their precise location for use in possible missile launches. We would chase at least two suspected Soviet subs in Norwegian waters during the time I was aboard.

Introductions over and assignment in hand, that evening Elaine and I boarded an overnight train. We took the famous Bergen Railway running between Oslo and Bergen, traversing the mountain plateau called the *Hardangervidda*. The mountains, steep valley walls, waterfalls, and hairpin turns were astonishing and the service equally so, at least for two Americans used to riding the much-maligned Long Island Railroad.

25

Welcome to the Norwegian Navy

In Bergen the KNM *Trondheim*'s Antisubmarine Warfare (ASW) officer, Lt. Kjell Olsen and his wife welcomed us. They brought us to their home and served us a hearty American breakfast of orange juice, scrambled eggs, toast and bacon. We didn't appreciate it at the time, because we didn't realize that Norwegians never ate such things for breakfast, unless, perhaps, if they were on vacation in England. Most Norwegians preferred a much different first meal of the day including various cheeses, canned fish, and dry bread accompanied with milk and strong coffee. We also failed to appreciate the degree of effort required to treat us so well with twin babies in highchairs competing for attention.

And speaking of coffee, the coffee in Norway was and probably still is a strong brew. Norwegians didn't use any filter, simply boiling up the coffee in a kettle. In the Norwegian navy the coffee was always made this way. It was a welcome beverage late at night or early in the morning on the bridge in the dark and cold.

One other interesting tidbit about coffee in Norway comes via the Sámi. The Sámi have historically been known in English as Lapps or Laplanders, the name possibly derived from an old Swedish or Finnish word. When out herding reindeer or traveling long distances over land, the Sami measured distances in "coffee stops." For example, one camping ground might be said to be two coffee stops distant. I learned this from some of my Norwegian colleagues one day while out hiking in the woods, a favorite Norwegian activity.

One Sunday afternoon in the hills surrounding a fjord in Northern Norway I was hiking with a couple of shipboard friends. We rounded a sharp turn in the path and found ourselves on the edge of a small clearing. We couldn't help but notice that we weren't the only ones there. No more than 20 feet in front of us stood a small herd of Norwegian *elg*. A Norwegian *elg* is not an American elk; it is an American moose. If you don't have experience with these very big and large-antlered creatures, which as sailors we did not, being confronted with a herd of them at

Around the year 1360, the German Hanseatic League established one of its offices at Bryggen (the wharf), a.k.a. Tyskebryggen (the German wharf), in the harbor at Bergen. The Hanseatic League went on to dominate trade for the next 400 years. Because the buildings were so close together and made entirely of wood, fires were a problem. Most of the buildings on today's Hanseatic Wharf date to 1702. Bergen, itself, was established around 1070. Today Bryggen is a UNESCO World Heritage Site (Grisha Brev/Bigstock. com).

close range and completely unarmed is intimidating. With no time to discuss moose safety practices and what might be done, we reflexively and immediately retraced our steps back around the corner from where we had come. To our great relief these moose, or *elg*, continued grazing and showed little interest in us.

Like the American moose, *elg* are not usually aggressive towards human beings, but males can be during the breeding season. They may also attack if they think their young are being threatened, or you're encroaching on their territory or you provoke them in some way. An *elg* attack can be deadly. An adult can run at a speed of 30 miles per hour, and weighs in the neighborhood of 1,000 pounds or more. They use their speed and weight to knock you down and then trample you with their hooves.

Another quick moose (*elg*) story: One Sunday, fellow ship's officer

Martin Gamnes and I were out hiking when we came across a lone moose, a safe distance away in a field. Just for fun, I mooed like a cow to see if it would react. The only reaction I got was from Martin who doubled up in a fit of laughter. Once he had recovered, I learned that he thought I believed the moose to be a Norwegian cow. To this day I think he's convinced I thought it was some Norwegian farmer's livestock. I could just hear the stories behind my back—"You know our American friend saw an *elg* today and thought it was a cow! He even mooed at it!"

But I digress. On July 1, 1973, I reported for duty aboard my first Norwegian ship, the KNM *Trondheim* docked at Haakonsvern.

The *Trondheim* was one of five Norwegian frigates and sister ship to the KNM *Oslo* (F-300) on which I would later serve. Captain Willy Andersen, who had trained as a U.S. Navy SEAL, was the ship's captain, and Bjornar Kipsgaard—who had earned his master's degree at the U.S. Naval Institute in Monterey, California—was the Executive Officer. The two of them were physical opposites—Andersen was short and wiry with close cropped blond hair and piercing blue eyes while Kipsgaard was tall and heavy set with big brown eyes and a thatch of dark brown hair. Each was intelligent and well educated with a personality that seemed to mirror his body type.

Other ship's officers, in addition to Olsen with whom I became close, included the weapons officer Lt. Tore Pettersen and the Navigator Lt. Jan Jensen. Quartermaster Chief Petty Officer Einar Basso also became a close friend and years later visited us at our apartment near Tyson's Corner in northern Virginia. Elaine and I became good friends with all of these men, their wives and children.

The Norwegian Navy put us up in furnished temporary navy housing that came with a panoramic view of the naval base. We stayed there for about two weeks before moving into a small, three-level town house that would be our home for the next two years. The address was Bregnestien 10A in Fyllingsdalen, part of a naval officer housing complex near Haakonsvern.

The Bregnestien house had a small basement, a ground level bedroom, bathroom, hallway, kitchen and dining room, and an upstairs living room and bedroom. A centrally located kerosene heater provided the heat. The hot water boiler was hung directly over the bathtub. The clothes washer was rough on clothing and there was no clothes dryer. No one had a clothes dryer. In winter we hung laundry in a wooden "drying closet" heated by electric heaters. The wastewater line was directly accessible through a hole in the bathroom floor. But there was plenty of room for the two of us; well, make that three of us. Not long after moving in we acquired a little gray cat we named Fred.

Before leaving for Norway, we had learned something about culture shock, at least that we should expect to experience it. No one could explain precisely what culture shock would entail, just that we would unexpectedly find some things surprisingly, even shockingly different than what we might be used to in the U.S. For example, well-constructed Norwegian houses came with exquisite views, but did not have some of what Americans consider basic conveniences, such as a telephone. (Of course, this was long before cell phones.) To make or receive a local phone call we had to visit a neighbor who lived four houses down from us. If we wanted to make a long-distance call, or an overseas call, we had to go to "Telephone Central," a special phone center in downtown Bergen and buy tokens to put in one of the bank of Telephone Central's pay phones. You could not get a telephone for your home because only so many telephones were permitted in a neighborhood. On average there was only about one telephone for ten homes. A neighborhood volunteer managed the phone. If you wanted to use it you had to ask permission from the homeowner phone manager and preferably schedule an appointment well ahead of time.

In the realm of social interaction, a typical American parting comment such as, "Stop by some evening for a drink," or "We have to get together again soon," were taken literally by our Norwegian friends. People showed up at our door the next night for drinks, or we promptly got invited for dinner. We rarely had a free night. Sunday afternoon was open house for everyone, no invitation needed. It was a time when anyone could show up and expect to be invited in for tea, or coffee and cake or what have you. As something of local celebrities—we were the only Americans anywhere in the area—we saw a lot of people on Sundays. Eventually we adjusted and often ended up enjoying the new customs or living styles.

Food products were usually good for a few surprising differences. One day we went to the local food store—tiny in comparison to an American food store—with mayonnaise on the grocery list. We knew Norwegians liked mayonnaise, but after searching the store we could not find it anywhere. Finally, we gave up and asked a clerk. "Here it is, sir, right in front of you," said he. Until that moment we had no idea people put mayonnaise in what looks like a toothpaste tube.

Shortly before leaving the U.S. we had purchased a small, bright red Buick Opel from a Washington, D.C., area dealer and had it shipped to

Oslo. Normally taxes in Norway approached 100 percent of the price of the car, but because of the status of forces agreement between Norway and the U.S. we avoided having to pay any import duties. However, were we to sell the car to a Norwegian when we left, the Norwegian buyer would have to pay the significant taxes due. At the end of our two-year tour, we ended up selling the car to a Norwegian Navy friend who had to pay the hefty Norwegian taxes. We had another friend in Oslo who owned a 1969 American-made Ford sedan she had purchased while living in the U.S. She was looking to sell it, but because of the tax burden she was asking more than $50,000 for it! I could never understand why the U.S. condoned the extremely heavy import taxes on American-built cars.

When our little Buick Opel arrived in Oslo, we returned there to drive it back to Bergen. While in Oslo the second time, we took the opportunity to purchase a number of boxes of Marlboro filter tips, my cigarette of choice at the time, as well as a case of Johnny Walker Red.

Like Americans in the early 1970s, many Norwegians smoked. They carried small pouches of loose tobacco and packets of cigarette paper and rolled their own cigarettes. Many of our Norwegian navy friends, like Lt. Tore Petterson, were so adept at rolling their own they could make a neatly packed cigarette with one hand in a strong wind. I saw him do it many times on the bridge of the *Trondheim*. I tried it several times but could never get the hang of it, even out of the wind using both hands.

The Norwegians rolled their own cigarettes because of the extremely high taxes on manufactured tobacco products. The cigarette taxes, like the alcohol taxes, were meant to keep Norwegians healthier. They surely had the opposite effect because of the absence of any filter on the hand-rolled cigarette. In Norway in 1973, a carton of Marlboro cigarettes cost almost as much as a bottle of Johnny Walker scotch. A gift of a carton of Marlboros to a Norwegian was greatly appreciated. The Marlboros were so valuable the Norwegians didn't smoke them, they saved them for honored dinner guests. They used manufactured cigarettes as we might good cigars, offering them to friends from a fancy cigarette box.

In any case, together with our scotch and American cigarettes, we headed back to Bergen on the main road, west over the mountains. A more scenic route one could not imagine. It was also a dangerous road with portions of it carved into steep cliffs and dropping hundreds of feet straight down immediately off the side of the road. If you suffered from acrophobia, you had better have someone else drive. Any fear of heights and you needed to keep your eyes closed for part of the trip. There were places along the road where you could stop and admire the breathtaking views, something we did several times. At its highest point, even at that time of year, the ground was snow covered. In fact, we were high enough, and far enough North, that the land was devoid of trees or green plants of any kind.

26

Deploying to the Arctic

No sooner had we arrived back in Bergen than it was time for my ship to deploy north. On the August 7, 1973, the *Trondheim* got underway from Haakonsvern for Northern Norway. We would be deployed north of the Arctic Circle until mid–December.

Elaine was left, with no language training whatsoever, to fend for herself in Bergen. The situation illustrates something of what people mean when they refer to the hardship that the families of military members experience. Not only was her husband deployed to inaccessible places north of the Arctic Circle, she was left alone with no friends or family in a remote environment in a foreign country, with no language ability, no radio, and one foreign language television channel that broadcast only a few hours in the evenings. She had no doctor, dentist, or even contacts other than a few of the Norwegian navy wives. She made friends with Bjørg Andersen, wife of *Trondheim*'s Captain Willy Andersen, and Mona Lilleheim, the wife of senior naval officer Johann Lilleheim, but there were no fellow Americans or any "unofficial" friends. The embassy in Oslo was at least twelve hours away regardless of the mode of travel one might choose. Also, remember that technology back then wasn't at all like it is today. For communication there was only the one neighborhood phone.

Also, this time Elaine would have no paying job of her own because there was no job to have. In the early 1970s, Bergen was not an "international" city nor even a particularly large town; it was almost entirely a Norwegian city, meaning there was little to no job market for Americans. We decided her "job" would have to be to learn Norwegian. So she signed up for a course at the University of Bergen.

When it came to my job, I was in for a rude awakening. My first few weeks aboard *Trondheim* were spent trying to adjust to a completely different methodology for driving a ship and, of course, in a language I wasn't even close to having mastered. Even if I had been good at the language in the classroom, the language used aboard ship was much different. For one thing, spoken Norwegian sounds very different depending on what part of Norway the speaker is from. A person from Kristiansand in the South sounds Danish, unlike a man from Bergen, who speaks with a much different "Bergensk" accent. Even among Norwegians people from Bergen are said to have their own language. Likewise, people from other parts of the country had different accents and pronunciations for many words. Then there was the need to learn the nomenclature for all the different machinery, equipment and activities for driving a ship at sea—the Norwegian *lingua nautica*. Just communicating quickly and easily with all the sailors on the bridge took more time to master than I had anticipated.

The language was not the only problem. Virtually everywhere in the coastal U.S., in the first week of August, the weather is relatively warm and mild, but not so at sea on the west coast of Norway. I went on my first bridge watch dressed as I would in the U.S., in a short sleeve khaki shirt and cotton pants. It was one of the longest four hours of my life. Afterwards it took me an hour to warm up. The temperature was in the mid-to-low forties, and in a sea breeze the wind chill makes it feel much colder. I hadn't realized that in Northern Norway autumn arrives in August and the first snows of winter by mid–September. The silver lining was that the Norwegians thought I was pretty macho for showing up in such a lightweight outfit, something even they would think twice about wearing. I did not make the same mistake twice.

It gets cold in Norway earlier than we might expect, but because of the Gulf Stream that runs from the Gulf of Mexico, up the east coast of the U.S., through the North Atlantic and into the Norwegian Sea, all Norway's fjords and ports remain ice free year-round, regardless of air temperature. In addition, south of 75 degrees north latitude (south of Svalbard, aka Spitsbergen) the sea is also ice-free year around. It is the Gulf Stream and absence of ice in the Norwegian and Barents Sea that gave the Soviets access to the North Atlantic and the Mediterranean for its huge surface and submarine fleet, headquartered in Murmansk. Only about 90 miles from the Norwegian border, the port of Murmansk also remained ice-free year around for the same reasons.

Like their storied Viking forebears, the Norwegians were tough when it came to cold weather. On numerous occasions I watched Norwegian sailors stand watch in the open as lookouts, dressed relatively lightly, while exposed to the coldest of wind and weather, and not uttering a word of complaint as they carried out their duties.

The Norwegians we got to know loved to be outdoors (*ut i naturen*)

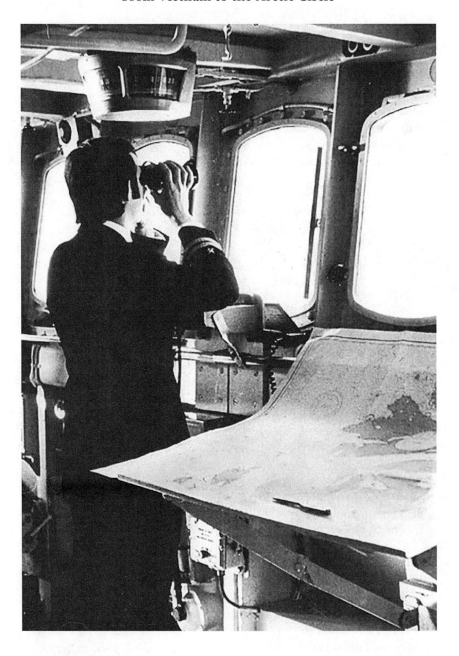

The author standing watch on the bridge aboard KNM *Trondheim* (Royal Norwegian Navy)

regardless of the weather. In the winter they went cross country ski-ing and in the warmer weather enjoyed hiking for hours in the woods, sometimes to pick wild mushrooms, sometimes to harvest wild berries but most often just to enjoy the beauty of nature.

The officers aboard ship exhibited no interest in stories about Vikings, but they loved to read westerns, especially westerns written by Norwegian authors. I read a bunch of them and enjoyed them. The narratives basically followed the spaghetti western ("codfish western?") format where the hero always beats the bad guy, as in Clint Eastwood's movies.

I quickly came to appreciate one fine tradition in the Norwegian Navy. Immediately after the ship anchored or secured to a pier, all the officers would gather in the wardroom for a shot of ice-cold Aquavit with a beer chaser. Only the duty officer did not drink. I grew to really enjoy the custom for the spirit of camaraderie it generated. Also, I never observed a Norwegian officer abuse the drinking privilege by taking more than the one shot of Aquavit and one beer. On U.S. Navy ships, booze of any kind is strictly forbidden.

Aquavit is a caraway-flavored spirit produced in Scandinavia, where it has been brewed since the 15th century. Of the more popular brands—the Norwegians favor *Linje Aquavit*. It is distilled from either grain or potatoes and is around 40 percent alcohol by volume. *Linje Aquavit* (literally translated as Line Aquavit) is named after the tradi-tion of sending oak barrels filled with aquavit on ships transiting from Norway to Australia and back again. Thus the aquavit passes the equa-tor (the line) twice before being bottled. The connoisseur believes the motion of the ship, the high humidity, the significant passage of time, and marked changes in temperature contribute to a better flavor. The beer chaser to the shot of aquavit was always Ringnes, a pilsner-style pale lager brewed in Norway. Norwegian beer is excellent, with Ringnes only one of several popular brands.

I also had to learn the Norwegian Navy's methodology for driving a ship. It is significantly different from our own. In the United States Navy, when maneuvering a large ship in inland waters, officers and crew on watch constantly chart the ship's position and discuss aloud when to alter the ship's course and/or speed. Most of the time the captain is on the bridge and often the navigator. While only one American naval offi-cer controls his ship's movement at any one time, he has a large support-ing crew to assist. Not so in the Norwegian Navy.

A significant part of the Norwegian naval defense plan calls for using to advantage the difficult coastline and intricate inland waterways. The idea is to move your ship or ships faster through the rocky maze, under the usual terrible weather conditions, than any opposing force might be able to move theirs. Key to this plan is giving the officers driving the ships enough ship-handling experience to be able to navigate their way through the difficult terrain and conditions at relatively high speed. The price for attaining that experience is the occasional grounding. In the Norwegian Navy a number of the senior officers were proud members of what they called "The Tulip Club." Any sailor will recognize that a propeller may look something like a tulip blossom after a grounding—the propeller being the first thing to make contact with the bottom. These experienced, Tulip-Club-officers were among the Norwegian Navy's best at managing the defense of their northern territory.

In the American Navy, the career of any captain whose ship runs aground is in serious trouble if not finished. This policy leads to commanding officers using only their best ship handlers as officers of the deck. Junior officers who don't learn quickly and easily are shunted aside. The U.S. Navy's policy leads not just to less ship handling training for junior officers but reduced initiative by commanding officers to take on situations that improve their own skills.

The thought occurred to me that driving a Norwegian ship put me at much greater risk of running a ship aground. Were I to do so, United States naval officers would investigate and ultimately judge my actions. In brief, I would be taking the risks but without the usual protections enjoyed by my Norwegian colleagues.

In the Norwegian Navy the officer who has the conn, or control of the ship's movement, did it almost completely by himself. Part of a Norwegian naval officer's training was to commit to memory the intricate channels within the Norwegian coastline and to know where to turn and when. This is no small accomplishment because according to the Norwegian Mapping Authority (NMA), the Norwegian coastline, including fjords and islands, is as much as 100,915 kilometers or an almost unbelievable 62,700 miles long! *The World Fact Book*, using a different measuring methodology, measures it at approximately one quarter that length; however, that still leaves more than 15,000 miles of rugged and intricate coastline to more or less commit to memory.

In my experience, along with being great ship handlers, the Norwegians are also great pilots. It's not just at sea that they have to battle the bad weather. Flying in and out of their many small airports often means they must face poor flying conditions.

26. Deploying to the Arctic

One incident stands out, a flight from Stavanger to Bergen on a return trip from London. As we approached the Bergen airport, we were buffeted by hurricane-force winds. Approaching the runway, the plane bounced around like a butterfly in a strong breeze. I had serious doubts as to whether the pilot should even attempt a landing, but in we went.

The passengers on the routes within Norway are almost all Norwegians. Norwegians can be slow to display emotion, especially fear reactions, and so while our flight into Bergen might have qualified as some kind of a wild amusement park ride, none of the passengers uttered a peep. The landing was perfect. As the plane hit the runway a huge Norwegian gentleman sitting next to me finished his beer and nonchalantly allowed, *"Ja, det var bra."* (Yes, that was a good job). I wanted to say, "Yeah, you got that right, we're lucky to be alive!" but restrained myself.

One of the qualifications for becoming a Norwegian officer of the deck underway is learning the locations of the numerous shallow water shoals, underwater rocks or skerries (the term skerry is derived from the Old Norse *sker*, meaning a rock in the sea), and promontories and how to sail them in the dark, in blinding snow squalls and in winds at hurricane force. The many offshore islands, rocks and shoals demarcate internal waterways through much of the Norwegian coastline.

Every Norwegian naval officer was also well schooled in "sailing on the lights," meaning he knew where the lighthouses and coastal lights were and how to use them to determine his location and thus where to turn. For example, with the Norwegian system it is possible to watch a navigation beacon change from a green sector to a yellow one, and another light turn from its yellow sector to a green sector, indicating it is time to turn into the green. This, too, took time to learn as the Norwegian coast has 212 lighthouses and another 4,800 or so navigational lights, all managed by the Norwegian Coastal Administration. I had to learn as much as possible about all that as well, otherwise I would effectively spend my two years in the Norwegian Navy as a tourist, someone not qualified to sail a Norwegian warship.

After a couple of months aboard the *Trondheim* I realized that becoming a qualified officer of the deck (OOD) on a Norwegian warship was going to be far more difficult than I had anticipated. I was learning the job, but not fast enough. I was at a point where I had serious doubts about my language competency reaching the necessary fluency level and my knowledge of the coast sufficient to sail it confidently. What finally put me over the hump came at an informal evening get-together aboard one of our sister ships. A couple of Norwegian naval officers from other

The author taking a bearing under the watchful eye of the *Trondheim*'s commanding officer Willy Andersen (Royal Norwegian Navy).

ships approached me and said they were surprised the U.S. Navy didn't send a more qualified officer. They said my Norwegian really wasn't very good and I didn't seem to know how to sail a ship very well. I was equally surprised and angered at their unvarnished comments. Maybe I should have been thankful. From that point on I gave up on the idea of giving up and became more determined than ever to learn all I needed to know.

A couple of months later, under the even-tempered tutelage of *Skipssjef Kommandørkaptein* Willy Andersen and his next in command *Kapteinløytnant* Bjornar Kibsgaard I achieved my goal and qualified as an Officer of the Deck (underway) in the Norwegian navy. It had taken me almost nine months to feel completely comfortable as a single, stand-alone watch officer, or officer of the deck, in any situation. It wasn't the easiest thing I've ever done, but I got there.

27

Life in the Far North

From early August until mid–December 1973, the *Trondheim* remained at sea north of the Arctic Circle, mostly patrolling the Norwegian territorial waters from Bodø just above the Arctic Circle to the Barents Sea and the Soviet border at the Norwegian town of Kirkenes. The ship also occasionally ventured out into the Norwegian Sea, on one occasion to search for a fishing trawler missing in the treacherous winter seas. To show the flag we sailed north to the islands of Jan Mayen and Bjørnøya (Bear Island) and the Svalbard (Spitsbergen) archipelago, about midway between the Norwegian mainland and the North Pole. North of the North Cape is so far north that from the end of October until mid–February the sun never gets above the horizon.

In Svalbard (Spitsbergen) we anchored in the bay of Isfjord on the west coast of the island, the largest and only permanently populated island in the archipelago. We went ashore at Longyearbyen (Longyear City). The world's northernmost town is named for its founder, an American named John Longyear who started coal mining there in 1906.

Once ashore we went to pay our respects to the local leadership—the island is administered by a governor—and to enjoy a pleasant lunch. The population of the city was approximately 2,000, primarily Norwegians, but with a number of other nationalities also present. The economy is surprisingly diverse with coal mining still the predominant industry. Tourism and scientific research are also increasingly important economic pursuits for the island's residents.

Because of Svalbard's proximity to the North Pole, people from many different parts of the world engage in research related to the Arctic environment. The Svalbard Global Seed Vault, officially established in February 2008, stores as many seeds as possible from the world's crop varieties and their wild relatives, refrigerating the seeds at 0 degrees Fahrenheit. The seed vault is designed to ensure against the loss of seeds in possible future crises.

The archipelago's polar bear population, at over 2,000 animals,

The *Isfjord* outside Longyearbyen in Svalbard. This photograph provides an excellent depiction of the frozen, remote terrain that is the archipelago. More than 50 percent of Svalbard is covered in glaciers. Whale men first used Svalbard in the 1600s and 1700s as a base camp. It has been part of Norway since 1925 (Rixie/Bigstock.com).

surpassed the human population. Known for being extremely quick, the bears can run up to 25 miles per hour. Very aggressive, these marine mammals are the largest species of bear in the world. Standing upright, an adult male may exceed ten feet in height and weigh more than 1,200 pounds; the world's record is more than 2,200 pounds. They are a mortal danger to anyone unlucky enough to get too close to one. The Norwegians posted warning signs—a white polar bear profile on a black background with a red triangle border—all over the island. Because of declining populations, in 1973 international law made it a crime to hunt, feed or otherwise interact with any polar bear. However, when we were there, it was still possible in the larger towns of Northern Norway to purchase classic, beautiful polar bear skin rugs, head included, at a very reasonable price.

Along with Longyearbyen, the main ports in Northern Norway all have a distinct personality. One of my favorites was Tromsø, located 217 miles north of the Arctic Circle. It is a cultural center for the region with a museum and many churches including the well-known Arctic

Cathedral with its modern design and magnificent stained-glass windows. The town also served as a long-time center for higher education receiving a significant boost in 1972 with the opening of the University of Tromsø. At the time it was one of only four universities in Norway, and the only one serving the northern half of the country.

As early as the 19th century, Tromsø became known as the "Paris of the North." The Norwegians with whom I spoke were unsure how the nickname came into being. Possibly it was because of the city's bright lights and metropolitan atmosphere in the heart of what is for much of the year a cold and dark environment. Another possibility might be that the university environment has long brought in many young people with their great energy, new ideas and enlightened ways of looking at things. A third might be that the town has long served as the epicenter of a spirited people in a frozen land north of the Arctic Circle.

Tromsø was of military interest. The once top-secret Norwegian Navy base Olavsvern was located just outside Tromsø, at the entrance to the Ramfjorden from the Balsfjord. Carved out of a mountain, the fascinating, high tech facility was built in 1967 at a cost of four billion

A section of the harbor in Tromsø at sunset. The city enjoys centuries-old wooden houses as well as beautifully designed modern-day buildings, like the famous Arctic Cathedral, built in 1965 (slidezero/Bigstock.com).

kroner. I was allowed to see the classified complex in 1974 when I was serving on the *Hvass* (P-972) and we moored to a dock in one of the channels inside the mountain. It was like a set from a James Bond movie.

With the end of the Cold War the base ceased being of vital defense interest, and in 2002 it was decommissioned as a navy base. In 2009 it was closed down completely. A few years later, in an ironic and highly controversial move, Russian research and development firms with Russian government connections rented the facility, purportedly for research purposes.

Tromsø, or more specifically the island of Haakoya just outside the city, is also the site of the sinking of the World War II German battleship *Tirpitz*. The *Tirpitz* had spent most of World War II in Norwegian territory. In September 1943 the *Tirpitz* in company with the smaller battleship *Scharnhorst*, shelled Allied positions on Svalbard. Shortly thereafter, on December 26, 1943, the British Navy sank the *Scharnhorst* just off the North Cape. On November 12, 1944, British bombers sank the *Tirpitz* with its eight 15-inch guns killing an estimated 1,100 men.

Another port favorite of mine was Narvik. The entire Narvik area is a captivating museum of World War II naval action. The Ofotfjord approach to the port city as well as surrounding waters are littered with sunken British, Norwegian and German warships from the fierce battles that took place during early World War II.

In 1940 Narvik represented a big prize for both the Germans and the Allies because it was an ice free port in the North Atlantic that could also provide valuable iron ore brought in by train from the mines in Kiruna, Sweden. Both sides saw it as important to deny control of Narvik and the supply of iron ore to the other. Thousands of men would lose their lives in the effort to win this tiny but strategic northern Norwegian town.

At the beginning of World War II Narvik citizens witnessed two major battles, the first on April 10 and the second on April 13, 1940. In the first, the British lost two destroyers sunk and one heavily damaged, but the Germans had two destroyers sunk, four destroyers damaged, an ammo supply ship sunk and six cargo vessels destroyed. The British 2nd destroyer flotilla commander, Captain Bernard Warburton-Lee, was killed in the battle and was posthumously awarded the Victoria Cross, the British Commonwealth's highest award for gallantry in the face of the enemy, for his role in leading the surprise attack on the Germans. For all of World War II, the British Government awarded only 181 Victoria Cross medals, and of that number only 23 went to members of the British Royal Navy and Navy Reserve.

From Vietnam to the Arctic Circle

In the second battle of Narvik, the Germans suffered the loss of eight destroyers and one U-boat, while the British suffered damage to only three of their destroyers. Most of the ships and men lost in these two battles remain where they went down.

Despite being defeated at Narvik and getting pushed back towards the Swedish border, the Germans eventually won out. In June 1940 the allies were forced to retreat from Norway following the successful German inva-sion and occupation of France, Belgium, the Netherlands and Luxembourg. The Germans would remain as occupiers until the end of the war.

Another port of long-time military interest was the little town of Kirkenes in extreme northeast Finnmark, on the coast of the Barents Sea and the border with the Soviet Union. It had a population of only about 3,500 hardy souls. Much of my fascination for the place came from the town's close proximity to the Soviet border and its remoteness, situated about 250 miles north of the Arctic Circle and further east than the city of Istanbul. I asked one of its stalwart citizens one day how she stood the freezing temperatures, the long dark winters and the limited opportunities for entertainment and recreation. She said that if she didn't take frequent trips to Mallorca, Ibiza and similar sunny Mediterranean islands she couldn't stand it.

The name Kirkenes—literally Church Nose or Church Peninsula—derives from the little town church built in 1862. Kirkenes Church stood stately and serene until the final days of World War II when it was bombed and burned down. The church spire was the only part to survive, and so after the war it was made a part of the new church.

For its small size, Kirkenes played a big role in World War II. The occupying Germans set up bases for the German Navy and airfields for the Luftwaffe there. Toward the end of the war, in fierce combat lasting from October 23, 1944, until April 26, 1945, Soviet and Norwegian forces managed to liberate all of Finnmark, the northernmost Norwegian county, from the Germans. The Soviet Army lost almost 3,000 men in the fighting.

In their retreat, the Germans pursued a scorched earth policy, burning down most of the homes, farms, businesses and infrastructure throughout Finnmark. Kirkenes had only eleven buildings that weren't totally destroyed. Throughout Finnmark, Norwegian civilians who could not hide or escape were rounded up by the Germans and shipped south.

To me, the most symbolically heroic thing about Kirkenes was another church, this one known as the King Oscar II Chapel. Located even farther east than Kirkenes, it sits alone on the coast facing the

Barents Sea. It is on a hillside at the mouth of the *Jakobselva* (Jacobs River) where this Norwegian-Russian border river flows into the Barents Sea. The little stone chapel is plainly visible from the sea. Standing as it does in barren land it looked to me from aboard ship as a kind of beacon of the West, a stunning demarcation between the corrupt Soviet communist ideology and Christianity and the attendant freedoms and prosperity of the West.

In 1869 the King Oscar II Chapel was built as something of a boundary marker to highlight the otherwise barren and indistinguishable border between Norway and Russia. King Oscar II (1829–1907), king of a united Norway and Sweden, visited the chapel in 1873, and so the chapel took his name. King Oscar II, a noted intellect in his day, was called "Europe's most enlightened monarch." To this day the King Oscar II Chapel is used for Lutheran services and other religious rites and celebrations.

In Northern Norway it was not easy to overlook the presence of the Soviet Union. Not far from Kirkenes is the Norwegian Army garrison of *Sør-Varanger* (South Varanger) on the Soviet border. The base, along with several border outposts, represented the Norwegians' first line of defense in the event of any Soviet incursion. The Norwegians would be vastly outnumbered in the event of any conflict, but they could at least sound the alarm for the rest of Norway and NATO. During a brief visit I saw the red phone that was directly connected to a red phone on the Soviet side in case either side had a need to discuss immediately any perceived provocation. I admired the courage of the Norwegian soldiers manning their small outpost prepared on a moment's notice to combat an overwhelmingly massive Soviet force.

The *Trondheim* left the more remote stretches of Northern Norway and headed south to Bergen in time for Christmas. Elaine and I enjoyed a very happy reunion sharing lots of stories about our four months spent apart. We also had a wonderful time entertaining and being entertained by our Norwegian friends. All were eager to show us how festive a Norwegian Christmas and New Year can be.

As in the U.S., for the most part Christmas in Norway means family reunions, going to church and, of course, opening presents. Norwegian children receive presents from the Julenissen (Christmas elf), whose origins are from a family of ancient mythical figures known as "nisser," who date from long before the birth of Christ. To this day Norway remains home to the "nisser."

The Julenissen, who in most Norwegian homes is more or less the

The author near the Soviet border in Northern Norway trying to look like a Norwegian sailor on liberty (author's collection)

equivalent of Santa Claus in American homes, is generous to young children. However, unlike Santa, the Julenissen is small, quick and comports himself more like an Irish leprechaun. He has a white beard and eyebrows, a plain red stocking cap, black knickers, white knee socks, a light jacket matching his red cap, and black clogs on his feet. His appearance is much like his farm and garden elf forebears. Of note is that he avoids chimneys and certainly doesn't go up and down them in the middle of the night. He also has no interest in reindeer husbandry.

Elaine and I decided to entertain our Navy friends with an American Christmas feast of roast turkey with all the trimmings, including corn on the cob which we managed to obtain from the small commissary in Oslo. The Norwegians rarely if ever ate turkey and never ate corn considering it "animal food," but they did not want to insult us by not having some, so they tried it. Most seemed to enjoy it saying they really don't know why no one eats it.

28

The Lost Ship

After several weeks in Bergen, it was time for *Trondheim* to once again deploy north of the Arctic Circle. The ship almost left without me. I had developed an infection in one of my teeth and simply ignored the discomfort. Besides, we didn't have a Norwegian dentist or the methodology for paying for one. On top of that I didn't want to miss a minute of our three weeks at home, including the Christmas and New Year's parties, searching for a dentist. But by early January the infection was winning, and I was in bad shape with a fever. One morning I couldn't get out of bed. Elaine called the ship, and Bjornar Kipsgaard, the Executive Officer, came to the house with Norwegian EMS people all dressed in white uniforms to take me to the hospital. Thanks to a resident dentist and some antibiotics I was healthy again in another couple of days, just in time to board the *Trondheim* for the sail north. The only lasting damage was that Elaine has forever reminded me of the time she had to call the men in the white coats to come and take me away.

By mid–January we were again north of the Arctic Circle making the rounds of the major ports, Harstad, Narvik, Tromsø and the like, and in early February participating in some joint exercises with other departments of the Norwegian military.

On Monday the 11th of February our participation in one exercise came to an abrupt halt. We learned that the 217-foot long British fishing trawler *Gaul*, with a crew of 36, was missing at sea. Her last known position was approximately 60 miles off the North Cape in the Barents Sea, not that far from our location.

By early morning of the 12th, we were off the North Cape on our way to the approximate area where the *Gaul* was last heard from to begin our search. The mission was to locate the ship, provide any assistance required, take onboard any survivors, or locate any trace of the missing vessel. The assignment would not be an easy one. It was mid-winter, cold and dark, the winds near hurricane force, and the sea roiling with waves of about 30 feet.

From Vietnam to the Arctic Circle

When the sea is as treacherous as it was, it is an awesome spectacle. The waves are so big and powerful it makes you wonder how the ship can withstand the onslaught. You have to brace yourself more or less constantly to keep from being tossed around like a rag doll. Many men became seasick, and you have to tie yourself into your rack to get any rest at all.

As I recall we sailed almost due north to a point about 100 miles off Bjørnøya (Bear Island) near the border between the Norwegian Sea and the Barents Sea, and using a grid pattern conducted a search of the area. We searched for days in the dark and miserable weather without seeing a sign of anything. The wind and sea conditions combined with the winter darkness made the chances of finding anything remote. We knew that even in an immersion suit, no human being could survive in such rough and frigid water for very long.

I remember scanning the raging sea and thinking, I'm not going to spot anything unless it's either very colorful or very large. The thought also occurred that were we to spot something, how would we go about recovering it? Sea and weather conditions made launching the ship's boat an impossibility. Even launching a life raft would be very risky. For someone to be in an exposed position anywhere on deck was to risk near certain death from being washed over the side. We continued our search because if we spotted something we might at least have a confirmation of what had happened and a position for possible further search when the conditions improved. Other British and Norwegian ships including our sister ship, KNM *Stavanger* (F-303), also reported negative results. There was no sign anywhere of the almost new—she was only 18 months old—stern trawler or any of her 36 crewmembers.

Some of my Norwegian officer friends said it is not all that unusual for small British and Norwegian fishing trawlers or other such craft to be swallowed up whole by the sea in a bad winter storm. They said sometimes the only confirmation of a loss is the finding of a small piece of a ship on the coast months, or even years, later. After several days of searching my friends thought that might prove to be the case with the *Gaul*. In fact, that was the case with the *Gaul*. A life ring from the ship was found at sea by a Norwegian ship about three months after she went down.

On Friday the 15th we received orders to give up the search and return to port to refuel and recover from a very difficult period at sea.

Subsequent investigation revealed that the *Gaul* probably sank sometime late on February 8 or early on the 9th. At 0930 on the 8th, she had reported to her home base that she was "laid and dodging" (meaning she was pointing into the wind and sea and trying to maintain stability) somewhere off the North Cape. At 1030 she reported again on her location and situation. She failed to make any report at 1630, her next scheduled call-in time. Other ships in her area at 1630 that day reported seas of between 20 and 27 feet and hurricane force winds. When she failed to call in on two more scheduled occasions, she was declared missing and the request was made for an organized search. She sent no distress call, or at least none was ever received.

A formal investigation launched in 1974 concluded the most likely reason for her loss was capsizing caused by extremely high seas. Anyone with experience in that area of the world and who has sailed in sea conditions such as what the *Gaul* experienced saw the findings as entirely reasonable. I could certainly second that. However, because she was a relatively large and modern vessel, the relatives of the lost crew and many others said they simply could not accept the findings. The president of the British Trawler Federation described the loss of the *Gaul* as "the worst ever single-trawler tragedy."

Because the disappearance of this big new ship occurred where it did and at the height of the Cold War, the conspiracy crowd quickly provided some alternative explanations. Near the top of the list was the idea she was somehow captured or sunk by the Soviets. The Soviets did it either by accident or because they suspected the *Gaul* was conducting espionage activities against Soviet forces in Murmansk and had to be taken out. Everyone knew the Soviets conducted espionage using their trawlers, so it made sense the Soviets suspected the West of the same thing.

If nothing else, these anti–Soviet conspiracy theories marked the degree of suspicion between Soviets and the West in 1974. People in Western Europe were well aware of the aggressive arms build-up by the Soviets under the General Secretary of the Central Committee of the Communist Party of the Soviet Union (CPSU) Leonid Brezhnev. They knew very well about the Soviet threat and their constant push for military domination around the world, just as we had seen demonstrated in the ports of Cuba.

In 1975 there came a breakthrough in the effort to determine what had happened to the *Gaul*. A Norwegian trawler snagged its fishing nets on an undersea obstruction in the area where the *Gaul* was suspected of having gone down. Nothing was done with the information immediately, but in 1997 a TV crew found the wreck where the Norwegian

trawler had snagged its nets. In 2002, human remains raised from the ship proved it was the *Gaul*. An exploration of the wreck revealed that some of the watertight hatches and doors and other openings were not closed.

In December 2004 the investigating board concluded that the open doors, hatches and the like compromised the ship's watertight integrity, and in a following sea the ship had taken water over the stern and flooded. In a vain attempt to bring the ship around into the sea, the bridge watch stander probably turned sharply to port, but the attempted sharp turn resulted in sending tons of floodwater rushing to the starboard side of the ship. The resultant instability caused by such a weight transfer led to the loss of control and caused the ship to heel sharply to starboard. Further flooding immediately took place until all buoyancy was lost and the ship sank, stern first. Probably it was all over within minutes. Even if someone had somehow managed to escape the sinking ship, the frigid water and storm-tossed seas would have meant death within minutes.

Thus the *Gaul* became another tragic tale in the history of the seas off the North Cape. The stories from World War II's Murmansk Run provide many examples of the ferocious nature of that body of water.

In the course of the war, beginning in late summer 1941, 41 Allied convoys sailed from the North Atlantic, around the North Cape to Murmansk and Archangel. The dangers inherent in the Murmansk Run were significant. Many Allied sailors lost their lives to German submarine attacks in the Allied effort to use this route to help supply the Soviets in their efforts against Hitler's Germany. Many of the allied runs occurred in the winter to benefit from the near constant darkness, but the trade off was the frigid temperatures, the strong storms and the waves reportedly sometimes as high as 75 feet. Sea spray could freeze on a ship's superstructure, creating a heavy coating of ice, causing instability and capsizing the vessel if not quickly removed. I can vouch that moving about the deck of a ship in such conditions is life threatening. Today the danger from German attack has passed, but the threat from the North Cape weather remains what it was: life threatening in the winter months.

Opposite: **The officers and men of the KNM *Trondheim* (F-302) assembled on the after deck. The author is seated in the middle of the front row wearing a white cover. The photograph was taken in spring 1974 while the ship was moored to the pier at Haakonsvern, the main naval base of the Royal Norwegian Navy located about nine miles south-west of the center of Bergen (Royal Norwegian Navy)**

From Vietnam to the Arctic Circle

After once again making the rounds of many of the ports in the North, *Trondheim* finally headed south returning to Bergen on March 21. The ship would remain in Bergen conducting small exercises, training new crew and preparing for the replacement of Captain Willy Andersen with Captain Kaare Rittland and shifting the crew from the *Trondheim* (F-302) to the *Oslo* (F-300).

Elaine and I were happy to be together again, but we knew my time in Bergen was limited before I deployed north once more from late summer to Christmas. Elaine had finished her studies at the University of Bergen and dreaded being alone again in the long, dark winter. She applied for a position at the American Community School in London and was hired. On her birthday, August 25, 1974, she took a small suitcase and a footlocker and flew to Heathrow with no idea of where she would live or even where the school was located.

Eventually, after living for several weeks in cheap hotel rooms and "bed sits," which were rooms with a hot plate and kettle, she and another new teacher from the United States, Rosemarie Buzzeo, decided to share a flat.

Rosemarie was staying in a temporary apartment owned by a Polish immigrant landlord named Taddeus Zawidzski. He offered them a larger, two-bedroom apartment in South Kensington, a fifth-floor walk-up. Dragging around her footlocker and suitcase for all those weeks was not easy! But with the help of their principal, Jim Page, a man Elaine said was beloved by both the parents and students, she and Rosemarie finally moved into their flat during the early part of October.

I visited Elaine in her London flat a number of times between the early winter of 1974 and the time we left Norway in the late summer of 1975. Rosemarie gave dancing lessons at a studio at night, so we mostly had the apartment to ourselves. The location was convenient to the underground and close to Hyde Park, Harrods Department Store, and the Victoria and Albert Museum. We did all the popular tourist sites virtually non-stop. I particularly enjoyed the break from my codfish diet with the wonderful food available from the food hall at Harrods, the roast beef at the world-famous Simpson's in the Strand, and the carveries in the big hotels.

However, as much as we enjoyed our brief stays together in London, we could not help but notice that England was in decline. Aside from the many still-prospering British businesses and institutions we enjoyed so much, some difficult problems were becoming more and more evident. Nationalized industries, inflation at 17 percent or more, rising unemployment, increasingly disruptive unions, large and growing budget deficits and excessive government regulation defined England in 1974–75. The poor state of the economy was bringing about increasing social ills such as worker unrest and deepening class and racial divides. Bombings by the Irish Republican Army had become a regular occurrence. Once, when Elaine was in Harrods, everyone had to evacuate during a bomb scare. The authorities rushed everyone, including ladies in curlers and flowing pink capes, out the door and into Brompton Road to wait until the all clear was sounded.

The city of London was dirty with uncollected garbage in the streets. The parks and streets were home to thriving rat colonies. There were power shortages, and constant labor strife had a growing negative effect on the average citizen's quality of life.

On February 11, 1975, Margaret Thatcher was elected leader of Britain's Conservative Party and became Prime Minister on 4 May 1979, the first woman to ever hold the office. The "Iron Lady" would remain in office until 1990, longer than any other prime minister in the 20th century. With a great deal of grit and determination, the "Iron Lady" turned England around, improving the lives of all her country's citizens. Elaine and I continued to visit London on and off through the 1980s and saw firsthand the positive outcomes her policies produced.

* * *

In late May 1974, the *Trondheim* got the call to make an official visit to Norway's Scandinavian sister nation, Iceland, during the week of June 10. KNM *Stavanger* (F-303) received orders to accompany us on the trip. I was excited to make the cruise for several reasons. First, I had never been to Iceland. Second, it was an opportunity to retrace the voyages of the Norse who first arrived in Iceland somewhere around 825 CE and who decades later would discover America. Third, it was a chance to see Eldfell, the volcanic cone that without warning was the source of one of the best-known and most recent volcanic eruptions in the world.

Eldfell (the name translates to Fire Hill) is on the Icelandic island of Heimaey about 15 miles off the southern coast of Iceland. Approximately 660 feet high, it was formed in an eruption that started on January 23, 1973. The lava continued to flow for the next six months, with volcanic debris burying about 70 residences and with 300 buildings burned in the island's harbor town of Vestmannaeyjar.

Around 825 CE, Vikings from Western Norway reportedly were attempting to reach the Faroe Islands when they sailed past and landed in Iceland. They liked what they found, and so settled the island, reportedly ousting a number of Irish who had arrived a few years earlier. From Iceland, Erik Thorvaldsson, a.k.a. Erik the Red, famously left for Greenland, becoming the first permanent, full-time Viking settler in Greenland. It was Erik's son, Leif Ericson, who in approximately 1002 CE explored the North American continent, eventually establishing a settlement at L'Anse aux Meadows on the northern tip of the Canadian island of Newfoundland.

We headed almost due west from Bergen past the Shetland Islands and then just south of the Faroes and on to Iceland. Our visit in Reykjavik also gave me the opportunity to invite Rear Admiral H.G. Rich, Commander of NATO's Iceland Defense Force (IDF) in Keflavik, aboard *Trondheim* for a tour, introductions and a cocktail party. The visit went very well; both the admiral and I enjoyed it very much.

In 2006 the U.S. military presence in Iceland came to an end. In March of that year the U.S. Ambassador to Iceland announced the U.S. would remove all elements of the Icelandic Defense Force (IDF). While Iceland and the U.S. remained close allies, on September 30, 2006, the American military ended its official presence in Iceland with the total withdrawal of all its forces.

29

Not Visiting Leningrad

We learned a great deal about Scandinavian history during my two-year assignment with the Norwegian Navy, particularly the modern history of Norway from the early days of World War II to the present. Norway's history with the Soviet Union was complicated, stemming back to what occurred during World War II.

For the duration of the Second World War, Germany occupied and devastated this small Scandinavian nation. In 1940 the population of Norway stood at only a little over three million. By the end of the war, 10,262 had lost their lives, and approximately 50,000 had been arrested, with 9,000 sent to prison camps abroad. By 1945, the Germans had reduced Norway's gross domestic product by half—a bigger decline than in any other German-occupied country.

Norway's government left Norway on June 7, 1940, establishing itself in London and remaining there for the duration of the war. It did not return to Norway until May 31, 1945. During that period the Germans set up a puppet, collaborationist government in Oslo led by the infamous Vidkun Quisling. Immediately following the war, Quisling was put on trial and found guilty of charges including murder and high treason against the Norwegian Government. He was sentenced to death and executed by firing squad at Akershus Fortress, Oslo, October 24, 1945.

Today the word quisling is used to mean a person who collaborates with an enemy occupying force.

In October 1944, the Soviet Union launched an offensive against the German forces occupying Norway's northernmost province of Finnmark. A small Norwegian contingent from England joined the Soviet forces. The Soviet general in command immediately incorporated the Norwegian troops into his battle plan, tasking the Norwegians with finding volunteers from the surviving population of Finnmark and organizing them into small combat units. The Soviets would provide their arms and other combat support.

Additional Norwegian forces also arrived from abroad. By April

From Vietnam to the Arctic Circle

1945, after six months of combat in the frigid cold and winter darkness, the Norwegians declared Finnmark free of the German army. It had not been an easy victory. The brutal German scorched-earth retreat caused terrible suffering and obliterated the little Norwegian coastal towns and villages. Surviving inhabitants were forced to flee further south or seek refuge in mountain caves or isolated mountain shacks.

The military operation in Finnmark lasted six months, from late October 1944 until late April 1945. During that time the Norwegians came to understand that the Soviets were interested in defeating the Germans and not in maneuvering to gain control of Norwegian territory. As the war ended, the Soviets, who had lost 3,000 men in the fighting in Norway, withdrew asking nothing from their Norwegian allies. Norwegians, especially those in the north, were grateful.

In 1945, Soviet Minister of Foreign Affairs Vyachislav Mikhaylovich Molotov had much to say about events in Finnmark. This is the same Molotov after whom the Molotov cocktail is named, the Finns having coined the nickname after the 1939 Soviet invasion of Finland. Even if the Soviet military leadership wanted Northern Norway for warm water naval and military bases, Molotov, and most importantly Soviet Prime Minister Joseph Stalin, undoubtedly weighed the potential benefits of the new military bases against rousing the anger of the U.S. and Great Britain for such an egregious violation of Norwegian sovereignty. In any case, the Soviets made many Norwegian friends, particularly in Northern Norway, because of the Soviet actions and decisions of 1944 and 1945.

The animus Norwegians felt toward their cruel German occupiers did not diminish after the German defeat, or even with the passage of decades. Almost 30 years later, the deep bitterness lingered. In the summer of 1973, just before I arrived, some of my Norwegian Navy colleagues told me that the West German Navy had hosted a NATO cocktail party in Bergen. None of the Norwegian officers would attend, until senior Norwegian Navy commanders issued direct orders for them to go. Even then, the officers thought seriously about not attending. Similarly, other Norwegian friends related stories to us about events they, or members of their families, had witnessed of decades old German atrocities, as if they had occurred only yesterday.

At a dinner party one of our Norwegian friends related a story about standing near a pair of West German tourists a few years earlier and overhearing one of them loudly and brazenly describe shooting Norwegians at a nearby location. Others at the party nodded their agreement. That such insensitive German tourist behavior was not unheard-of and helped to keep the Norwegian resentment fresh and alive. In the U.S. we often hear of the German effort to be ever mindful of the atrocities of World War II, but in the mid–1970s we did not hear that in Norway.

The basis for lingering Norwegian resentment against the Germans following World War II seems obvious. What is less well known, at least here in the U.S., is the receptiveness of the North Norwegian population to those who helped liberate them from the terrible German occupation. I learned that immediately following the war, a good many Norwegians felt it would be difficult to support NATO forces that included West Germans in opposing their Soviet liberators.

For postwar Norway, the German occupation had numerous political and military ramifications. Foremost of these was Norway's decision to become a founding member of NATO and its commitment to maintaining armed forces large enough to provide a realistic deterrent to any future military threat. Ironically, with the onset of the Cold War, that threat became manifest in Northern Norway's old liberating ally, the Soviet Union.

Mountains in the Lofoten archipelago provide a dramatic backdrop for this small fishing village. Fishing has been a mainstay of the area since the Viking times (Anet landa/Bigstock.com).

From Vietnam to the Arctic Circle

Thus, one can understand the Norwegian government's concerns about lingering Soviet influence, particularly with those from Northern Norway. The Norwegian government understood the importance of "showing the flag," that is, showing off its military to the people it would protect. Part of the reason the Norwegian Navy deployed to Northern Norway was not just to be visible to potential enemies and detect possible Soviet submarine intrusions—of which there were many over the years—but also to be visible to, and interact with, the local population. I found that in the mid–1970s, the people in Northern Norway were as pro–NATO and pro–American as anywhere else in Norway. Despite the Soviet assistance at the end of World War II, they understood the importance of NATO and the huge role the U.S. played in keeping the western democracies safe from communist aggression.

To have an American naval officer serving aboard a Norwegian warship took some diplomatic courage on the part of the Norwegian authorities. Senior Norwegian naval officers with whom I spoke said the Soviets rarely missed an opportunity to tell them that, as NATO members, they were little more than a tool of the American military establishment. According to the Soviets, the Norwegian military did what the Americans ordered. So, the Norwegians understood that the Soviets would view their having a U.S. naval officer officially serving on one of their biggest ships as more proof of American control of Norwegian naval forces. While the Norwegians certainly did not kowtow to the Soviets in any meaningful way, as a tiny nation on the border of a massive nuclear superpower, some discretion in official matters needed to be observed. Peaceful relations with the Soviets necessitated avoidance of situations that might appear to the Soviets as though they were being poked with a sharp Norwegian stick.

In early 1974 Norway received an invitation from the Soviets for an official visit to Leningrad (now Saint Petersburg) by a Norwegian naval vessel in the early to mid–September timeframe. The KNM *Oslo* (F-300) was selected to make the visit. Earlier in the summer the crew of the *Trondheim* had transferred to the *Oslo*, so it was *Kommandørkaptein* Kaare Rittland who would command the ship for the visit. When I learned of the visit, I immediately thought such a port call was a wonderful opportunity. Not only would I get to set foot in the Soviet Union and see it for myself, I would do it in the still beautiful Baltic port city of Leningrad, once the capital of Imperial Russia. It was to be a once-in-a-lifetime opportunity to see the Hermitage, the Winter Palace and many other world-famous sights.

29. Not Visiting Leningrad

By that point I had become so integrated into the Norwegian navy it didn't occur to me that others might not see it the same way. The Norwegian high command understood how my presence on the frigate would be perceived by the Soviets. Orders came down for me to be temporarily reassigned to the 25th TKB (Torpedo Gun Boat) Squadron in Bergen for the duration of the official visit to Leningrad. I was disappointed, but I understood the Norwegians' reasoning, and there was nothing I could do about it anyway.

I had been very naïve about the visit to Leningrad. As it turned out, none of the officers went on any organized tours of the city sites, no one purchased fun souvenirs to bring home—although I did get a couple of "From Russia with Love" postcards from my buddies—and no one got treated to anything by any unofficial Soviet. Instead, the visit revolved around alcohol. Morning, noon and night, official gatherings featured endless toasts and rounds of straight vodka. Toasts required draining the glass. My Norwegian officer and chief petty officer friends who, of course, were used to drinking alcohol socially, said it was literally sickening. Some of my friends said they could not even remember most of the visit.

Another surprise was the lack of quality of the official gifts the Soviets provided. The mementos were made either of cheap plastic, cheap cloth or a combination of the two. Most of the items, some with Russian writing, looked like favors from a child's birthday party. There was an endless supply of inexpensive plastic and enamel pins, buttons and badges celebrating any and every Soviet event imaginable. My friends said that despite their construction from very cheap materials, the Soviets seemed quite proud of their offerings.

To a man the Norwegian officers said they would never go back again, not because the Soviets treated them badly or were hostile, but because of the constant drinking, the poor quality of difficult to obtain consumer items, and the Soviets' generally primitive lifestyle. And this was in the beautiful city of Leningrad, not some small town in the Siberian outback. We never really heard much in the West about these significant societal deficiencies, with most people believing, like my Norwegian friends, that Soviet citizens enjoyed a standard of living not far below that of many West European countries. My Norwegian friends were astonished at what they found to be the reality of daily life in Lenin's communist paradise. When the Soviet Union collapsed 17 years later, our intelligence analysts more or less failed to see it coming.

The Shetlands,
Back North, Sailing Subs

While KNM *Oslo* visited Leningrad the Norwegian Navy temporarily reassigned me to the 25th TKB Squadron in Bergen. The squadron was about to make a port visit to Lerwick, the main town in the Shetland Islands in northern Scotland. The Shetlands are only 230 miles due west of Bergen and in decent weather a pleasant sail. We were fortunate to have calm seas and an easy ride both coming and going. During the transit I couldn't help but think of the Vikings who sailed these waters while carrying out their raids and trading forays. They did not have far to sail; in fact, with a favorable wind it was only about a day's journey. One day more would bring them to Aberdeen, only 210 miles or so to the south of the Shetlands. The Shetlands and Western Norway have had a long and close relationship. The name Lerwick even derives from Old Norse.

Lerwick's "old town," on the coast of the North Sea, featured many 17th-century buildings, almost all still occupied today. In Norway and much of Europe buildings hundreds of years old are still very much in use. In America, if a building is 200 years old it's usually on some historical registry and untouchable.

For centuries, fishing was the backbone of the Shetlands economy. It was still a big part of the economy at the time of our visit. But the economy had started to benefit from the exploitation of the rich oil reserves in the eastern Shetland Basin with Lerwick providing workers for the offshore oil platforms. In 1975, the massive Sullom Voe oil terminal began construction employing thousands more people. Lerwick's economy boomed with greatly increased port traffic and use of the town as an oil industry service base.

The stark contrast between Leningrad and Lerwick, geographically and ethnically not far apart, was remarkable. On the one side was the decaying socialist society with much of its citizenry deprived of meaningful livelihoods and pacified by endless supplies of cheap alcohol. On the other side the capitalist free market offered its citizens a chance to contribute meaningfully to society while bringing a promising future for workers and their families.

*   *   *

No sooner did the *Oslo* return from Leningrad than it was time to deploy once more. At 0330 on Friday, September 27 we slipped our mooring lines in Haakonsvern and went to sea. We were to proceed to Bodø then Harstad and finally Kirkenes on the Soviet border before turning back again along the north coast. We were not scheduled to return to Bergen until just before Christmas.

The autumn season meant long dark days—pitch black from a little after two in the afternoon until just before ten in the morning. From 10 a.m. to 2 p.m. the sun sat on the horizon. Daylight consisted of two hours of sunrise and two hours of sunset. The fall also brought bad weather, usually at or below freezing with high winds and snow showers. The constant contact with the same men in such an environment sometimes made tempers short and personality conflicts inevitably worse than they might have been otherwise.

By November, I had become good at handling a Norwegian frigate. In fact, I was considered the best, or the second best, officer of the deck aboard ship. It had become routine for the C.O. to designate me to bring the ship into port.

On Friday evening, November 8, we were docked at the secret Olavsvern Naval Base, not far from Tromsø, along with a couple of Norwegian submarines and miscellaneous other ships. Some of the submariners came aboard for a late meeting and a few beers in the wardroom. I had the watch. In the late afternoon we received a message telling us to get underway for Tromsø and to spend the weekend there. Because I had the duty and hadn't had anything to drink, Captain Rittland told me I should get the ship underway and proceed north up Balsfjord toward Tromsø. He said he would join me on the bridge when he had finished his meeting with the submariners who would sail with us.

Once underway we learned that the normal Grøtsundet waterway leading to our pier on the east side of Tromsøya (Tromsø Island) was closed, and so we would have to take the "back way." I don't recall the precise route we took, but I believe it was around the west side of Tromsøya and then south on Grøtsundet. It involved traveling through narrow and shallow waterways, passing under the Sandnessund Bridge, and then docking against the strong current. It was a much more diffi-cult sail than a simple northerly course through Grøtsundet. Our navi-gating of the unusual route in the pitch dark went perfectly.

As the ship passed the north end of Tromsøya headed for the dock, I noticed Captain Rittland on the bridge. "That was fine," he said, "Why don't you go ahead and make the landing, too." Our navigation officer had said we could expect a slack tide meaning the current would be next to nothing. But he had made a mistake. The tide was running out and was quite strong. We also had a steady wind blowing us off the dock making the landing of this more than 300-foot long ship a more chal-lenging assignment. Make the landing too slowly and you lose control; make it too fast and you may not stop in time. Another difficulty was that we had never before moored to the small, cramped, poorly lit pier that had been assigned to us.

I knew I could handle the conditions just as well as, if not better than, anyone else and so aggressively pursued our landing. The land-ing went perfectly—it could not have been done better. Afterwards Cap-tain Rittland appeared from a dark corner of the bridge together with the submariners who unbeknownst to me had joined the captain on the bridge not long after we had left Olavsvern to observe. All of them came over and congratulated me on what they said was an excellent job of ship handling. These submariners were some of the same officers who had so pointedly criticized me a year earlier. They remembered that and so did I. Their honest congratulations had the effect of making us all feel the emotional reward that comes with accomplishment and its appro-priate recognition.

The man who made this possible was Kaare Rittland. He knew my level of competence on the bridge. He also knew that I'd had a tough start with a few of the officers in the Norwegian Navy and that there were Norwegian officers such as our visiting submariners who liked to denigrate the American's abilities. He had the confidence in me to bring these guys up to observe, and fortunately his plan worked. It silenced the critics.

I made note on November 27 that I'd brought the ship in the last five times in a row and a total of twelve times within the recent past. Except for Rittland, only one other ship's officer had landed the ship, and he had done it only three or four times in good conditions. After what seemed like a slow start aboard *Trondheim*, I was very pleased to finally be back to the level of competence I enjoyed sailing a warship in the U.S. Navy.

30. The Shetlands, Back North, Sailing Subs

It was not long after the landing in Tromsø with the submariners aboard that I accepted an invitation to go aboard one of the Norwegian navy's 15 submarines for a routine four-day patrol in the open waters off the North Cape. I had been asked a couple of times previously if I wanted to experience life aboard these remarkable boats but had demurred for a variety of reasons. After my second time turning down the invitation, a few of the submariners—we ran into the sub crews regularly in various ports—began to kid me about being afraid. I'm sure some of the teasing comments had been tried out on others before me. They also hinted at problems the Norwegian Navy had with getting and retaining competent personnel to man all its Kobben class submarines, the smallest operational submarines in the world.

My sub sailor friends had lots of stories about how uncomfortable it is for everyone locked up inside these small, coffin-like ships, especially for people with little tolerance for confined spaces. They said some sailors suffered claustrophobic attacks as soon as the main hatch was closed, others after long periods underwater, and still others when some unusual event or noise triggered their attack. Whenever a sailor suffered such a debilitating mental issue the ship would surface, providing conditions permitted, and return directly to port for the sailor's debarkation and reassignment elsewhere.

So, I decided I owed it to myself to experience firsthand what sailing in these tiny submarines was really like and accepted their invitation to go out on a four to five-day patrol under the Norwegian Sea. I soon learned the Kobben class boats had some unusual characteristics that made shipboard life challenging for any sailor.

Everyone has some idea how cramped the quarters are in a submarine. Even the big American nuclear missile boats are not without serious space limitations. But these Norwegian *Kobben* class ships were only 155 feet in length and a mere 15 feet wide. For comparison's sake, some ancient Viking longships were considerably wider than a Kobben class boat, and only 30 feet shorter. The narrow-hulled USS *Chehalis* (PG-94) was almost 10 feet wider!

Space aboard ship was at an absolute minimum. In some spaces sailors had to squeeze past one another. The wardroom where we ate and slept was not much larger than your average clothes closet. The table and bunks folded and fit neatly inside everything else. The crew shared only one head, and that was in the forward part of the ship mounted between racks of torpedoes. Privacy, like space, came at a premium.

From Vietnam to the Arctic Circle

On the surface, the subs were slower than a Viking longship, at a max speed of only about 10 knots. Submerged they went only a little faster, up to 17 knots. Their propulsion came from two 1,100-horsepower diesel engines and one 1,700-horsepower electric motor. Their armament consisted of eight 21-inch torpedo tubes located in the forward section of the ship.

Creature comforts aside, the ships proved highly effective for operations in Norwegian coastal waters. Not only were they small, they were very quiet. Perhaps most important of all, the Norwegian officers who sailed them were highly knowledgeable of their coastal environment. The Norwegians could maneuver around the plentiful underwater obstacles far more quickly and effectively than any enemy.

The Norwegian underwater terrain came with as many irregularities as the mountainous fjords above the surface. Underwater outcroppings, hidden rock formations, unexpected shallows, deep-water drop offs and odd currents were abundant. To avoid a potentially catastrophic problem it was vital for the Norwegian submariner to know his underwater geography. Even then there were occasional surprises when small geographic anomalies were not on the charts. One of the officers explained to me that sometimes the local fishermen find a shallow spot, or rock, or other subsurface irregularity that makes for a good fishing spot. They keep it to themselves rather than reporting it. In fact, while I was on one of the frigates, we received word that a Kobben had banged into an underwater rock because it had not been noted on any chart—this despite the locals having some familiarity with its location. Fortunately, it was a glancing blow and there were no injuries or serious damage sustained.

Another important factor in protecting the Norwegian subs from enemy detection was the extensive and frequently changing layering of the unique coastal waters. Layering is where water of one salinity and temperature, and therefore density, lays on top of a layer of water of a different salinity and temperature. Generally speaking, the fjords receive run off from the mountains which provides a top layer of fresh water, followed by a mixed layer of fresh and salt water, then various density levels of colder salt water. Because the speed of sound varies through each of these layers of water, detecting the position of a submarine using sonar becomes difficult. Without getting too scientific, this layering can even create dead zones where sound waves are blocked, and sonar effectively blinded.

Speaking of water temperatures, I think I was most surprised by the temperature inside the submarine. While underway the temperature inside the boat was not much above freezing because of the frigid waters in which the ship was operating. Because it was so cold inside the boat, everyone dressed in a well-insulated snowsuit. You ate, slept and stood watch in your snowsuit.

On the frigates we frequently ran anti-submarine exercises with a Kobben, usually in the open waters of the Norwegian Sea. Even there the sub was almost always difficult to find let alone track. We were inevitably surprised at the end of each exercise when the sub would surface only a few hundred yards away from us.

Not every hour was spent in the open sea. We spent a few enjoyable hours one sunny late winter afternoon floating on the surface in one of the smaller and more sparsely populated fjords of Finnmark. For about an hour we fished for cod by hand line off the deck of the sub. On deployment the Norwegians aboard the frigates did this about two to three times a week using the cod they caught for the next few days' breakfast, lunch and dinner. You just haven't had breakfast until you've had cold cod porridge and coffee at 7 a.m. in a rough sea.

* * *

In 1974–75 Norway's number one enemy was the Soviet Union. For Norwegian submariners that meant contributing to keeping track of the huge Soviet sub fleet right next door in the Barents Sea and Murmansk. Soviet subs routinely transited past the North Cape for patrols in the North Atlantic and elsewhere in the world's oceans. Occasionally they also surreptitiously entered Norwegian waters, including up the fjords, to reconnoiter the area, learn the underwater terrain and test Norwegian defenses.

Despite the overwhelming difference in numbers of ships, the Norwegians held two significant advantages over the Soviets. All the Soviet subs were much larger than the Norwegian subs, and they were far noisier. In the submariner's fight to find one's opponent before he finds you, these were substantial shortcomings. I learned firsthand that the Norwegians could hear and see the Soviet boats without the Sovs even being aware the Norwegians were there.

I was only aboard for four nights, but that was long enough. The boats usually went out on patrol for a matter of days, but never more than two weeks or so. They told me the record for being underway was something like 16 days. Everyone agreed that would be a very long time living under those conditions.

From Vietnam to the Arctic Circle

I left thankful for the Kobben class experience but happy to return to shipboard life above the surface. I had to admit to my submariner friends that it takes something special to sail uncomfortable little boats like that on a permanent basis.

31

The Sami

Anyone who travels around Northern Norway learns about the Sami, the indigenous people who inhabit Northern Norway, Sweden, northern Finland and the Kola Peninsula. I learned more about them one evening when the ship I was on suddenly had to come to a stop and then take a detour.

We were about to enter a fairly narrow strait in Northern Norway when one of the lookouts reported something in the water dead ahead. There was nothing on the surface search radar, so we went immediately to our field glasses. We saw what looked like small sticks poking out of the surface of the water. As the ship drew nearer, we saw hundreds of heads with antlers on the top of them, moving through the water. A herd of migrating reindeer was crossing the strait, probably soon to be followed by Sami herders. A strange but not unusual sight in the far north during periods of reindeer migration, it prompted a fascinating discussion by several of my Norwegian friends of the Sami and their unique way of life.

In early December 1974, the *Oslo* found itself in the port of Alta not far from the North Cape. Captain Rittland organized a visit for the ships officers and chief petty officers to *Kautokeino Kirke*, a Sami church in the Finnmark area of Northern Norway some 70 miles distant. Early one snowy Sunday morning we took a bus south on the E45 Road into the mountains to the heart of Lapland and the picturesque little town of Kautokeino not far from the border with Finland.

The geographical distribution of the Sami evolved over time. Most probably they moved west from the Ural Mountain region of Russia during the Bronze Age, eventually settling in the Finnmark area and the Kola Peninsula. Their livelihood came primarily from hunting reindeer and other land animals and fishing. Those Sami who lived off the land moved with the seasons, never forming permanent communities.

Almost all the Sami are of the Lutheran faith, having converted to Christianity in the 19th century. They observe the major holidays of the

Christian calendar. Advent, the weeks prior to Christmas, brings out a good number of the faithful. Thus, our visit to Kautokeino at that time was propitious for demonstrating the Norwegian government's solidarity with the Sami in their united place of worship. It was not always so.

Like other indigenous minorities, the Sami faced centuries of discrimination and abuse from the larger and more dominant Scandinavian and Russian cultures. Over the years much of their language and culture was lost to laws that were created to deny them rights to their own land, beliefs, language and livelihoods. For example, Sami languages, and Sami song-chants, called *yoiks*, were illegal in Norway for almost two hundred years, from 1773 until 1958.

While the countries the Sami inhabit have done much over the past few decades to help preserve the Sami people and their culture, they now face new and increasing threats to their way of life from tourism, climate change, commercial development and other aspects of modern life. The Norwegian government has tried to make up for past wrongs; for example, the Sami now receive special protection and rights under Norwegian law. In both Norway and Sweden, reindeer husbandry is legally protected as an exclusive Sami livelihood. In Norway only ethnic Sami have the right to engage in reindeer husbandry in reindeer pasture territories set aside for only them. Today reindeer meat, hides, leather and assorted goods made from the antlers are a profitable business with about 3,000 people engaged in reindeer herding.

To be appropriately attired for services at the Kautokeino Lutheran Church, Captain Rittland, myself and the other Norwegian officers wore our dress blue uniforms with only the gold of our ranks decorating our clothing. For their Advent Sunday morning service, the Sami wore their *gakti*, their colorful traditional clothing.

Gakti is worn both in formal settings such as at church or while working. Their outfits are adorned with bands of bright red, blue, green and yellow on a royal blue wool background. The men's jackets are baggy in order to carry their possessions in inside pockets. The women are similarly dressed with their skirts decorated like the men's tunics. The men also wear a broad leather belt low on their hips. The belt combined with the long baggy jacket gives them the appearance of having massive chests and short legs. Many also wear the warm and comparatively light reindeer-skin coats and boots with the traditional curled up toes.

In the deep fluffy white snow, the little red painted, freestanding wooden church stood out like a red buoy in an ice-covered bay. From all directions the Sami came by foot to the church, trudging through the deep snow in small family groups

While some of the Sami have Asian facial features, I found most of those attending this service had bright blue eyes, a slightly more diminutive stature than average and fine, reddish blonde hair. Their physical attractiveness combined with their colorful clothing created a unique, striking appearance.

The inside of the church matched in spirit the colorfulness of its parishioners. Well lit and with high ceilings, the warm ambience of the sanctuary was a refuge in the cold and snowy hinterland.

The sight of 100 or so Sami sitting in pews together with one American naval officer and fifteen Norwegian officers had to be unusual to say the least. I couldn't help but smile at the thought of an official U.S. naval presence in Kautokeino, one of the more remote towns in the world.

Unknown to most Americans is that there are an estimated 30,000 people living in North America who are either Sami, or descendants of Sami. Most have settled in areas that are known to have Norwegian, Swedish and Finnish immigrants such as Minnesota, the Upper Peninsula of Michigan, North Dakota, and Washington State. Descendants of these Sami immigrants often know little of their heritage. Some say that's because their ancestors hid their original culture to avoid discrimination from the far larger Scandinavian population. Of course, in the America of old it was not unusual for immigrants of any nationality to try to blend into mainstream America as quickly as possible, which meant eschewing the language and culture of the past.

For me, interacting with the Sami in their traditional environment and experiencing their Lutheran church service was unforgettable.

On the return ride to the ship the bus made a quick stop at the Juhls Silver Gallery located a mile or so outside of town with a great view of Kautokeino. The building itself is a recognized architectural gem because it blends so remarkably into the local landscape.

We were fortunate to have Frank Juhl give us a personal tour of his gallery. Frank was originally from Denmark, and his wife Regine, from Germany. They founded their gallery and attached workshop in 1959. At the time their move to open a silver shop in Kautokeino was a very risky proposition because of the remoteness of the location; there weren't any paved roads in or out. Over the years they expanded their gallery adding more rooms while maintaining the structure's environmental integrity.

Over the years the Juhls' shop has become well known for its exclusive Scandinavian jewelry designs made by silversmiths on the premises. In addition to the jewelry, the shop also sells unique silver spoons and other utensils in the Sami tradition, many of them silver renditions of objects carved from bone or other materials.

The silver renditions of everyday Sami spoons captured my attention. Some were copied from Samisk designs and others inspired from original Samisk works. These sterling silver utensils were true works of art that reflected the Samisk culture of the far North like nothing else. The sterling silver spoon I purchased is a treasured family heirloom to this day.

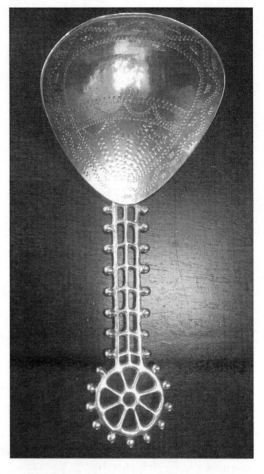

Nils Juhl's handmade sterling silver spoon based on a Sami design purchased by the author in 1974 at the factory in Kautokeino, Norway (courtesy Elaine Kiesling Whitehouse).

32

The Turn

It was finally time to return to Haakonsvern. The plan called for us to cast off from the pier in Bodø at 0800 on Monday, December 10, arriving back in Haakonsvern late in the afternoon of the 12th. To keep that schedule we would have to sail the inland waterway at a relatively high speed, a task that can be problematic for a host of reasons at this time of year.

On December 11, I had the 2000–2400 bridge watch. Overcast with no moon the night was pitch black, the temperature around 25 degrees Fahrenheit, and wind about 15 knots with a threat of brief but intense snow squalls. At around 2230 (10:30 p.m.), with the ship at 20 knots, all was well. After three months away everyone wanted to get home as soon as possible, and so the captain ordered that we should proceed with "all deliberate speed."

One potential hazard with the inland route is that sheer rock walls—steep mountains dropping straight into the water—often border the channel. While these features block the worst of the wind and the high seas, they can also hide approaching ships or small storms and snow squalls. Radar does not go through, or over, rocks and so you are sometimes blind to what is on the other side or what might be coming.

On this evening, as the *Oslo* was approaching a starboard turn that was marked by a large buoy, two things happened. First, the captain came out of his cabin and onto the bridge to ask how things were going. Second, and only a minute or so later, a blinding snow squall descended down a mountainside onto the waterway. Like the sudden appearance of a heavy fog bank on a roadway, the squall immediately reduced visibility to almost zero. The radar became useless because thick snow blocks it completely. We suddenly couldn't see anything.

The captain looked at the chart on the navigation table and could see that we were close to where we needed to be to make the sharp right turn. If we did not succeed in executing this turn properly, the ship would speed directly into the face of a sheer mountain wall. However,

Sognefjord is on Norway's west coast about 50 miles north of Bergen. Known as the "King of the fjords," it is more than 4,250 feet deep at its deepest point and more than 125 miles long (Grisha Brev/Bigstock.com).

the location was also such that if we turned too soon, we risked running aground or even hitting the mountain wall to the right of us. At 20 knots, slowing would do little good so close to the turn. The sudden snow squall persisted, and we were effectively operating in the blind. We had to make the turn and make it accurately or we were dead.

I was standing out on the starboard wing of the bridge in the wind and snow straining to sight the buoy on the right side of the channel marking the spot to commence the sharp right turn. The captain joined me. Shouting to be heard over the noise of the wind and sea, he asked if I knew when to turn. I replied honestly, "No, I do not." The captain got something of a rueful smile on his face and simply replied, "Neither do I." In that instant we shared the thought that despite being blind somehow, we just had to get this right. The alternative would be disaster.

After my exchange with the Captain, I knew the decision on when to turn remained mine. Our dire situation blocked everything out of my mind, everything except trying to determine when to commence the turn to starboard. Somehow my brain calculated where the *Oslo* must be based on the time of our last known position and how fast we had been going. I could visualize the chart in my mind and where the ship was on the chart! Based on that vision and with the captain standing beside me in the driving snow, I ordered the helmsman to commence the turn. Within a matter of less than a minute, suddenly the buoy marking the right side of the channel appeared in the near impenetrable darkness passing by very close to the starboard side of the ship.

I had no rational explanation for how I had somehow managed to "know" when to turn. It was as if I had allowed some outside power to take over in the *in extremis* situation and save the ship from certain disaster. After the buoy passed safely to starboard the captain looked me in the eye, and this time with a smile of relief said quietly, "Thank you. I think I'm going to turn in." Only he and I would ever know how close we had come to catastrophe.

The remainder of our passage down to Bergen passed uneventfully with *Oslo* arriving on schedule. Once again, the Christmas break was a welcome respite for all from the monotonous yet demanding routine of deployment in the far north. Elaine and I took the opportunity to take a few days off to go cross-country skiing in Voss, the renowned sports resort about an eighty-minute drive into the mountains from Bergen. The area is a scenic wonder with the village surrounded by high mountains, wooded valleys, fjords, rivers, waterfalls and lakes. We stayed at Fleischer's Hotel with its rustic charm and breathtaking views of the area. We both took to cross country skiing, like our Norwegian friends, enjoying just being out in nature. Our visit to Voss was one of the rare times we had the opportunity to enjoy together some of the most beautiful nature in the world.

Following our trip to Voss we flew to London to spend the rest of our Christmas holiday in Elaine's apartment in South Kensington. On January 5, I took a flight back to Bergen.

At 0800 on Monday, January 13, 1975, KNM *Oslo* cast off from the main pier in Haakonsvern for another deployment to the north. I had hoped to remain in Bergen in preparation for joining my new command, but Captain Rittland insisted I remain aboard for the trip north—my fifth time for the journey. The plan called for me to remain aboard *Oslo* until Sunday, January 19, when I could fly south to Bergen in time to report for my new assignment on the 20th.

While the transit between Bergen and Bodø could be challenging, there were also many parts of it with spectacular scenery and rare natural beauty. One such place was a mountain known as Torghatten (Hat Mountain) located about halfway up the coast. Captain Willy Andersen had first pointed it out to me, and related the winsome legend behind it.

From Vietnam to the Arctic Circle

The granite mountain of Torghatten takes up most of the island of Torget. From a distance of many miles, you can see a near-perfectly round hole straight through the middle of the mountain. Of course, in legend-rich Norway, there is an ancient folk tale to explain how the hole came to be. According to the legend Torghatten was formed when a troll named Hestmannen (The Horseman) shot an arrow at Lekamøya, a beautiful young girl, who had rejected his advances and was running away from him. The Troll-King of nearby Mount Sømnafjellet (Somna Mountain) saw what was happening and in the nick of time threw his hat in front of the arrow. The Hestmannen's arrow went right through the hat forming a hole and saving Lekamøya from harm. Then with the sunrise, the hat turned to stone, which still stands to this very day.

Modern science explains the 520 foot long, 66 foot wide and 115-foot high Torghatten hole somewhat differently. Norwegian geologists say it was not formed by a couple of trolls but is a natural formation created by ice, melting water and gravel during the ice age. However, everyone prefers the folk tale explanation to the scientific one.

By the end of the week of January 13, KNM *Oslo* was in Ramsund Naval Station west of Narvik and by Friday the 17th docked at the pier in Narvik for the weekend. That same evening the wardroom hosted a *mess aften* in my honor.

What was a *mess aften*? Once in a great while the wardroom enjoyed a four-star filet mignon dinner with all the trimmings. The first time I experienced such a dinner it came as a complete surprise. One Saturday the *Trondheim*'s executive officer, Bjornar Kipsgaard, told me that the evening meal would be in full dress uniform. I was to come to the wardroom at 6 p.m. appropriately attired. I had no idea what to expect, and Kipsgaard would not further explain. I guessed perhaps a visiting official or senior officer or some other such person requiring us all to look our best.

The evening began with cocktails followed by seating at the wardroom table, which was beautifully set for a formal banquet with crystal glassware, china dishes, silver cutlery, linen napkins and the like. Once everyone was seated one of the two stewards appeared dressed in formal attire to begin serving the wine and the first of many courses. The main course consisted of large portions of specially purchased filet mignon.

Dinner speeches are a fixture in any Norwegian dinner party, civilian or military. My first *mess aften* aboard the *Trondheim* began with a speech given by the ship's Captain Willy Andersen. As the senior officer present, captain of the ship, and de facto "host," Captain

Andersen provided the requisite dinner party speech *Velkommen til Bords* (Welcome to the table). Throughout the meal he would call on various officers to stand and give brief, extemporaneous speeches on a variety of subjects. At the end of the meal came the last and most important speech: the *Takk for Maten Tale* (thank you for the food speech). Despite not being forewarned, as a newcomer and the resident American naval officer, I was expected to speak, which I did, essentially thanking my friends for their welcoming of me. Finally, after all was said and done, the two stewards who had taken the entire day to prepare and serve the meal were called in and formally thanked for their exceptional effort.

After dinner, formalities went by the boards. More drinks led to joke telling, unusual games, individual displays of physical prowess, cigar smoking and other such things one might expect a well fed and mildly inebriated group of men to do. Eventually Captain Andersen

Oil painting of KNM *Oslo* (F-300), presented to the author by Kommandorkaptein Kaare Rittland upon the author's departure from the *Oslo* to join the 24th TKB Squadron. The heavily armed 317-foot-long ship was commissioned on 29 January 1968. She ran aground in Norwegian waters on 24 January 1994 with the loss of one officer's life. On January 25 she was taken in tow. She sank shortly thereafter (courtesy Elaine Kiesling Whitehouse).

retired for the evening, which was the signal that the rest of us could begin to leave as well.

So, aboard KNM *Oslo* I was flattered to have a *mess aften* given in my honor. Some of the officers from KNM *Stavanger* moored next to us also attended. I greatly appreciated the evening, especially the complimentary words spoken by Captain Kaare Rittland. The wardroom formally inducted me into a special order entitling me to wear a small gold ball on a maroon ribbon with my dress uniform to any further such functions. They also presented me with an engraved ship's plaque with my name and dates of service aboard *Oslo*. However, I was most touched with the presentation by Captain Rittland of an approximately 30-inch by 20-inch oil painting of the *Oslo* underway in a Norwegian fjord. It is a beautifully painted piece by a talented Norwegian artist that Rittland had been given by one of his friends when he took command. I've always recognized that it took a lot for him to give me that personally meaningful work. Captain Rittland and I had become quite close; I appreciated the confidence he had shown in me, and I knew he would never forget our narrow escape from disaster when somehow I had ordered the correct turn at just the right moment as we hurtled through a blinding snow squall in that narrow fjord the month before.

33

Riding Norwegian Gunboats

By early 1975 I had spent a year and a half primarily on frigates. It was time for me to transfer to a gunboat, an important part of Norway's maritime defenses. I was pleased and excited when senior Norwegian naval officers in Oslo decided to assign me as the commanding officer of a fast attack boat. However, before that could happen someone in a more senior position overruled the decision. I was an American naval officer, not a Norwegian naval officer, and the law would not permit a non–Norwegian citizen command of a Norwegian warship. While unstated, there were also the political sensitivities, both internal and external, to having an American officer captain one of their warships. On January 20, 1975, the transfer to the 24th TKB (Torpedo Kanon Boat) Squadron took place as planned, but with me as the executive officer (second in command) of KNM *Hvass* (P-972) one of the squadron's Storm Class fast patrol boats.

These Norwegian-designed and built fast attack boats were considerably smaller than the *Chehalis* with a displacement of only 138 tons (*Chehalis* was 247 tons), a length of approximately 120 feet and a beam of about 20 feet (*Chehalis* was 165 feet and a beam of 24 feet) and a draft of almost 6 feet (*Chehalis* took only 5 feet of water).

The Norwegian Navy built its fleet of 20 fast attack boats between 1965 and 1967. Two 7,200-horsepower Maybach diesel engines powered the boats, which could do well over 30 knots. They carried a crew of about 20 men. A squadron consisted of 4 or 5 boats each with its own captain plus a squadron commander.

The boats rarely operated independently. They almost always sailed as a squadron. Their small size did not preclude a powerful punch. The boats had a fully automatic 3-inch gun on the main deck forward and a 40 mm on the main deck, just aft of amidships. Most of the boats were also equipped with the Norwegian-built and highly effective Penguin surface-to-surface, medium range, anti-ship missile. Boats that had been retrofitted had 6 deck-mounted box launchers on the aft end with

Norwegian Navy Storm class missile gunboats in formation in coastal waters. These are the boats on which the author served as executive officer (Royal Norwegian Navy).

three launchers to a side. They were called *missilkanonbåter* (MKB) or Missile Gunboats in English.

I also sailed on the Tjeld-class torpedo boats. They were only a little over 80-feet long, with a beam of less than 25 feet and a draft of just under seven feet. The two turbo-charged diesel engines allowed speeds of over 50 miles per hour. Each boat carried a lot of firepower, with 4 individual torpedo tubes, two to a side, one 40 mm gun amidships and one 20 mm. To me, the open-air bridge and weapons systems made these boats less than optimal weapons platforms in the cold weather conditions of Northern Norway. The U.S. Navy used the same design, calling them *Nasty* class patrol boats. The 20 boats operated by the U.S. Navy, PTF-3 through PTF-22, were used in Vietnam's riverine warfare.

Norwegian Navy tactics called for taking full advantage of their operating environment. Besides speed and maneuverability in challenging waterways, the crews employed camouflage netting. Gunboat crews practiced attaching their ship to a steep rock face (sheer rock faces approachable by shallow draft vessels were common) and then placing camouflage nets over the entirety of the ship. A trained crew could accomplish the entire process within a matter of minutes. When they were finished—providing you didn't know precisely where they were—it was impossible to see them with the naked eye. Photos taken from both air and sea proved they could be made virtually invisible. Another gunboat tactic was to sail the four boats in the squadron side by side, such that a sailor could carry a cup of coffee from one ship to the next. On radar screens, the four boats would appear as one, deceiving the enemy about the number and size of ships opposing them.

Creature comforts aboard these ships were hard to come by even for the officers. Short on space, all the officers ate and slept in the small wardroom and shared one small head. As usual, shipboard food focused on the ubiquitous cod with an occasional chicken, meat or other fish dish substitute. One of my least favorites—fortunately a rarity—was "*maake egg og* (horse) *mussel*," literally one sea gull egg and one mussel.

Norwegian *Tjeld* class TKBs (Torpedo Gun Boats) underway in side-by-side formation (Royal Norwegian Navy).

I could never finish mine. If you've never had seagull egg, don't. It tastes as you might expect given a seagull's diet. The horse mussel is big and tough—up to seven inches in length and several inches across—and, unlike its Prince Edward Island cousin, demands an acquired taste.

Often the seas were so rough as to preclude eating anything you couldn't hold onto with one hand while you held on to the ship with the other. At other times the food just wasn't something an American would consume in quantity—raw or salted fish for example—very nutritious and low in fat! In the two years I was in the Norwegian Navy, I went from approximately 185 pounds to no more than 155 pounds. I weighed less than I did in high school.

Approximately twice per week we would fish for cod off the side of the ship using handheld drop lines with three or four hooks. A cod will bite on a bright shiny hook with no bait attached. The cod were so plentiful that it wasn't unusual to pull up three or four on a single line. No fish I know fights less than a cod, so it was not that hard to pull up so many cod on one drop.

Aboard ship cod-themed meals included boiled cod heads, cod livers in cod liver oil with carrots (more of a sauce), codfish pudding, cod roe cakes (one of my least favorite—compressed beach sand has a comparable texture and flavor), canned cod fish balls, salted cod in bacon fat gravy (tough in a rough sea), cod tongues, dried salt cod, and dried smoked cod. Often we enjoyed boiled fresh cod with boiled potatoes and boiled carrots all cooked in a single pot. It was great for the cook because all he needed to do was bring a large pot of water to a boil and throw in the dinner. The cook would sometimes make cod fish pudding from the leftovers and serve it for breakfast, which came as something of a breakfast surprise the first time I had it. Usually breakfast was your choice of various kinds of Scandinavian cheese such as *brunost* (brown cheese), *nøkkelost* (cumin cheese), or Jarlsberg, sardines in olive oil or tomato sauce, other canned fish, crisp bread and, of course, strong coffee.

Other main meals included one of my favorites *hval biff* (whale meat served in a brown gravy), raw herring and onion with beets, baked chicken pieces and steak. Norwegian chickens are fed chicken meal made from cod. It makes the chicken meat taste just like—you guessed it—cod. I would have loved a picture of the look on my face the first time I bit into cod-chicken. What a surprise! Another everyday dinner might include dried, smoked cod soaked overnight and then boiled for the dinner table. Before the cooking process begins the dried, smoked cod closely resembles asbestos roofing in color, smell and texture.

33. *Riding Norwegian Gunboats*

The Norwegians knew full well that some of their staples left many non–Norwegians less than enthused. A story often told was of a shipment of their dried, smoked cod donated to a Sub-Saharan country suffering widespread famine. A couple of months after receiving the shipment the Africans requested the Norwegians never again send them roofing materials as it smelled terribly and decomposed after no more than a couple of rainstorms.

On occasion, Norwegian Navy food could be excellent. One day when I was on a gunboat in Northern Norway we came across a wild salmon fisherman. We purchased five or six beautiful fish from him. I thought for sure we'd be eating well that night, but not so. The guys took the fish, gutted them, strung a line through their gills and hung them in a cool and unused paint locker in the aft section of the ship. Four or five days later we ate them, and they were delicious, the best salmon I've ever eaten. Their only failing was that the meat near the head of the fish that had been exposed to the air in the paint locker tasted very faintly of oil based paint.

In the dark, snow and wind we sailed these boats at high speed through the narrow and shallow channels along the intricate and sometimes treacherous Norwegian coastline. The high speed, shallow draft vessels gave the Norwegian naval officers a chance to show off their impressive inland piloting skills and in-depth-knowledge of the difficult terrain. We also sailed in hurricane force winds and the rough seas of the open water, on occasion needing to seek shelter in a fjord or strait to avoid catastrophe.

Once we were participating in NATO exercise and the opportunity came up for me to spend a day on a West German gunboat. After the first hour the thought kept recurring, how did the allies ever beat the Germans in World War II? The difference between the behavior of the German sailors and that of the Americans and the Norwegians was night and day.

On the bridge of the German gunboat no one spoke at all unless giving an order or acknowledging one. There was no small talk, no lounging around drinking coffee, only attentive silence from sailors who looked like they were dressed for inspection. When the captain spoke, he did so in a quiet voice. There was no need for him to speak loudly. If he gave an order, the response was instantaneous compliance. Also, everything on the bridge was clean, polished and in order, no old cups and ash trays lying around, no navigation charts in a pile, no field glasses hanging from a chair, or caps and jackets tossed in a corner.

I greatly enjoyed the food served on the West German gunboat. I'm afraid I embarrassed myself at the wardroom evening meal. The dinner was roast pork with red cabbage and beans. I ate as much as the German officers combined. It was served with meticulous attention to detail, perfectly cooked, served hot and delicious. It was one of the few dinners I can truly say I'll never forget.

It was food, I think, that made me want to visit Paris for Easter in 1975. Elaine and I stayed at the Hotel Baltimore on the Avenue Kleber in one of the most beautiful districts of Paris, close to the Champs Elysées, the Arc de Triomphe and the Eiffel Tower. Everything we had heard about French cuisine proved true. Every restaurant served delicious meals. We also enjoyed the unforgettable sights, the Notre Dame Cathedral the most magnificent of all. What a terrible loss that it suffered that devastating fire. A tour of the Archaeological Crypt that lies beneath the Cathedral Square provided a look at life in Paris from its earliest years to the present. It is a memorable, *in situ* presentation of what Paris was like in centuries before.

* * *

My 24th TKB Squadron deployed to Northern Norway on the April 20, 1975. The route north was the same as for the frigates. Our first stop north of the Arctic Circle was Bodø with a steady drive north and east from there toward Kirkenes on the Soviet border, arriving by the middle to end of May. The weather was especially cold for May. The wind was blowing hard, it was barely 40 degrees and snow still covered the ground. Ironically the sun was out all the time, bright even at midnight.

The small size and shallow draft of the boats permitted us to show the flag in many small, remote fishing villages all up and down the Arctic coast. The small number of men aboard the gunboats combined with the poor sailing conditions also made stopping and tying up somewhere overnight a good idea. The people in these isolated places were always happy to see us and eager to interact. We frequently entertained the local citizenry aboard ship, and they entertained us ashore. Such socializing was a big part of our job, and while it sounds like lots of fun, it was also wearing in its own way for both officers and crew.

The Norwegian policy of showing the flag as often as possible everywhere in the North helped the people in these remote locations to feel patriotic and proud to be citizens of Norway. With the Soviets only a few miles away, signs of the Norwegian military commitment to

A Norwegian fisherman's cabin on a promontory in the Lofoten Island chain. The scenically spectacular islands lie on the north side of the broad Vestfjord that lies north of the Arctic Circle. Vestfjord, which originates far inland near the town of Narvik, is known for its codfish industry, scenic beauty and strong winds and heavy seas in the winter months (denbelitsky/Bigstock.com).

the people of Northern Norway was a vital part of Norwegian national security.

Frankly, I was surprised that not once did I experience any negative reaction to my presence aboard ship from any of the many Norwegians with whom we had contact. Given the years of very negative media coverage of the American military in Vietnam, and the not infrequent criticism of the U.S. military from some Americans, I was doubly surprised not to hear negative comments about our armed forces. On the contrary, the vast majority of Norwegians with whom I spoke were eager to express their thanks to the U.S. for helping to make the world a better and safer place. At least in Norway in the early 1970s, the U.S. was held in very high esteem.

Also, the timeframe for my observations was not an especially good one for U.S. political and military developments. On April 30, 1975, the North Vietnamese and the Viet Cong occupied the presidential palace in Saigon, effectively marking the end of our losing effort in Vietnam, and President Nixon had resigned in political disgrace less than one year before. I was asked many times to explain why Americans wanted to banish President Nixon when he had done so much to end the war, open up China and counter the Soviets.

By early August, I found myself back in Bergen, preparing for our return to the U.S. Part of the process was to visit the Naval Attaché's office at the Embassy in Oslo for a review of my fitness report, the Naval Attaché's endorsement of my request to resign, and to say good-bye to the office staff.

In a letter dated June 12, 1975, to the Secretary of the Navy via the Chief of Naval Personnel, the Naval Attaché, Captain David W. De Cook had endorsed my request to resign my commission stating in part the following:

> Lt. Whitehouse's performance in Norway under the PEP program has been outstanding. He has been a fine envoy from the U.S. Navy and has established an excellent reputation all the way up through the Inspector General of the Norwegian Navy. Only his nationality has in fact precluded his command of a Norwegian FPB—an honor he was in fact recommended for. I feel it is through his example that the program has been expanded this year to include a U.S. Naval Aviator and a corresponding Norwegian Air Force officer of very fine reputation.

34

A Change of Course

I was pleased that the Navy wanted to keep me, even trying its best to accommodate my desire to take a break from sea duty. My Bureau of Naval Personnel detailer had offered me a position as a navigation instructor at the Naval Academy, an offer I was tempted to accept. However, I knew that to continue on a competitive track, I needed to go to Destroyer School in Newport, Rhode Island. I also knew that on completion of the course I would have to go back to sea again for at least a couple more years and maybe longer. Such a life made it difficult for Elaine to have a career. But the biggest shortcoming with sea duty and never being at home was not being around to start a family. Both Elaine and I wanted children and we weren't going to get it done through long separations. On the other hand, we both loved the travel and adventure the Navy afforded us. The Navy was modernizing, and opportunities for good officers were plentiful. We both also loved serving our country and felt we were making a real contribution. So we were torn about what to do.

The thought occurred that maybe I could get another job where we could use what we had learned about political systems, foreign languages, living in foreign countries and the pervasiveness of Soviet aggression. More than seven years earlier, in my senior year at Brown, I had taken a one-semester course on modern American history taught by former CIA Executive Director, Lyman B. Kirkpatrick. Kirkpatrick had been an Office of Strategic Services (OSS) officer during World War II, and joined the CIA at its creation in 1947. He had risen rapidly through the ranks despite being confined to a wheelchair after a bout with polio in 1952. He served as a senior official with CIA until 1965 when he joined the faculty at Brown. Kirkpatrick was a powerful speaker. His presentations about the role of the OSS and CIA in trying to keep America safe from foreign enemies intrigued me and captured my imagination in a way that nothing had before.

So at the age of 29 we decided to make a big change. By the end of August 1975 my request to resign from the Navy had been accepted and, after almost eleven years, I was a civilian once again. I applied to the CIA and after a lengthy hiring process began an exciting career doing what I had thought about for years. We had our son not long after that. The move to the agency worked out well for all of us. While I have never worked with more honest, hard-working, decent people than those in the U.S. and Norwegian navies, I have never regretted my change in careers. My many years spent working as a case officer in the CIA's Directorate of Operations could not have been more rewarding.

Appendix

Soviet Socialism and Its Influences Today

"What are we fighting for?" my close friend Dave Lerner asked me in his letter after the loss in combat of our mutual friend Spencer Lund. Conversely, what are we fighting against? needed to be asked. The finger has pointed to the Soviet Union and its heinous communist system, so a little more detail about that abominable construct is appropriate.

What do you know about the Soviet Union? If you are someone over age 50 you may know quite a bit. If you served in the U.S. military or government during the Cold War, when the Soviet Union was our enemy and was dubbed the "Evil Empire" by Ronald Reagan, you are a "Cold Warrior." But once the Soviet Union was officially dissolved on December 26, 1991, attention started to turn to other parts of the world. The Middle East and Far East became focal points, and after the first World Trade Center attack in February 1993, global terrorism began to become a primary concern.

So how did the communist nation of the Soviet Union evolve? The story is long and fascinating, and beyond the scope of this work. But in brief, it started out with Russia, an isolated country that was not part of the European Renaissance, remaining under a feudal system. While the rest of Europe became industrialized, Russia continued to be a country of the very few rich and the masses of very poor.

Nicholas II of Russia and Alexandra of Hesse, Germany, and their five children were the last imperial family of Tsarist Russia. While the people of Russia suffered and starved, the family lived a life of luxury. After the Revolution of 1917, the imperial family was sent into internal exile in Tobolsk, Siberia. There, on July 17, 1918 in a cellar room where they believed they were waiting for transport to a safer location, they were all shot and/or bayoneted to death. The assassination of the tsar, tsarina, Alexei, their son, and his four sisters marked the end of tsarist Russia and the beginnings of the Soviet Union.

After the Russian Revolution in 1917, a scholar named Vladimir Lenin instituted the Marxist system of communism, and the Soviet Union was born. The official date of the formation of the Soviet Union was December 30, 1922.

One of Lenin's goals was to increase the food supply for the peasants. Lenin promised them that they would receive land they would own themselves. He was certain that when peasants were free from government control, more crops could be grown, a capitalist principle.

Lenin died in 1924, and after a brief power struggle Joseph Stalin took over. Stalin, a brutal man, used terror to keep himself in power. Under his regime, people who did not follow the party line or were heard criticizing the government, literally disappeared overnight.

Stalin's policies were an economic disaster for the Soviet Union. He instituted "collective farms" in which the independent plots of land designated by Lenin were consolidated. Stalin thought he would be able to control large farms more easily than small ones. However, the peasants resisted the collectivization. They wanted to retain their autonomy, but Stalin tried to use force to get them to farm the large plots. Peasants were forced out of their homes, killed, imprisoned, or disappeared. Their farms were abandoned and fell into ruin. Millions of people starved to death.

This was the condition of the Soviet Union for much of its existence. Some leaders tried to institute reforms, but with limited success. Nikita Khrushchev, the leader who ultimately succeeded Stalin, was the first General Secretary who tried to institute reforms in the agricultural sector of the Soviet economy. He also acknowledged the atrocities of Stalin in his famous and fascinating "Secret Speech," which he delivered at the 20th Congress of the CPSU in February 1956. In this speech he denounced Stalin, enumerating his abuses and atrocities and his failures during World War II. Khrushchev also famously declared, "We will bury you!" in 1956, at the same time he called for "peaceful coexistence" with the United States.

Leonid Brezhnev, Nikolai Podgorny and Alexei Kosygin succeeded Khrushchev in 1964 with Brezhnev eventually becoming preeminent. The years under Brezhnev were ones of political and economic stagnation and an aggressive foreign policy combined with an enhanced military presence. Brezhnev remained in power until November 1982. It was not until 1985 that true change began to come to the Soviet Union. On

March 11 of that year Mikhail Gorbachev became the General Secretary of the Central Committee of the Communist Party of the Soviet Union. With his advocacy of *glasnost* (openness) and *perestroika* (economic restructuring) he was the first Soviet leader to bring meaningful change after decades of stagnation. Along with U.S. President Ronald Reagan he was responsible for the end of the arms race and the Cold War.

The Soviet Union was the largest country in the world. It occupied 8,570,000 square miles, nearly a sixth of all land on earth, and was twice the size of the United States. Different sources give the number of ethnic groups in the Soviet Union as ranging from 104 to 250 in its fifteen republics, each with its own language and traditions. These regions and ethnic groups did not feel loyalty to the government of the Soviet Union, but they paid lip service to it out of fear.

The term "Socialist Republics" is also a misnomer, for the country was neither socialist nor did it consist of republics, which implies democracy. Ruled by the Communist Party of the Soviet Union (CPSU), the country was in fact a strict, centralized dictatorship. Even today a favorite trick of the far left is to give completely misleading names to oppressive programs and policies. So, what exactly, are socialism and communism and why do they not work in practice?

Socialism is an economic system in which there is virtually no private property. With socialism, the government controls and decides everything, including distribution of services. From our personal experience we came to understand what it's like to live in a country with socialist programs, with their exorbitant taxation and resultant under-the-table economy. Citizens cut deals off the books, and use black markets, bartering, gift giving, etc., in order to avoid the excessive taxation. Per my earlier comment, my Norwegian Navy friends used to complain that they had the worst employer possible – the Norwegian Government. The government knew exactly how much they got paid and so there was no avoiding the confiscatory tax rates. We don't read about it in the more leftist elements of American media, but in other socialist European countries like Norway there is always a robust, widespread, untaxed and publicly unacknowledged underground economy. The socialist European nations have plenty of very wealthy people, all proficient in hiding their money from the taxman.

When we were in Norway, people routinely paid "under the table" for many goods and services. We bartered for the installation of our washing machine with a bottle of liquor and a carton of cigarettes, or paid cash in dollars for other services. It was how the socialist system worked. People bartered goods for virtually everything including the "free" medical care. A transaction where you received a receipt marked "paid" usually meant at least twice the price of an "off-the-books" deal.

The underground economy extends to medical care, which the government controls. Socialized medicine may sound great in theory, but is not so in reality, often it's not good at all. We had several friends who, rather than be treated by Norwegian doctors, spent a lot of money to travel to London for still-available private medical care. When we were in Norway, you had to wait for an appointment for routine care. On one occasion Elaine needed minor surgery for which she waited months, while the condition grew worse. Finally, an acquaintance of ours made arrangements for her to move to the top of the list in order to have the procedure done, and a "gift" was given in return. Thus, the irony is that while socialism and communism kill productivity through government control, taxation and regulations, the under-the table economies have developed a kind of private enterprise that is the free market basis of capitalism. In other words many socialist countries survive because of their under-the-table, secret capitalist system.

I once had a conversation with a young Norwegian doctor who was serving as the ship's doctor aboard the KNM *Trondheim* (F-302) I asked how he became a doctor. He said it was easy. All he had to do was take a test with one hundred multiple-choice questions. He scored higher than the test's cutoff score and so was accepted into medical school. Others who scored similarly also qualified to receive the necessary medical training and became doctors. He complained that Norwegian medical training relied too heavily on West German medical expertise and that instruction was in German. As a result, many Norwegian doctors spoke fluent German but did not have much expertise in English. From personal observation I knew he was correct. Of all the Norwegian professions with which Elaine and I came in contact, the medical field had the least number of competent English speakers. Maybe that has changed since then.

Elaine and I experienced socialism as I described it – an economic system in which there is virtually no private property. Communism can be thought of as a radical extension of socialism.

After the Revolution of 1917, communism became the ideology of the Soviet Union, or Union of Soviet Socialist Republics. With communism there is no free market enterprise at all, except "under the table." In communist countries, corruption becomes rampant, shortages of everything prevail, and there is a huge disparity between the elites and

Left to right: the ship's doctor and the author cutting the author's birth-day cake, a traditional Norwegian blotkake (cream cake). The photograph was taken on November 4, 1973, in the wardroom of the KNM *Trondheim* (F-302) (Royal Norwegian Navy).

the average person. Free exchange of information is suppressed and the government censors heavily. Freedom of expression is squelched. In the Soviet Union the main Communist newspaper was *Pravda*. The non-communist newspaper was *Izvestia*. *Pravda* translated to "the truth" and *Izvestia* meant "the news." The now-tired Soviet joke was, "There's no truth in *Pravda* and no news in *Izvestia*."

The communist system had disastrous results for the people of the Soviet Union. Today one needs look no further than Cuba and Vene-zuela to see the disasters of the "modern" socialist/communist system. China is another socialist problem state with its increasing authoritar-ianism, repression of the Moslem Uyghurs in reeducation camps, and expansionist moves in Hong Kong, Tibet, the South China Sea and elsewhere.

Karl Marx, in his *Communist Manifesto* that described and advo-cated the economic theory of communism, did not predict its real-life effects. It advocated rule by the working class where competition does not exist, and the government decides who needs what and who pays.

The society then becomes "classless." The system is based on the theory of "from each according to his ability to each according to his needs" whether or not the individual with the "ability" agrees to it or not. The communist party, the *only* party, controls all political and economic activity. Economic planning is centralized meaning communist party chiefs dictate all economic and financial plans and policies. In the Soviet Union, only about six out of every 100 people were members of the communist party. Its senior members became the society's powerful and wealthy elite. Today only about six percent of the Chinese population belongs to the ruling Chinese Communist Party (CCP).

After the fall of the Soviet Union, picture books for U.S. children about the Soviet Union ended up in the discard pile of school and public libraries. Studies of the USSR were dropped from high schools or were given only perfunctory attention. By 2015, when Elaine was substitute teaching high school history on Long Island, not one of her students knew or had even heard of the USSR, Soviet Union or the Union of Soviet Socialist Republics. Just think, America's number one enemy for more than fifty years and they had not even heard of it. Indeed, the second most popular Democratic candidate to run for president of the United States in 2016, Bernie Sanders—who ran again for president in 2020—is an avowed socialist who believes in equal outcome for all. In 1988 he even honeymooned in the Soviet Union, a highly unusual, even scandalous move by any American citizen at the time. Today, few know much about the Soviet Union, and so Sanders' Soviet honeymoon is ignored.

Many people, particularly younger people, like the concept of equal outcome in which everyone has everything the same. It sounds noble. Doesn't the Declaration of Independence state, "We hold these truths to be self-evident, that all men are created equal..."? But do people focus on what this phrase really means? Does it mean that it is the job of the government to make everyone equal? No, it does not. The phrase was meant to convey equality of opportunity, not equality of outcome.

Many of the aspects of socialism and communism mentioned above may seem far removed from the United States, but there are other characteristics that have, indeed, influenced the United States. For example, Karl Marx described religion as "the opiate of the masses" and used his atheism to support his communist ideals. Following Marxist dictates, the Soviet Union did not recognize any religion. In *Critique of Hegel's Philosophy of Right,* Marx wrote that religion is only an illusion that should be abolished:

Religious distress is at the same time the expression of real distress and the protest against real distress. Religion is the sign of the oppressed creature, the heart of a heartless world, just as it is the spirit of a spiritless situation. It is the opium of the people. The abolition of religion as the illusory happiness of the people is required for their real happiness. The demand to give up the illusion about its condition is the demand to give up a condition which needs illusions.

Today we see organized attempts to remove any reference to God from the public square. Religious symbols in public places, particularly those of the Christian religion, are attacked as unconstitutional, a violation of everyone's First Amendment right that says, "Congress shall make no law respecting an establishment of religion, or prohibiting the free exercise thereof...." Some members of the modern American intelligentsia lecture us that any reference to God must be removed from all public displays, from monuments to mottos, and many public schools are forbidden from going anywhere near mention of religion or the role of religion in our western history.

The August 31–September 1, 2019 *Wall Street Journal* carried an opinion piece by Tunku Varadarajan on feminist Camille Paglia. Paglia is a professor of humanities and media studies at the University of the Arts in Philadelphia who instructs undergraduates. In the piece, Paglia recalls teaching a class of undergrads a few years ago. She was teaching *Go Down Moses*, the famous spiritual, and realized that none of her students recognized the name "Moses." She said, "I thought: Oh my God, when Moses is erased from the West, what is left of Western civilization?" In the same article Paglia is quoted as saying:

> Everything is so easy now. The stores are so plentifully supplied....Undergrads who've studied neither economics nor history, have a sense that this is the way life has always been. Because they've never been exposed to history, they have no idea that these are recent attainments that come from a very specific economic system. Capitalism has produced this cornucopia around us, but the young seem to believe in having the government run everything.

A famous quote attributed to the American writer and philosopher Jorge Agustín Nicolás Ruiz de Santayana y Borrás (George Santayana) from his 1905 book *The Life of Reason* says, "Those who do not learn from history are doomed to repeat it." Indeed, it is vital that America learns the lessons of the Cold War, and the lessons provided by the failed socialist/communist regimes in the Soviet Union, China, Cuba and Venezuela.

For years polls have shown that a majority of Americans recognize the debilitating problems that come with the failed socialist policies of

Appendix

the Soviet Union and other former Cold War powers. Yet despite the recognized dangers, many are now listening to American socialists who passionately claim they are not in the mold of the Soviet Union, or China, Cuba or Venezuela. They say this is a different country and a new day, and their policies can lead to a new, more equitable sharing of wealth that will make a better world for all. Let us share the excessive wealth of the elite with the poor and less privileged for the betterment of all!

We can only continue to remind people of the demonstrably undesirable results of the tired socialist ideas and policies. We need to be vigilant because, as American journalist and author Sydney J. Harris said, "History repeats itself, but in such cunning disguise that we never detect the resemblance until the damage is done." I pray we all see that truth.

Author's Service Record

September 1964: Sworn in as Midshipman 4th Class, Naval Reserve Officer Training Corps (NROTC), Brown University, Providence Rhode Island.

May 1965: Promoted to Midshipman 3rd Class.

May–July 1965: 3rd Class Midshipmen training cruise aboard USS *Wasp* (CVS-18) home ported in Boston, Massachusetts. June 24–July 1 one-week TDY to Fleet Air Wing Five, Naval Air Station Brunswick, Brunswick, Maine.

September 1965–May 1966: Midshipman 3rd Class, Brown University NROTC Unit.

May 1966: Promoted to Midshipman 2nd Class.

May–July 1966: 2nd Class Midshipmen training cruise including 3 weeks at Corpus Christ Naval Air Station, Corpus Christi, Texas, and three weeks Marine Corps training at the Naval Amphibious Base, Little Creek, Virginia.

September 1966–May 1967: Midshipman 2nd Class, Brown University NROTC Unit.

May 1967: Promoted to Midshipman 1st Class.

May 1967–July 1967: Midshipmen 1st Class training cruise aboard USS *Corry* (DD-817), home ported in Norfolk, Virginia.

September 1967–June 1968: Midshipman 1st Class, Brown University NROTC Unit.

June 1968: Commissioned as an Ensign in the United States Navy at a ceremony on the campus of Brown University. Received orders to report aboard the USS *Buck* (DD-761) home ported in San Diego, California.

July 1968: Reported for temporary duty at 32nd Street Naval Station prior to reporting for duty on the USS *Buck* (DD-761), San Diego, California.

July 1968: Reported for TDY at Naval Air Station North Island for 10-week Drone Anti Submarine Helicopter training course on San Clemente Island.

Author's Service Record

September 1968: Reported for duty aboard the USS *Buck* (DD-761) in dry dock at the Hunter's Point Naval Shipyard, San Francisco.

October 1968–April 1969: On completion of sea trials in waters off San Francisco the USS *Buck* participated in REFTRA and a variety of pre-deployment exercises in the waters off San Diego.

April 1969: Deployed for WESTPAC and duty in the war zone aboard the USS *Buck* (DD-761). Served as *Buck's* Drone Anti-Submarine Helicopter (DASH) officer.

May 1969–November 1969: USS *Buck* (DD-761) in the war zone. Duties included naval gunfire support in South Vietnam and plane guarding at Yankee Station.

July 1969: Promoted to Lieutenant (junior grade).

November 1969: USS *Buck* (DD-761) returned from WESTPAC to the 32nd Street Naval Station, San Diego.

December 1969–July 1970: USS *Buck* (DD-761) participated in a variety of training exercises, drills, and inspections in the waters off San Diego. Served as Buck's 1st Division officer and Officer of the Deck (underway).

July 1970: USS *Buck* departed San Diego for WESTPAC and the war zone.

August 1970–December 1970: USS *Buck* (DD-761) in the war zone. Duties included naval gunfire support in South Vietnam and plane guarding in Yankee Station. Served as *Buck's* 1st Division officer and Officer of the Deck (underway).

December 1970: Transferred from USS *Buck* (DD-761) in Yokosuka, Japan for duty as Executive Officer aboard USS *Chehalis* (PG-94) home ported in San Diego, California.

January 1971: Reported aboard USS *Chehalis* (PG-94) in San Diego, California.

June 1971: Designated a Surface Warfare Officer by the Bureau of Naval Personnel in a letter dated 16 June 1971.

June 1971: USS *Chehalis* (PG-94) departed San Diego via Acapulco, the Panama Canal and Cartagena, Colombia for her new home port in Little Creek, Virginia.

July 1971: USS *Chehalis* (PG-94) arrives in Little Creek, Virginia, to join Coastal River Squadron 2 (COSRIVRON 2).

Promoted to Lieutenant July 1, 1971.

July 1971–February 1972: *Chehalis* participated in a variety of East Coast port calls including Salem, Massachusetts, and the U.S. Naval Academy, and naval exercises and inspections while remaining home ported in Little Creek, Virginia.

January 14, 1972: Took command of the USS *Chehalis* (PG-94) from Lt. R.G. Martin at the U.S. Naval Amphibious Base, Little Creek, Virginia.

February 22, 1972: Turned over command of the USS *Chehalis* (PG-94) to Lt. Dennis Crosby at U.S. Amphibious Base, Little Creek, Virginia. Returned to duties as Executive officer.

February 1972: USS *Chehalis* (PG-94) deployed to Guantanamo Bay, Cuba for a classified and open-ended assignment.

March 1972–June 1972: USS *Chehalis* (PG-94) conducted independent operations in the coastal waters of Cuba, Jamaica, Haiti and the Bahamas. Made port calls in Ocho Rios, Jamaica, Port au Prince, Haiti, and Great Inagua Island, Bahamas.

June 1972: Transferred from USS *Chehalis* (PG-94) at Guantanamo Bay Cuba to the Foreign Service Institute, Roslyn, Virginia, to attend a nine-month course in Norwegian language and culture.

May 1973: Graduated from the Norwegian Language and Culture course at the Foreign Service Institute, Roslyn, Virginia, with a certificate in Norwegian studies.

June 1973: Departed Norwegian Language training in Roslyn, Virginia, for two-year assignment in the Royal Norwegian Navy.

June 1973: Reported for duty in the Norwegian Navy at the Office of the Naval Attaché, American Embassy, Oslo, Norway.

June 1973: Reported aboard KNM *Trondheim* (F-302) docked at Haakonsvern, Norway's main naval base in Bergen, Norway. Assigned as Operations officer with requirement to become a qualified Officer of the Deck (underway).

August 1973–December 1973: Deployed in Norwegian territorial waters north of the Arctic Circle aboard KNM *Trondheim* (F-302). Ship's duties include anti-submarine warfare and Norwegian border protection.

December 1973–January 1974: In port at Haakonsvern, Norway's main naval base in Bergen Norway.

January 1974–March 1974: Deployed in Norwegian territorial waters north of the Arctic Circle aboard KNM *Trondheim* (F-302).

March 1974: In port at Haakonsvern, Norway's main naval base in Bergen Norway.

June 1974: KNM *Trondheim* (F-302) in company with KNM *Stavanger* (F-303) paid an official visit to Reykjavik, Iceland.

July 1974: Together with the entire ship's crew transferred from KNM *Trondheim* (F-302) to KNM *Oslo* (F-300).

Author's Service Record

September 1974: TDY to the 25th TKB Squadron in Bergen for official visit by the squadron to the Shetland Islands, Scotland while KNM *Oslo* made an official visit to Leningrad, USSR.

September 1974–December 1974: Deployed north of the Arctic Circle aboard KNM Oslo (F-300). Ship's duties include anti-submarine warfare and Norwegian border protection. Served as Officer of the Deck (underway) and operations officer.

December 1974: In port at Haakonsvern, Norway's main naval base in Bergen Norway.

January 1975: Deployed north of the Arctic Circle aboard KNM *Oslo* (F-300).

January 1975: Return to Haakonsvern for transfer to the 24th TKB Squadron as the Executive Officer of KNM *Hvass* (P-972).

April 1975: Deployed north of the Arctic Circle with the 24th TKB Squadron aboard the KNM *Hvass* (P-972). Duties included Norwegian border protection.

August 1975: Return to the Norwegian Naval Base at Haakonsvern for transfer back to the U.S. Navy via the U.S. Naval Attaché's Office, Oslo, Norway.

August 1975: Honorably discharged from the U.S. Navy at U.S. Naval Station, Washington, D.C.

Medals: National Defense Service Medal; Vietnam Service Medal (2 bronze stars); Republic of Vietnam Campaign Medal; Armed Forces Expeditionary Medal; Navy Commendation Medal.

Bibliography

Books

CIA World Fact Book, Washington, D.C., 2021.

Coleridge, Samuel Taylor. "The Rime of the Ancient Mariner." *Lyrical Ballads*. London: R. Briggs and Co., 1798.

Goscha, Christopher. *The Penguin History of Modern Vietnam*. New York: Penguin, 2017.

Howell, Nathaniel R. *Islip Town's World War II Effort*. Islip, New York: Buys Brothers, 1948.

Melville, Herman. *Moby Dick; or The Whale*. London: Richard Bentley, 1851.

Tornoe, Johannes K. *Early American History: Norsemen Before Columbus*. Oslo, Norway: Univeritetsforlaget, 1964.

Newspapers, Magazines, Articles, Papers and Journals

Brooklyn Daily Eagle

Foreign Affairs

Frank E. Evans Association, Inc. Newsletter

Life Magazine

The New York Herald Tribune

The New York Times

Newsday

Norske Torpedobaater 1873–1973

Report of the Office of the Secretary of Defense Vietnam Task Force (The Pentagon Papers).

The Soviet Military Buildup in Cuba, June 11, 1982 (The Heritage Foundation).

"The Soviet Navy's Caribbean Outpost," *U.S. Naval Institute Magazine*. September 2012.

The Suffolk County News

Tin Can Sailors

Wall Street Journal

Television

CBS Evening News, February 27, 1968.

Websites

airandspace.si.edu
atlasobscura.com
bahamasgeotourism.com
bbc.com
britannica.com
britishseafishing.co.uk
brownwater-navy.com/vietnam/seafloat
cfr.org backgrounder US-Cuba Relations
fodors.com
Gemini 4 Astronautics.com
gunboatriders.com
gyrodynehelicopters.com
history.com
history.navy.mil
HonorStates.org
kystverket.no/en/EN_Maritime-Services
lifeinnorway.net
military.wikia.org/wiki/Operation_Seal
ordsnationalgeographic.com
militarytimes.com
navsource.org
nordnorge.com > aktivitet > juhls-silver-gallery
nytimes.com/1970/09/26/archives/us-warns-soviet-not-to-bur174ahc.org
rarediseases.org/mal-de-debarquement
rbth.com
reuters.com
SFGATE.com
United States Naval Institute.

Bibliography

usni.org.
ussfee.org (Frank E. Evans Association, Inc.)
valor.washingtonpost.com/politics/ 2019/05/02
whc.unesco.org
wikia.org

Letters

Whitehouse, John and Elaine, personal correspondence 1968–1975.
Lerner, P.O. 3rd Class David, personal correspondence.

Firsthand Sources

Skip Leeson
P. R. Martin
R. Martin
Mike Sobyra
Gene Van Orden
Elaine Whitehouse
Henry Whitehouse
John H. Whitehouse
John H. Whitehouse, III

Index

Index

Index

Index

Index

Index

Index

Index

Index